# Diplomacy
# Lessons

Similar titles from Potomac Books:

*First Resort of Kings: American Cultural Diplomacy in the Twentieth Century*
Richard T. Arndt

*Defiant Superpower: The New American Hegemony*
Donald E. Nuechterlein

*War and Destiny: How the Bush Revolution in Foreign and Military Affairs Redefined American Power*
James Kitfield

# Diplomacy
# Lessons

*Realism for an Unloved Superpower*

John Brady Kiesling

Potomac Books, Inc.
Washington, D.C.

First Paperback Edition 2007
Copyright © 2006 Potomac Books, Inc.

The opinions and characterizations in this book are those of the author and do not necessarily represent official positions of the U.S. government.

**Library of Congress Cataloging-in-Publication Data**
Kiesling, John Brady, 1957–
  Diplomacy lessons : realism for an unloved superpower / John Brady Kiesling.—1st ed.
    p. cm.
  Includes bibliographical references and index.
  ISBN 978-1-59797-017-4 (hardcover : alk. paper)
  1. United States—Foreign relations—2001- 2. War on Terrorism, 2001—Political aspects. 3. Diplomacy—Philosophy. 4. Realism—Political aspects—United States. 5. Great powers. 6. United States—Foreign public opinion. 7. Kiesling, John Brady, 1957 8. Diplomats—United States—Biography. I. Title.
  E902.K54 2006
  327.73009'0511—dc22
                          2005034119
ISBN-13 978-1-59797-110-2

Printed in the United States of America on acid-free paper that meets the American National Standards Institute Z39-48 Standard.

Potomac Books, Inc.
22841 Quicksilver Drive
Dulles, Virginia 20166

First Edition

10 9 8 7 6 5 4 3 2 1

To the new generation of the U.S. Foreign
Service, whose faith in their country
and curiosity about the planet
will bring new pride to a proud profession.

# ★ *Contents* ★

# ★ *Acknowledgments* ★

This book would not have been written without the faith of a small army of wonderful people who read my letter of resignation to Colin Powell and found some way to assure me that I had something important to say. I was skeptical then that the world needed any more books. I am still skeptical, but apparently the time and toil of writing a book are society's minimum price for challenging any aspect of its conventional wisdom. I thus owe particular thanks to Todd Schuster, who offered his services as my agent at a time when the book was only a shadowy possibility, and to Sandra Shagat, who took on most of the agent chores as my book draft moved into less marketable territory. Lisa Camner of Potomac Books asked the pointed questions that forced me to make the book less obscure than diplomatic instinct would prefer.

I owe a lasting debt to a series of long-ago professors and fellow students, particularly to Erich Gruen and to ancient history seminar-mates Joe, Ann, Richard, and Lisa at Berkeley, who taught me to piece together the fragmentary evidence the world gives us. Stephen Miller introduced me to the colors of dirt and the texture of Greek village life, the "real world" in microcosm. The Hellenic Studies Program of Princeton University, led by Dimitri Gondicas and Mike Keeley with backing from two wonderful former Foreign Service bosses, Bob Keeley and Dick Jackson, offered academic refuge for precious months after I resigned. Princeton gave me some of the history and academic breadth I had missed as a diplomat. Anne-Marie Slaughter of the Woodrow Wilson School gave me the precious opportunity to lecture to a world-class academic public and to teach gifted undergraduates in a fail-safe environment.

To Joe Scholten, Anne Cusick, and Maggie, to Greg and Nitsa Mattson, to Greg and Pam Thielmann, and to Pam and Becka I owe delightful days or weeks of Washington refuge. To Nicholas Pisaris, Elisabeth Sifton, and others who read draft chapters, I am grateful for the insightful comments and eloquent silences.

My diplomatic inspirations tended to come in pairs. In thanking Clint and Marilyn Smith, Sam and Sallie Lewis, John and Helen Davis, and Monty and Toni Stearns, I leave unacknowledged other fine diplomats whose careers it is in the U.S. national interest not to undermine. Greek friends—fellow diplomats, journalists, politicians, academics, and ordinary folk—proved their friendship by being honest in expressing their firm disagreement with policies it was my diplomatic duty to represent to them.

Foreign service life puts great stress on families. My parents and siblings have seen less of me than we would like, but Einstein's "spooky action at a distance" seems to apply. My daughter, Lydia, by discovering her own curiosity about the world, has made me very proud.

Finally, to Regina, who gave me the courage to be a better person than anything in my previous diplomatic career suggested I could be, my undying gratitude and love.

# ★ *Introduction* ★

This book is a plea for the profession of diplomacy. I spent twenty years as an officer in the U.S. Foreign Service, part of the vast, mostly invisible mechanism that keeps ordinary Americans safe and prosperous. It was both an honorable career and a subtle and difficult art. Every few years I uprooted my family, learned a new language and new faces, and tried to solve my small part of the huge puzzle of how Americans can best thrive in a world they share with 6.5 billion strangers.

When I resigned in protest at the end of February 2003, U.S. diplomacy had lost its role as primary defender of U.S. interests overseas. An ideology of contempt for foreigners had prevailed in Washington, and the U.S. military was preparing bloody regime change in Iraq. The damage to U.S. interests was obvious even before the war began, and not only in the blackening of America's image overseas. Repairing that damage would take years of brilliant work by every diplomat America had.

By resigning instead of continuing to serve, I took on a moral responsibility to the millions of Americans who embraced my resignation as an act of patriotism. As the fiasco of Iraq gradually became apparent, Americans wanted to understand what U.S. power could realistically accomplish. Hence this book: the product of twenty years of trying to make sense of my country's and my own diplomatic successes and failures.

"Realism" is used as a dirty word in U.S. foreign policy, a synonym for selfishness and indifference to human suffering. The White House and the Pentagon are full of proud idealists with the moral courage to torture and kill in the name of freedom. When I joined the Foreign Service, I too thought I was an idealist. The United States

1

was a moral superpower, and we diplomats had a moral duty to use our country's wealth and power to make the world peaceful, prosperous, and democratic. Now, with the benefit of twenty years' experience, I am a State Department realist.

Realism—hard-nosed calculation of cost and benefit to the American people, based on an accurate understanding of human nature and the workings of power—dictates that the United States cannot affordably defend its selfish interests except by presenting itself to the world in moral terms. By the unsophisticated moral calculus that prevails in every human society, the means America uses are indistinguishable from the ends it pursues. World peace, prosperity, and democracy are goals the American people should pursue with selfish persistence, but we cannot attain those goals except by patient, curious, generous diplomacy that starts with the humble moral obligation to save more lives than we destroy.

America cannot save everyone. It has neither the legitimacy nor the skills even to try. Conflict and competition are key organizing principles of every human society. We may someday evolve away from them, but for now the international system is based on some two hundred disunited states run by two hundred problematic governments. Each of those governments rebuffs powerful outsiders as a way of holding on to the precious political legitimacy it needs to govern.

But isolationism is not a moral or even a sensibly selfish option for a state uniquely endowed with the rare power—including military power—to save lives thousands of miles from its shores. The United States uses its power most effectively in strengthening states and governments, not in subverting or supplanting them. When we harness the international institutions we created for the purpose, our power is multiplied. When we act on our own, we weaken an international system that, in the long run, offers the only realistic hope of locking struggling new nations into rules of conduct that will someday bring freedom and dignity to their people.

This is not meant to be a partisan book. Every government and political party in the world shapes its foreign policies to serve sometimes-squalid local political interests. I respected both George H. W. Bush and Bill Clinton for their diplomatic talents. They understood that the United States does not have the luxury of pretending the consequences of a self-centered foreign policy will remain safely remote. The current Bush administration may be learning that lesson as well.

Condoleezza Rice took office as America's diplomat in chief in January 2005 with a pledge to restore U.S. diplomacy to its central role in U.S. foreign policy. The swagger and name-calling subsided. The State Department began to rebuild frayed ties with foreign governments and the international organizations on which our broader security depends. Senior U.S. diplomats sat patiently and professionally through weeks of frustrating nuclear negotiations with North Korea. Such changes of direction are encouraging, but a more radical transformation is necessary.

As national security adviser, Dr. Rice was a loyal and disciplined bureaucrat. Diplomats and bureaucrats need each other, but they are different animals. The U.S. bureaucratic game takes place within a narrow space of a few thousand civil servants and the politicians who persuade the taxpayers to pay their salaries. Success and failure are judged by pay grade and by the size of a line item in the federal budget. Bureaucrats thrive by offering politicians whatever version of reality best meets their political requirements of the moment.

Diplomacy takes place on a larger board, and success and failure are measured by one standard only: the enduring security and prosperity of the American people. America's interests are not those of tomorrow's headlines or the next presidential election, but rather the future of our children and their grandchildren in a world they will share with nine billion other humans who crave the same things we do. Good diplomacy will identify, for a president brave enough to listen, the minimum foreign policy sacrifices required to lock our rivals and partners as firmly as we must into global rules of competition by which ordinary Americans can prosper.

A diplomat's analytical approach does not offer miraculous solutions to the world's woes. It will, however, help thoughtful voters separate fact from fantasy in the promises made by their leaders. In leaving out any discussion of economic and environmental diplomacy, I am acutely conscious that this book is a personal and incomplete contribution to one of the world's most ancient and essential debates. I wrote what I knew best and what I brooded on most.

Like most of my colleagues, I learned diplomacy the hard way, by the mistakes I made. If I exaggerate the failings of U.S. diplomacy, it is for didactic purposes. In any case, I hope my personal history of Pyrrhic victories will inspire a generation of gifted, patriotic young Americans to take the Foreign Service exam and launch themselves into the world to do better than I.

No other profession combines the collective wisdom of a superpower with the training and mandate to speak to the most interesting people on the planet in their own languages. No profession could have offered me finer colleagues. No other career, ultimately, could have given me the self-confidence I finally mustered to send a letter to Secretary of State Colin Powell to inform him that President Bush, his boss and mine, was doing grave damage to American interests by misunderstanding the nature of the world America aspires to lead and even ought to lead.

# 1

# ★ *A Diplomat's Rebellion* ★

*"I make mistakes, but I am on the side of Good," the Golux said,
"by accident and happenchance. I had high hopes of being Evil
when I was two, but in my youth I came upon a firefly burning
in a spider's web. I saved the victim's life."*

*"The firefly's?" said the minstrel.*

*"The spider's. The blinking arsonist had set the web on
fire."*

*The minstrel's uncertainty increased . . .*

James Thurber, *The Thirteen Clocks*

A diplomat should take a long view of the national interest. I
spent the summer before I joined the Foreign Service as a field archaeologist, supervising a dozen local workmen digging in the ruins
of Aphrodisias in western Turkey. While I scribbled notes in my tiny,
illegible handwriting, my men ripped through a Turkish farmhouse
to uncover a new piece of the Roman city below. Excavation director
Kenan Erim had spent two decades filling the village museum with
statues, but the glory of his site and the short attention span of his
donors required a steady flow of new discoveries. Soon enough a
pick hit marble, the headless statue of a late Roman emperor. The
mud he lay in was clingier than we thought, and he cracked in two
as we lifted him. Archaeology is more destructive a profession than
we care to advertise.

For almost seven hundred years Aphrodisias had been a glorious marble city in a fertile valley, with broad streets, grand colon-
nades and fountains, and statues everywhere. A wall of inscriptions
in bureaucratic Greek documented the city's special privileges:
Aphrodisias was sacred to the goddess Aphrodite. Julius Caesar, the
Roman dictator, now a god himself, had claimed her as his ancestor.
This made the Aphrodisians cousins to the imperial dynasty. Their
city prospered mightily as a result.

Some self-serving myths can be milked for centuries, but reality always intervenes eventually. Neither the formidable Roman legions nor Aphrodite herself saved the grandest city of the ancient district of Caria from becoming, thirteen hundred years before I reached it, a muddy village in the middle of nowhere. Fertile farming valleys need constant, organized human intervention not to revert to malarial swamps. As the Roman Empire unraveled and its citizens were murdered, raped, enslaved, or reduced to poverty, grand proclamations from the capital had no power over the water table. The Roman streets became pools for croaking frogs. The marble statues of emperors and priestesses waited in the mud for Kenan Erim's picks and shovels.

Aphrodisias was my last dig. In April 1983, with a fresh master of arts degree in ancient history, newly married to a fellow archaeologist, I drove with my wife from California in her Volkswagen Beetle and took a dingy room at the Highlander Motor Lodge in Arlington. The next day I put on my one suit and joined thirty-three colleagues in the fifteenth A-100 junior officer training class at the State Department's Foreign Service Institute. We eyed one another nervously in an ugly high-rise in Rosslyn. This was my first real job. How would my liberal Silicon Valley childhood and my obsolete classical education help me in this world of neckties and conventional conformity?[1]

U.S. diplomacy is, as it was for our defunct Roman predecessors, a trade learned by apprenticeship. Our seven weeks in the classroom were a bureaucratic crash course in the structure and private language of the U.S. foreign affairs hierarchy, plus a two-week immersion course in visas and passports. Our two-hour session on diplomatic etiquette, spiced with obsolete lore regarding gloves and calling cards, seemed by comparison like precious real-world training.[2]

The British ran an impressive empire for 250 years with diplomats and administrators educated, like their ancient Roman predecessors and like me, with tales from Plutarch on the lives of the great men of Greece and Rome. This was an education based on morality and power. The ancient authors whose works survived two thousand years of brutal shifts in intellectual fashion were the ones who taught that it was good to be brave, to tell the truth, to treat subordinates decently, to spare the innocent, and to be generous to the conquered. The ancient Greeks were naive in their belief in divine retribution, but they were not naive in their recognition that trampling on human moral sensibilities led to bad ends. Romans were scarcely starry-eyed idealists. Their world was full of violent death and betrayal. They recognized better than most American leaders that foreign suppliants have a more urgent interest in successfully lying to an alien superpower than that same superpower has in discerning the truth. A liberal education—literally the education befitting a free man—helped an honest man discern the truth. A wise leader did not lie, especially not to himself.

I can confirm in retrospect, after twenty years serving my country, that Plutarch and Thucydides were not a bad introduction to the moral and intellectual challenge of keeping Washington, D.C., from decaying, like Aphrodisias before it, into a swampy wasteland of broken columns. Human beings, even politicians and bureaucrats, are animals with deep moral sensibilities, and their behavior has changed little since the fifth century BC.

In May 1983 I took my oath to support and defend the U.S. Constitution as a foreign service officer of the U.S. Department of State. Like the ancient Romans, I take oaths seriously. Unlike the Romans, who understood perfectly well how precarious their unwritten constitution was, I had no idea that protecting the U.S. Constitution was a full-time battle even in peacetime. The democratic trappings of the Roman constitution were routinely ignored or subverted by the very people chosen to defend it. Looking at my smart, idealistic new colleagues, it never occurred to me that the same might ever be true in America as well.

Working for a superpower has many advantages. Reading the classified cable traffic and intelligence reporting from open and secret sources all over the world, I felt better informed than my foreign diplomatic colleagues, certainly on any issue that mattered to the United States. As a U.S. diplomat, I became a valuable contact almost automatically. Even as a young and ignorant junior diplomat I could presume to speak to foreign cabinet ministers and ambassadors, and they would answer me.

This taste of omniscience encouraged me to adopt the knowing, cynical style of my fellow diplomats. Our job was to understand local politics and the petty, personal motives that lurked behind them. Underneath our cynicism was a powerful sense of mission. Most of us simplified the complex world: what was good for America and for us personally was also good for humankind in general.

As I rose up the Foreign Service career ladder—through postings in Israel, Morocco, Greece, Armenia, and three assignments in Washington, D.C.—I too had no serious doubts that the meetings I attended, the information I gathered, the reports I wrote, and the diplomatic persuasion I attempted all fit into an effort that made the American people safer and richer by nudging the world in a positive direction. I took for granted, and so apparently did we all, that America's interests were served by promoting peace, prosperity, and human rights abroad as well as at home. Not everything America did was noble, unselfish, or even competent, but American power had a benign-seeming logic that I could defend to any foreigner I met with enthusiasm, a clear conscience, and logical arguments.[3]

## *Return to Athens*

My career advanced as it was supposed to. After sixteen years and four overseas postings I was judged worthy to become the political counselor at the U.S. embassy in Athens, Greece. I had reached the threshold of senior management as chief of my Political Section, running the little team of foreign service officers that kept the ambassador and the U.S. government informed on political developments in Greece as they affected U.S. interests.

I arrived in Athens on July 2, 2000, in the waning days of the Clinton administration, just in time to sweat in my dark suit through the embassy's July 4 reception for three thousand of America's nearest and dearest friends in Greece. I had known Nick Burns, my ambassador, from my very first Foreign Service assignment in Tel Aviv, when he was my counterpart in Cairo next door. He was a supremely energetic, ambitious, capable professional, socially gifted and self-confident.[4] Burns was happy to put my fluent Greek and local knowledge to work.

My window into Greek politics was wide, thanks to the politicians, journalists, and diplomats I had befriended there as a junior political officer in 1988–92. I had a toehold in the American archaeological colony in Athens. Maintaining my web of working relationships with the Athens foreign policy community kept me at the office, diplomatic receptions, or professional round-tables until late almost every night.

In 2000 the issues that kept the Political Section busy were absorbing and morally almost irreproachable. We worked with an excellent, progressive foreign minister named George Papandreou. Born in the United States to an American mother, educated at Amherst, son and grandson of Greek prime ministers, Papandreou was a problem solver determined to end the state of near war that had existed between Greece and Turkey since 1955. He was determined, as well, that Greece would use its membership in the European Union (EU) and its economic strength to become the stabilizing power in the Balkans. The United States supported these goals with enthusiasm.

I spent much of my first year in Athens quietly consulting with

Papandreou's advisers and diplomats as the United States and its EU partners leaned on Serb leader Slobodan Miloševic to step down following the fraudulent Yugoslav elections of September 1999 and then brokered a solution to the ethnic conflict between Albanians and Macedonians in "the Former Yugoslav Republic of Macedonia." I was involved in unpublicized efforts to persuade Greeks and Turks to risk direct negotiation over their Aegean disputes and in building support for the United Nation–sponsored package deal to solve the Cyprus conflict by bringing Turkey into the EU. On a bilateral level, we had a status-of-forces agreement to negotiate to protect the U.S. military personnel at the base in Souda Bay and a terror war to manage against Greece's tiny domestic terror group Revolutionary Organization 17 November (17N, see chapter 11).

### *The November 2000 Elections*

I am ashamed to admit how little attention I paid to U.S. domestic politics, even in a presidential election year. I was completely absorbed in the diplomat's intellectual challenge of determining what combination of arguments and personal relationships would do the U.S. government's business in Greece at lowest cost. Successful diplomacy depended, in Greece or anywhere, on close study of personalities. Nevertheless, I preferred to pretend we Americans, from the president down, were interchangeable players on the same united team: America's team.

Any good bureaucrat would laugh derisively at this point. I had never understood why Ambassador Frank Wisner insisted the India Desk fax him at U.S. Embassy New Delhi each new "In the Loop" political gossip column from the *Washington Post*. I looked down on embassy colleagues who spent every spare moment comparing notes about who did what to whom in each office in Washington. Absorbed in my Greek puzzles, I could not be bothered. I was loyally serving my political masters in Washington, and I assumed that changing those masters would not change America's national interests or the appropriate tactics to advance those interests.

I watched the 2000 presidential debates at the ambassador's residence, a breakfast gathering with an invited Greek audience of journalists, politicians, and academics. I was pro-Gore, but not with much partisan enthusiasm. President Bill Clinton had over time become an excellent diplomat, eventually outstripping his competent but less charismatic predecessor, George H. W. Bush. The Republicans who controlled the House of Representatives denied funding to any U.S. foreign policy initiative that might burnish Clinton's reputation. Strapped for cash, the State Department had no choice but to embrace multilateralism and backroom diplomacy because they were cheap. Vice President Al Gore's "reinventing government" campaign contributed to the shrinkage of my Political Section by a third from its Cold War peak under President Ronald Reagan. Still, Gore stood for continuation of the sensible internationalist policies that, under Bush the elder and Clinton, had kept the United States the undisputed world leader and a magnet for the world's brains and capital.

The Greeks in the audience all shuddered when George W. Bush smirked about having executed convicts as governor of Texas. I shuddered with them. The death penalty is defensible as domestic policy, maybe. Indifference to the prevailing moral sensibilities of foreign publics is not. Such gaffes, if continued, would make Bush useless as a symbol of American democratic values to the overseas audience.

Still, overall the stakes of the election seemed low. Bush bobbled the names of foreign leaders, but we all do. U.S. interests survived Reagan's 1982 mistake of hailing the people of Bolivia on his official visit to Brazil. Like most other Americans Bush didn't understand the difference between states and nations. Nation building is a messy ideological process the United States does well to stay out of, while state building is a dreary duty for any prudent superpower, like building sewage treatment plants. His promise of a humbler foreign policy implied that he intended to listen to foreigners long enough to figure out that America's unique history was a poor guidebook for the rest of the world.

### The New Administration

Greek schadenfreude was intense as the 2000 Florida vote-count fiasco unfurled. I told anyone who listened that the end result was a tribute to the strength of the U.S. Constitution and Americans' commitment to their institutions. I hoped that I was right and that the new president would be brighter and better than the sordid maneuvering that elected him.

I respected new Secretary of State Colin Powell instinctively, as did most State Department employees. I paid little attention to Defense Secretary Donald Rumsfeld, except to note that, unlike his Clinton-era predecessors, he was more interested in defeating his inside-the-Beltway bureaucratic competitors than in tending to America's security alliances. I paid no attention at all to ultraconservative political appointee John Bolton, our new undersecretary for arms control and thus a key architect of U.S. international security policy.

Bush's public, brutally inept repudiation of the International Criminal Court (ICC) and the Kyoto Climate-Change Protocol was the first unmistakable signal that diplomacy had ceased to be the preferred language of the United States abroad. Diplomats faithfully obey the president the voters give them. I quietly took on the ICC fiasco—it was better to sacrifice my credibility than my ambassador's. Armed with official instructions to demand that U.S. citizens be exempt from ICC jurisdiction, I gamely went to the Greek Foreign Ministry. I discovered immediately that those instructions left me naked. The key Greek official, the head of the Ministry of Foreign Affairs Legal Division, had been part of the ICC negotiation process for a decade and had heard the official Bush administration line firsthand, from U.S. officials considerably senior to me. She felt personally betrayed by how the United States, which once championed the ICC as the logical and moral response to atrocities such as Bosnia and Rwanda, had reversed its position once Bush took office. She had factual arguments from the negotiating history to demolish the populist drivel the new political appointees had sent out as America's talking points.

America's position was a disgraceful one: the U.S. Congress had embraced a pressure group of cynical populists with a Goebbelsian lie that UN black helicopters were poised to take away America's freedom. Taking a page from the rhetoric of friends like Slobodan Miloševic, the ex-ruler of Serbia, Congress decided to demonstrate the virility of its concern for "national sovereignty" by passing a law to shield America's future war criminals from legal scrutiny by the international community.

I was diplomatic about it. I reassured the Greeks that America was not endorsing war crimes. The ICC treaty made clear that each country has the right and responsibility for trying its own war criminals, with the ICC acting when the criminal's home state failed to act. America had a track record of punishing war criminals, its own as well as others'. America remained firmly committed to bringing all such criminals to justice. Still, Greece and the EU needed to find a way to accommodate U.S. concerns, or the United States would walk away from its international peacekeeping commitments and cut off military assistance to all but key allies.

Personally, however, I was certain that America's pusillanimity on the ICC was stupid as well as immoral. Americans benefited handsomely from international law because the United States had written much of it. Now the United States was hacking away at the moral and political foundations of its own creation. Why would anyone else accept international law as a legitimate argument for self-restraint when the United States would not? America's alternative to law and diplomacy was the ugly threat of U.S. military might, but the U.S. military—unlike the president and Congress—at least understood how expensive an alternative it was.

The ICC threat to U.S. citizens was far-fetched. To eliminate that threat, my colleagues and I dutifully squandered diplomatic capital bullying or bribing states to sign symbolic agreements. In Greece, the effect of Congress's American Service Member Protective Act was to make our service members less safe than before. The odds were always remote that any of the hundreds of uniformed Americans at our base in Souda Bay would ever be accused of being international war criminals. It was certain, however, that each year young, frisky American military personnel would be arrested by Greek authorities for brawls, traffic accidents, or misunderstandings with shopkeepers. We had just negotiated a sensible new status-of-forces agreement that waived criminal jurisdiction for such incidents back to the U.S. military justice system except in cases of "major political importance" to Greece. Furious at our ICC stance, the Greek foreign and justice ministries ruled that almost every fistfight by a U.S. service member was a crime of sufficient political importance to require trial by a Greek court. Greek jails have improved, but the average American seaman would be better off taking his chances with the ICC.

The ICC debate was a tiny part of the diplomatic work of protecting U.S interests in Greece. U.S. policy toward southern Europe was still mostly in the hands of the professionals. Our goals remained the sensible ones of regional stability, shared prosperity, and human rights. We continued behind the scenes to encourage Greek-Turkish reconciliation. More publicly, we worked to reunite the divided island of Cyprus through a federal constitution brokered by the UN and made palatable by EU membership for both Cyprus and Turkey. We blackmailed the Greeks, through a damning public report and the threat of humiliating sanctions, into giving some legal protection to foreign women and children trafficked into prostitution by local pimps. Washington's interest in our shared war against the 17N terror group remained high, unhealthily so, but we and the Greek government conducted our diplomatic business smoothly and unobtrusively during the first eight months of the new U.S. administration.

## September 11, 2001

Ambassador Burns left in August to become U.S permanent representative at NATO. The battle for the NATO slot was intense because both the State Department and the Defense Department have vital bureaucratic interests in Brussels. Part of the personnel trade that got Burns the job was the appointment of a new U.S ambassador to Greece, Tom Miller, an equally energetic and ambitious but less-gifted career diplomat who had burnished his weak conservative credentials by playing tennis with Donald Rumsfeld. Miller was not due in Athens until October. My counterpart at the U.S. embassy in Sarajevo, where Miller was then ambassador, warned me that my next two years would be difficult.

On September 11, thirty seconds after CNN reported the crash of the third airliner into the Pentagon, the embassy security officer, ████████████████, the defense attaché, and I sprinted simultaneously to the office of Chargé d'Affaires (acting ambassador) Mike Cleverley, all with the same advice: we must assume that global war has been declared against the United States. It was time to alert the Greek air force and government and to evacuate the embassy of all but a handful of essential personnel. We stayed (who would ever tell his colleagues he was less essential than they?) and waited for the other shoe to drop. We are still waiting.

The hypnotic television footage of the Twin Towers collapsing over and over again horrified Greeks no less than it horrified Americans. Greeks reassured themselves that America, unlike Europe, had been asking for it through its arrogant behavior.[5] But they were nervous; America was a wounded elephant. Would we trample the world flat in pursuit of our flea-sized tormentors? Greeks, like most Europeans, were anxious to calm us down and prevent a "clash of civilizations" with their Muslim neighbors. After 9/11 no reasonable U.S. request would be refused.

It never occurred to me that America might choose to behave like a wounded elephant. As I thanked Greek contacts for their condolences and reassured them that the United States would react responsibly, I was calm enough personally. We had been struck a painful blow, but one it would be almost impossible to repeat. Al Qaeda was a far less capable adversary than the doomsayers claimed. Meanwhile, the murder of twenty-eight hundred innocent people erased the legitimacy that al Qaeda's suicidal bravery was supposed to win them with ordinary Muslims. The gut-wrenching sight of men and women falling to their death from the towers gave the United States the right to demand—not merely request—effective counterterrorism cooperation from the whole world. The 9/11 murders were, practically if not legally, all the international mandate the United States needed to enter Afghanistan and destroy al Qaeda there.

Invading Afghanistan was a self-evident response to 9/11, one no democratic politician could deny an angry American people. The invasion could not be a cure for international terrorism—no such cure exists—but America could force radical groups to disperse to countries where, unlike Afghanistan, local police existed to watch them. The war, I felt certain, would do no more harm to the Afghan people than they had already suffered at the hands of the blind bigots who ruled in Kabul. If the United States was patient and generous enough, it might do some actual good to this long-suffering country.

Most Greeks, including journalists who ought to have known better, were incredulous about U.S. motives for ousting the Taliban. I was confident the U.S. government had no illusion that occupying Afghanistan would be fun and profitable (Rumsfeld dragged his feet at first, fearing Afghanistan would distract the president from Iraq). Grand geostrategic visions for Afghanistan were a mirage or worse. America's task there was to snuff out al Qaeda and leave behind, as best it could, a functioning Afghan government that would not let terrorist groups come back.

Greece's military chiefs pressed the embassy to tell them what Greece could do to help. We never got them an answer. I was irritated that the Pentagon could not be bothered to authorize us to pass on at least a polite "No thank you," far less a list of specific U.S. requests, to Greece's offer of assistance. The only explanation that made sense of this unresponsiveness seemed petty and vindictive: The Office of the Secretary of Defense was enforcing Secretary Rumsfeld's bureaucratic reflex to squeeze the State Department out of the counterterrorism business. When America has no allies, it needs no diplomats to tend those alliances.

Greeks agreed almost instantly to the one thing we asked, to give American ships and aircraft blanket clearances to the Middle East through the vital U.S. air and naval base at Souda Bay. Beyond that, Greece had little that met America's precise requirements for a special operations–led unconventional campaign conducted by anti-Taliban Afghan warlords. But a president armed with common sense and common courtesy would not have allowed the Defense Department to block a positive answer. Accepting foreign help when it is offered spontaneously is a fine relationship-building strategy. Greek domestic politics are a huge barrier to sending troops overseas. The political cover 9/11 offered allowed the Greeks to make a muscular commitment to the United States that had been politically impossible before the attacks and would soon become impossible again. Whether Rumsfeld agreed or not, the United States would be trapped doing state building in Afghanistan for an extended period. By contributing a small contingent and taking a few casualties, Greece would lock itself psychologically into the state-building coalition.

No analyst believed that killing Osama bin Laden would end the threat of terrorism. The U.S. international security apparatus had a more complex and ambitious duty, to debunk the yammering about a clash of civilizations while demonstrating to the participants in dozens of vicious private wars that killing Americans would be fatal to their cause. But that was not the thrust of the president's message to the American people, a message that reached the outside world simply as "wanted dead or alive."

The Pentagon launched in 2002 its then-secret maritime interdiction initiative in the Mediterranean. As the defense attaché and I puzzled over the instruction cable, we concluded that it had been drafted as bureaucratic showboating. The program would preposition U.S. Navy SEAL teams with fast boats at strategic points to intercept commercial shipping in the Mediterranean that might be hauling terrorists or their supplies. But this was not a pressing problem the United States needed to deal with. On the rare occasions when terrorists decided to stow away in cargo ships rather than fly legally and comfortably, our intelligence was almost certainly not going to be good enough to catch them. Even if the Navy caught actual terrorists, it had no criminal jurisdiction to deal with them. For that reason alone, it was wiser to let local coast guards do the work ██████████████████████████████████████████████████████████████████████ ███████████████████████████████████████████████.[6]

Because of its geographic position and huge merchant fleet, Greece was a necessary partner in maritime interdiction. We asked pointed questions by classified e-mail to attempt to clarify the legal basis on which the program would function, but it was not our business at the embassy to challenge policy. My political-military deputy worked quietly and capably with the Greek Foreign Ministry to help make maritime interdiction missions possible. The enthusiasm of the Greek military and coast guard for sexy secret operations overcame the legal qualms of Greek diplomats. Our SEAL teams, with their Greek partners, eventually boarded some number of suspect vessels and discovered some number of economic migrants en route to a new life in Italy.

The State Department had its own exercise in bureaucratic wishful thinking. It would ban international financial transfers by terrorists and close down their bank accounts. Greek bankers dutifully combed their files for names that matched those the embassy had given them. Most terrorists have common names, and few of them are as dependent on international high finance as bin Laden's wealth had led the United States to assume. The four-figure cost of a terrorist attack can be raised locally in cash donations. Shutting down the informal *hawala* networks for moving money between the Middle East and Europe made good business sense to Western Union, which charges hefty fees for immigrants to send remittances home to their families. Greek banking authorities came up empty, however, in their searches for terrorism funds. Other countries inflated their seizure statistics by shutting down pro-Palestinian Islamic charities that had irritated the Israelis. These were trumpeted in the United States as major counterterrorism successes.

Still, the overall U.S. goal was entirely sensible: to mobilize the international community to cooperate effectively against terrorism, both through the freer exchange of law enforcement and intelligence information and through establishing better controls over the international movement of illegal people, weapons, and money. This was a difficult task given how bad bureaucrats are in sharing information even with rival bureaucrats in their own government. Building trust with U.S. foreign partners was indispensable if the superpower hoped to succeed. But America's diplomacy did not seem to be aimed at building trust abroad. It focused on looking macho at home.

I was mystified early in 2002 when U.S. embassies around the world were instructed to force the removal of Jose Bustani, an aggressive Brazilian diplomat the Clinton administration had handpicked as head of the Organization for the Prohibition of Chemical Weapons (OPCW) five years before. Around the world U.S. diplomats demanded an emergency OPCW executive committee meeting to fire Bustani, using the implied threat of withholding U.S. dues. The talking points sent by the Political-Military Affairs Bureau of the State Department offered vague allegations of mismanagement but nothing that would justify an urgent meeting to remove him. I could not enlighten the Greeks as to our true motives.

Bustani claimed in his public defense—plausibly since we had no rebuttal to offer—that he had committed the crime of attempting to hold U.S. chemical companies to the same chemical weapons inspection standards the United States insisted on for everyone else. He had compounded that arrogance by urging that Iraq become a member of the Chemical Weapons Convention and thus subject to international inspection of its suspected chemical weapons facilities. The United States, he darkly implied, feared that such inspections might undermine the international consensus for invading Iraq.

Bustani's allegations may or may not have been correct. I learned after I resigned that Bustani had fallen foul of John Bolton, the neoconservatives' mole in the State Department. Judging from later press reports about Bolton's unsavory bureaucratic habits, I assume ███████████████████████████████████████████ ███████████████████████████████████████████.

At least one of Bolton's motives was simple and primitive, to remind the world by beating up an insufficiently respectful victim that the U.S. government was still the dominant ape in the jungle.[7]

## *Shadows of War*

When bureaucrats of any single country get together behind closed doors they ritually sneer at foreigners as arrogant, ill-informed, cynical, corrupt, and selfish. This is a solidarity-building exercise, not factual analysis. Foreigners are statistically no dumber or more self-seeking than Americans, and some foreign diplomats are very smart indeed. My colleagues from the Belgian and Dutch embassies wagged their eyebrows at me and smirked with great expressiveness at our monthly gathering of the "Number Two Club" of Athens diplomats, shortly after Bush announced in his 2002 State of the Union address an "axis of evil" linking North Korea, Iran, and Iraq. They were too polite to say openly that if the United States was fantasizing the secular Arab Saddam Hussein making common cause with the Persian Shiite mullahs, then the U.S. government knew not even the most basic facts about the Middle East. I gamely insisted that we understood the Middle East perfectly well and that one should not overanalyze rhetorical flourishes intended for a U.S. domestic audience. I assumed I was telling the truth.

In August 2002, with Cheney's speech to the Veterans of Foreign Wars, I learned to my horror that war with Iraq was on the way. Exhortations to invade Iraq had been a fixture of the pro-Israel ideologues of the American Enterprise Institute (AEI) since the mid-1990s, most notably in the infamous 1996 Project for a New American Century, but President Bush the elder had known better and so had Clinton. Now the rhetoric emanating from the White House parroted that of the AEI. I was appalled. These people clearly had no concept of the world they inhabited.

The world is awash in self-appointed Middle East experts. Four years as a junior officer in Tel Aviv and Casablanca, a few words of Arabic, a few more of Hebrew, and travel in Egypt and Turkey did not qualify me to discuss the intricate details of tribal politics that make a given Middle Eastern country comprehensible. Still, any U.S. diplomat polite enough to chat for a few minutes with Middle Eastern diplomatic colleagues at receptions was keenly aware that U.S. government policies had no credibility with any major Middle Eastern population.

Winning a war against Saddam did not worry me. The Iraqi military was weak and poorly led, and ours was superb. But I did know something about democracy building from Romania and Armenia. Implanting democracy takes more than good intentions and a team of eager young consultants. In countries where America enjoyed some legitimacy as an ally, we could create a set of powerful incentives for democracy, for example, the lure of NATO and EU membership. Then local democratic leaders could use that outside influence to win a decisive domestic political advantage over their oligarchic and military competitors. In remote Iraq, a bitterly divided tribal despotism armed to the teeth, America had no such leaders and no such incentives.

Watching the slaughter in Bosnia in 1992–95, I had come to believe firmly in the need for international humanitarian intervention. My colleagues and I in the Office of Eastern European Affairs at the State Department had been given an award in 1994 for advocating U.S. military intervention in Bosnia. I insisted on one simple condition for that intervention: that the United States could expect to save more lives than it was likely to destroy.

Saddam had slaughtered tens of thousands of his rebellious subjects over the decades without the United States feeling any need to save them. By 2002, however, Iraq was wretched but relatively peaceful. Nothing suggested that Saddam contemplated crimes outrageous enough to outweigh the horrors any war brings. Unlike in Bosnia, where the United States had intervened in an ongoing civil war to protect an already bleeding population from its neighbors, in Iraq U.S. occupation would itself be the trigger for a bloody war of all against all. The presence of foreign troops on Iraqi soil would legitimize the armed zealots. U.S. marines would be haunted by the prospect of gunning down fourteen-year-old children armed with hand grenades.

There remained the national security argument that Saddam and al Qaeda were somehow in league to destroy us. Any hardheaded person who looked at the balance of power in the Middle East knew that whatever suicidal hatred Saddam might harbor toward the United States he kept firmly to himself. His army, destroyed by Desert Storm and thirteen years of draconian UN sanctions, was no longer a threat to U.S. interests, not even Saudi oil. Osama bin Laden and Saddam Hussein were polar opposites ideologically and practically. They neither trusted one another nor had any rational interest in working together. After 9/11 the best either could expect from covert terror cooperation was guaranteed destruction at U.S. hands.

Unless America could make a credible case to the world for that nonexistent Iraqi threat, it would cast itself as the villain in a war of aggression. Plenty of Greeks already saw the United States as evil. Convincing the rest of them, and whole world with them, did not serve American interests. I began to lie awake at night, speculating wildly. Rumsfeld and Cheney (I was underestimating Bush, or perhaps overestimating him), intentionally or not, were giving aid and comfort to America's enemies, pressing for an unnecessary war that would inflame hatred of America around the world.

In September the military mobilization orders for the Persian Gulf began to leak out, confirming the clear message President Bush gave the UN General Assembly on September 12. Military traffic through Souda Bay, already elevated because of operations in Afghanistan, increased dramatically. Nothing in the regular State Department cable traffic, however, gave any indication that Bush and British Prime Minister Tony Blair had already, in April 2002, committed their two countries to military regime change in Iraq.

My embassy colleagues and I did not discuss the coming war, even after it became front-page news in the Greek press in mid-September. It was not a comfortable topic. To criticize the war would directly or indirectly challenge the moral accommodation each of us had made to our profession. I did not trust all my colleagues. Some would see the war as a bureaucratic opportunity. In any case, maintaining a loyal front to my subordinates was my duty. My dissent was personal. They were fine people, and I did not want to disrupt their ability to thrive in the State Department.

In late September, still with only the vaguest instructions from Washington, we began to explain to frantically opposed Greeks why the coming war would be just and necessary. A leading neoconservative showed up at the embassy on October 9, invited by the Public Affairs Section to speak at a Greek political conference. Our cultural officer arranged for me to meet and brief Joshua Muravchik, a resident scholar from AEI, in my office. Intentional rudeness is hard to coax out of a diplomat, but I was rude without being coaxed. After describing Greek outrage about the war, I told him that anyone who believed America could democratize Iraq, Iran, and Syria by force was living in a fantasy world. Outraged by a reporting telegram I had read in September, I charged that Israeli prime minister Ariel Sharon was egging the president on to war. Muravchik smoothly and politely disagreed, but I was shaking when he left. Muravchik was wise enough in his speech to the Greeks to speak in general terms about America's more muscular and unilateral new foreign policy. My Greek contacts shook their heads at what they read elsewhere about the AEI's program of Arab "freedom" at U.S. bayonet point.

On October 10 I drove to the Foreign Ministry with my ambassador to meet Foreign Minister George Papandreou. I was carrying a manila folder with a sealed envelope that held the printout of the Iraqi weapons of mass destruction (WMD) report from the unclassified Central Intelligence Agency (CIA) website, along with a copy of the official British white paper (the "dodgy dossier" cribbed in part from someone's doctoral dissertation). This was all the State Department had given us from the intelligence community in response to our urgent plea for evidence of Iraq's imminent threat to world peace.

Papandreou was an important man for us to convince because on January 1, 2003, Greece would take over the rotating presidency of the EU. Papandreou would then chair the EU foreign policy meetings that shaped Europe's response to our call for war. The ambassador winked as he reminded me not to mention that the CIA report was unclassified. I rolled my eyes. Papandreou was a trusting man, but we could not fool him for very long. At some point Papandreou or his experts would realize that what we had given him to justify the war was crap.

The reports looked solid enough on first glance. They fell apart only when you spent twenty minutes online (and yes, in 2002, thanks to Secretary Powell's overruling of the State Department's computer security zealots, we diplomats could at last search the Internet from our desks!) to read the old published reports of the UN weapons inspectors. Sooner or later the Greeks would probably realize that key U.S. arguments—for example, the thousands of liters of culture medium "unaccounted for"—left out vital facts and dates to make it sound as if drums full of Iraqi anthrax were missing and still dangerous. The inspectors from the UN Special Commission (UNSCOM) had known better.

The language of the secret U.S. National Intelligence Estimate (NIE) of October 2002 confirmed my sense that America had no good reason to go to war. Saddam might or might not have chemical and biological weapons capabilities, but the United States had no credible evidence of these weapons to share with foreigners. The best the CIA could come up with on Iraqi nuclear programs was a statement that, given fissile material by a third party, Iraq could build an atomic bomb "within several months to a year." So could Swarthmore College, my alma mater. And the State Department's own intelligence analysts added footnotes to the NIE distancing themselves even from that meaningless conclusion.

America operates under a solemn treaty commitment to the principles of the UN Charter. To wage war, the United States was compelled under international law to convince the Security Council (UNSC) that Iraq's nuclear capability posed an imminent threat to U.S. security and to world peace. If the NIE was America's best shot at proving even to itself that Saddam was a threat to the world, the world would conclude that no such threat existed. The foreign policy costs of an illegal war would outweigh any conceivable benefits of overthrowing Saddam.

I grasped at straws to persuade myself that the U.S. military mobilization would turn out in the end to have been a brilliant tactical gambit to bring in a new UN inspection regime to defang Iraq conclusively and avoid war. In two or three heated debates with Papandreou's advisers, I used the argument effectively: if Greeks wanted to prevent war, the only tactic that would work was united, unwavering international pressure on Saddam Hussein, pressure that forced him to comply fully with UN inspections.

I relaxed when President Bush bowed to British prime minister Tony Blair's plea and agreed to go to the UNSC. Passed 15 to 0 in November 2002, Resolution 1441 was a brilliant diplomatic compromise between America's determination to go to war and the rest of the world's determination that war should be a last resort. Greeks embraced 1441 with relief. With the UN dagger at his throat, Saddam would agree to turn his country inside out for the inspectors. And indeed he did.

The UN inspections resumed four years after President Clinton had suspended them. Iraq turned over every WMD document it could find, a huge, pathetic pile of documents the previous UNSCOM inspectors had already seen. The United States announced in triumph that this pile was proof of Iraqi bad faith, but no proof of good faith was possible. The inspectors found nothing in any of the places where U.S. intelligence insisted weapons would be found. Their leader, Hans Blix, offered very polite, discreet criticism of the intelligence the United States provided. But Washington does not take criticism well, even from careful Swedes.

Foreign Minister Papandreou was liked well enough that Secretary Powell would take his phone calls. Papandreou's EU presidency role gave him added clout. He started working Greece's contacts with the Arab world, trying to persuade the Arab League to join a delegation to ask Saddam to step down and save his country. Obviously, this was a long shot, given Saddam's brutal history, but

Papandreou telephoned Powell to seek his support. I was prepared for skepticism. I was not prepared for the reporting telegram I read. Powell made clear that the U.S. government would not lift a finger to help Papandreou or the Arab League promote a peaceful exit for Saddam. Only one conclusion was possible. President Bush was interested not in Iraqi regime change per se, but only in regime change by the U.S. military.

It is a bad day when a U.S. diplomat finds himself agreeing with the French. President Jacques Chirac's effort to preserve international legality and the exclusive right of the UNSC to decide peace or war was self-serving and sanctimonious. Nevertheless, both logically and morally, Chirac's position was stronger than ours. Peaceful alternatives had not been given a genuine chance. Going to war without a proven threat to world peace would gravely weaken the UN and the rule of law in general. The military occupation of Iraq, Chirac knew from his own experience in Algeria in the late 1950s, would be a bloody mess.

As Secretary Powell, at British insistence, made his February 2003 pitch for a second UNSC resolution authorizing the war, I prayed that UNSC members like Mexico would stand firm against U.S. pressure. This was fairly likely, since President Bush had destroyed his relationship with Mexican president Vicente Fox during 2002. It looked as if the United States could not put together a working majority in the UNSC. But rooting against your own country's diplomacy is a dangerous form of madness. How could I stay a diplomat?

## Getting Angry

The management style of my new ambassador had raised my hackles. Tom Miller woke up hours before the rest of us, read everything that came from Washington, and used his superior knowledge of Washington's likes and dislikes to keep control of the mission. My comparative advantage at the embassy was as an expert in things Greek. My ambassador knew Greece well enough to consider advice from his subordinates unwelcome interference. Communication between us dwindled.

To be fair, Miller did not need much advice from his subordinates. The mistakes he made that better diplomacy would have prevented were of minor importance to U.S. interests in Greece. His crass pose, a defense mechanism like the Goth outfit of an insecure teen, cost the United States some respect, but plenty of Greek politicians were much crasser than he. His limited linguistic talent was not a real liability. The new generation of Greek leaders all spoke fluent English, and the Greek public was better off not hearing the talking points Washington sent us. My own more diffident and high-flown style was neither a decisive improvement nor something Miller could possibly adopt.

The first year was rocky but survivable. I had worked for difficult bosses before. Normally I would have taken refuge in the thought that my tour in Athens would soon be over, in June 2003. But then the war began to dominate our work and thinking. From the occasional sidelong glance I was fairly sure that Miller also knew the war was a mistake. But he gave no sign of worrying as he delivered our disingenuous talking points on Iraqi weapons programs and links to terrorism. I concluded, watching him, that the only audience that mattered to U.S. Embassy Athens was back in Washington. The bottom was falling out of foreign attitudes to the United States, in Greece and around the world, but that was not a problem we needed to report or try to remedy.

I was demoralized, not by losing arguments over diplomatic tactics but by what those losses seemed to imply for the diplomatic profession generally. Miller was the product of a Washington bureaucratic environment that prized traits I did not have. Maybe he was right, and a busy superpower had no time for diplomatic niceties or the detailed local knowledge that was central to my professional self-esteem. He was certainly correct in recognizing that Greece would not interpose itself, even as EU presidency, between the United States and Iraq. Miller urged a second UNSC resolution to authorize the war but held back from saying that Greece would block use of Souda Bay without it. I quietly edited his telegram to make these conclusions clearer, but no diplomatic skill or local expertise could turn Greece into a decisive argument against U.S. unilateralism.

I realize in retrospect that I let myself be bluffed into believing Miller's was the superpower diplomacy of the future. Self-promoters and "good managers" thrive in the Foreign Service or any organization, but Secretary Powell was not a bully. Plenty of senior State Department officials recognized the ineffectiveness of swagger and arrogance. A good chess player would foresee that the inevitable debacle in Iraq would push the pendulum back toward the diplomats. But it was hard to be a dispassionate analyst. If simply riding out the world's anger was America's diplomatic strategy for the future, my sources of professional pride and happiness had dried up. Speaking to foreigners in their own language was a waste of time because Washington had nothing it wanted to hear from them through me and would offer no valid arguments I could use to convince them.

My ambassador's exalted position protected him from the Greek criticism that mounted higher and higher as the war grew nearer in January 2003. I had no such protection. Greeks were furious about the war. The street demonstrations were getting larger and more vehement. Greeks who had never marched were marching. The swastikas defacing the U.S. flag were no longer the work of a few extremists. Ordinary Greek housewives resented that their comfortable world had become violent and frightening again so suddenly. The ancient, threadbare Greek Communist Party was recruiting young members again. I was bitter that the America I served was becoming odious to Greek friends whose opinions I respected. The Greek media were full of sound and fury, and for the first time in my experience, half of it was accurate.

## *Dysfunction*

I found myself taking Greek anger at the United States personally and became increasingly depressed. Depression is dangerous. It makes us sluggish and vulnerable to bureaucratic predators. I had predators to watch. My deputy, though he yearned for the visible trappings of power, was willing to wait me out decently. His mate was gifted in the office politics that in Greece it is undiplomatic to call "Byzantine." Then there was Diplomatic Security (DS).

DS has an unenviable job, to protect the State Department and its secrets from terrorism and theft. It is less well equipped than the FBI or CIA for rooting out spies or penetrating terrorist cells and no more talented or successful. It tends to focus on tasks that are measurable within the narrow confines of the embassy. One such task is to make certain that classified material is locked away. DS enlists the bored young marines of the Marine Security Guard detachment to search offices after hours and leave an ominous pink slip when classified material is found unsecured.

DS likes tidy desks and tidy minds. My cluttered desk accurately reflected the untidiness of the political universe in which diplomats operate. I was careless enough times over twenty years to accumulate a worse than average number of pink slips. In a locked office on a locked floor of a walled embassy full of armed marines, a Political Section safe left open did little harm. But protecting classified material is a serious obligation, and I did not do enough to seem serious about it.

Repeated security infractions are a source of bargaining chips for DS in its struggle with the political officers who dominate the upper management of the State Department. A history of mishandled classified documents can be used by DS to block promotions or assignments. Our chief security officer in Athens was counting the days to his lucrative postretirement career in corporate security. His deputy belonged to that school in DS that is not overly scrupulous in how it accumulates its bargaining chips.

Late in 2000 unlucky coincidences and devotion to duty caused a newly arrived junior officer to leave a Greek photocopier technician briefly alone in the Political Section suite, an area barred to unescorted foreigners. My concern as her supervisor during the damage assessment interview that followed the incident was to protect a gifted subordinate from any career consequences (and her subsequent career has indeed been brilliant). It never occurred to me that a bigger target was in DS sights. I learned only after the report was filed that I had been secretly written up for negligence. When I appealed, months after the incident, I had no way to prove that DS had submitted a false account of my testimony.

My punishment was a letter in my file that would make me ineligible for promotion for one year. It was too soon to hope for promotion anyway, so I went back to work, angry at the injustice but too busy to brood over it. I would have appealed further if I had realized that the rules had changed. DS had exploited the debacle of a laptop computer, improperly loaded with other agencies' secrets, that had disappeared from the most sensitive area of the State Department building. No one in DS was punished for its part in letting uncleared contractors do the work. Instead, DS persuaded the secretary of state to impose retroactively a point system for punishing everyone else.

Late in 2002 DS pink slips began to sprout around my desk like mushrooms. It did not seem to matter how carefully I scoured my office before I left work each night: the marines found the "SECRET" hard drive of my computer on the floor beside the safe; a memo marked "CONFIDENTIAL" appeared in an unclassified folder in my desk. Almost certainly the lapses were my fault, the result of working too late with too little sleep, but I no longer had absolute faith in the integrity of the system I worked for. I had DS change the combination of my safe. The embassy doctor gave me a free box of the antidepressant Paxil. I carried it around unopened in my briefcase for a month, debating the role of depression in my diplomatic character. I caught bronchitis in early February 2003; this did not help my mood.

## The Final Days

The showdown in the UNSC, Secretary Powell's impressive but misguided effort to make the Iraq War legal through a second resolution authorizing the U.S. invasion, was upon us. Watching Powell as he addressed the UNSC on February 5, I concluded that he believed what he was saying. The evidence he presented, however, was indirect and inconclusive. It would not convince foreign skeptics, certainly not the Muslims we needed to convince, of the purity of our motives for invading Iraq. Powell did not know, as he gave his presentation, that the CIA had already disavowed his key evidence.[8]

On February 6 my certainty that postwar Iraq would be a disaster was briefly shaken. A conflict resolution specialist named David Phillips came through Athens. I had worked before with this articulate scholar-entrepreneur on Track II academic contacts to promote Armenian-Turkish reconciliation. I stopped coughing long enough to have him over for drinks at my apartment with the staff of the Political Section. Phillips told us a remarkable story of the working groups of Iraqi exiles that the State Department had put together to map out the postwar future of Iraq. The compromises Kurds, Sunnis, and Shiites had reached in those meetings were amazing diplomatic accomplishments.[9]

For twenty-four hours, Phillips's beautifully articulate confidence that we had a plan for postwar reconstruction caused me to think that perhaps my government knew what it was doing. Then I got skeptical again. The Iraqi exiles were excellent people, but they could not speak for ordinary Iraqis any more effectively than my Romanian exiles had for ordinary Romanians a decade ago. These deals would not hold up once they returned.

On February 12 a memo arrived from the Bureau of Personnel in Washington to warn me that if any more security infractions occurred my security clearance would be suspended while a review panel in Washington considered my case. I showed it to our local DS chief, along with the pink slip that preceded it by six hours. Bureaucratically, the timing was good. Eager to stay out of the State Department, I had volunteered to go out as the political counselor in Kabul, Afghanistan. The suspension would catch up with me just as I left Athens in July to start ten months of Dari language training. In language school the suspended clearance would not be a problem. I would have to abase myself to a security review board. Given my past record and the shortage of qualified volunteers for the Kabul post, the board would treat me as it had a colleague of mine in a similar predicament. It would chide me, enroll me in a two-day information security refresher course, and send me off to Afghanistan for the redemption I welcomed.

I was too humiliated to think like a good bureaucrat, however.

I went to the ambassador. Miller took my unhappy news calmly. The moment I left, he dictated a memorandum to document for his files that he had counseled me to avoid security infractions. As a dispassionate analyst, I should have admired his instinct for covering his bureaucratic backside. Instead, when I read my copy of the memo the next morning, anger and contempt overflowed in me. It was a salutary feeling.

## *Making the Leap*

Over the long months that I struggled alone with my professional conscience over U.S. policy, I was bleakly aware how limited my influence was. Sitting awake at 4:00 AM with my laptop on my knees, I could never explain why the secretary of state should heed a Dissent Channel message from Athens (see chapter 6 on dissent). My expertise in Greek politics entitled me to assert that the Greek public would be furious if America invaded Iraq without UN approval. So what? The United States could survive perfectly well without the good opinion of the Greeks, an opinion U.S. cold warriors had forfeited three decades ago by embracing an incompetent military dictatorship. The risk of Greek terrorist attacks on U.S. interests was too small to notice. U.S. commercial interests in Greece would suffer modest harm, but our business presence there was tiny anyway. Having just spent more money than they could afford on arms deals, Greeks would have forgotten their anger by the time they were able to buy more fighter aircraft.

The overall national interest argument, blindingly obvious though it seemed to me, was one I had no bureaucratic standing to make. Invading Iraq would reduce rather than increase the safety of the American people. Arab nationalism and Islam guaranteed a destructive backlash to any U.S. attempt at state building. But I was neither an Arab expert nor a democracy expert, simply a foreign policy generalist with some experience of both. Our official experts were silent. The decision for war had been made by the president, and no message I sent to Colin Powell would give him any leverage to get that decision reversed, even if he secretly agreed with me— but he did not.

Anger finally sharpened my wits. I suddenly understood that if a successful career in U.S. diplomacy required me to become like my ambassador, the price of that career was too high. If I resigned as a diplomat, however, I would be free to put to proper use the skills I had learned.

Resignation had never entered my mind before, not once in twenty years of sometimes dissenting views, but the longer I thought, the more compelling the idea seemed. I had been miserable for the past eighteen months because I measured my self-worth only by my career. I was helpless to speak out effectively because I was bound by the rules of a bureaucracy that freely violated its own rules. Diplomacy as we were conducting it now did not serve the interests of the American people. Our efforts simply made it easier for the U.S. president to violate the principles on which America had thrived as a great power. I certainly could not stop the coming war with Iraq. I could, however, marginally increase the political cost the warmongers would pay for the harm they wreaked on America's image and interests. Resigning would transmute my misery into something positive for the world. I would become a champion of the version of U.S. diplomacy I believed in, the kind that has some chance of working.

Outwardly nothing changed with my epiphany. But I suddenly felt happy and confident. A few minutes later I went to a meeting I had scheduled with the chief adviser to the Orthodox archbishop of Athens. In two days, on February 15, 2003, Greeks would join the rest of the world in the largest anti-U.S. demonstration in a generation. My goal in seeing Father Thomas was to improve the odds that the archbishop would not succumb to the temptation of riding this popular wave, as he had ridden others (such as Greek opposition to the 1999 NATO bombing of Serbia) in the past. I had not discussed the meeting with my ambassador. I knew from other contacts that Miller and the archbishop did not have an effective relationship. If he visited or even telephoned, this gesture would become public and seriously counterproductive. Based on a couple of prior conversations at embassy receptions, I trusted Father Thomas to deliver the message accurately and to keep it confidential. But I did not trust my ambassador to delegate the task safely to me if I asked him.

It was odd, ninety minutes after I had decided to resign over Iraq, to be sitting with an Orthodox priest, explaining to him in fervently formal Greek that, by the Church's doctrine of just war, Iraq was a war of necessity, a war of self-defense. But I felt as convincing as I had ever felt in my life. Forgotten bits of classical Greek vocabulary surfaced from undergraduate days to give my argument a veneer of philosophical plausibility. I had come to terms with myself morally. Now I could wield an argument I did not believe, convinced that this meeting would do some good for the U.S. taxpayer and even for the world, by helping keep the Greek Orthodox Church from giving divine sanction to Greece's growing anger at the United States.

Maybe my meeting did some good. In any case it was a prudent and timely gesture of respect for the political power of the Church. The archbishop was careful, and the Church stayed out of the protests. Though individual priests took part, at least as many quietly rejoiced that America would be smiting the infidels.

I was an impeccable diplomat all that day. Invited to lunch by my Turkish embassy counterpart Atilla, I probed him on the problems the war was creating for Turkish domestic politics. He suggested obliquely and diplomatically that Deputy Defense Secretary Paul Wolfowitz had badly bungled his visit to Turkey by ignoring the changes that had taken place since the days when the Turkish military routinely overruled the civilian government. That afternoon I accompanied the ambassador to a meeting with Kostas Karamanlis, then-leader of the official opposition, to talk about the war and the protests. I said nothing to anyone about my decision. At dinner that night I finally told my partner, Regina. She was overjoyed, not that I would be unemployed but that I would now stop gnawing at myself.

Purely by chance I had given myself a week for prudent second thoughts. Desperate to get away, I had volunteered as an Organization for Security and Cooperation in Europe election observer in the Armenian presidential elections. I took the February 14 Armenian Airlines flight to Yerevan. The Armenians seemed caught up in their post-Soviet troubles and almost indifferent to the upcoming war. Their indifference was a relief after Greek anger.

I climbed into a U.S. embassy SUV for the drive south over the snowy passes to the mining region of Kapan. My former political assistant Alla, an Austrian UN contractor, and I went from one poor village to the next, talking to voters, local officials, and the schoolmaster who maintained the brave little local museum. We spent the night of the vote count in a grimy, freezing elementary school on the edge of Kapan, watching the election commission chairman try to obfuscate the unmistakable evidence of vote manipulation. No, I had not been underestimating America's ability to impose the blessings of democracy (see chapter 10).

I flew back to Athens late enough on February 21 that I could collect my mail at the embassy and disappear for the weekend without revealing to anyone my unchanged decision to resign. My second year in Armenia, a geographic bachelor by then, I had spent nights and weekends putting my knowledge of archaeology and Armenian to work on an English-language guidebook. This was my donation to Armenian economic development via the U.S. Embassy Yerevan website. On Saturday I sat at the computer and updated the text with the past week's travels. It was a blissful day of escapism.

On Sunday I composed my letter of resignation. I remembered

the text flowing smoothly and easily from the heart, but Regina re-minded me later how many hours I crouched silent and motionless over my laptop.

On Monday, February 24, I informed Ambassador Miller and my immediate boss Mike, the deputy chief of mission (DCM), of my decision. The ambassador nodded. I would be happier as an aca-demic, he said. The DCM was upset. He had devoted his life to his career and to a wonderful Foreign Service family that seemed in-separable from it. He could not imagine anyone walking away vol-untarily. That afternoon I called my career development officer (CDO) to find out what would happen to me. I was relieved to learn that my pension was not gone completely. In 2017, at age sixty, I would be eligible to collect 38 percent of the salary I was earning in 2002, but half would go to my ex-wife. My CDO e-mailed me the papers to fill out.

I went home that night and reread my letter of resignation, a policy analyst's cold critique of policy. By long tradition that letter is always addressed to the secretary of state, but I remembered then that Secretary Powell was not my only audience. The American pub-lic was struggling from outside to understand whether our slide into war with Iraq would make them safer or not. They would not under-stand the grimy logic of national self-interest unless I used the lan-guage of American character and values. I sat down again to try to put my diplomat's heart into the letter.

On February 25, 2003, I faxed my letter of resignation to the State Department (see appendix A). To make sure that Secretary Powell would read it, I copied it into Dissent Channel format and hit the send button. Now they owed my misery a reply.[10]

My intent had been to empty my embassy apartment, leave quickly, and say nothing until I was free to speak out as a private citizen. Nagging at the back of my mind was the knowledge that efficiency reports were due in mid-April. Promotion in the State Department is an "up-or-out" competition with all other officers of the same rank and specialty. The careers of two officers under me would be in the hands of a promotion panel. My DCM called to ask me to stay and draft their efficiency reports. My official date of resig-nation, we agreed, would be March 7. Until then I would be in limbo, and war was coming.

Limbo is an ugly place. The DCM, trying to persuade me not to resign, had said that no one would know or care if I resigned. After I resigned, I called an old boss, a dissident former ambassador, who offered the same melancholy assessment. In my new bureau-cratic isolation, the suspense was too difficult to bear. I called a friend in New York. At his daughter's bat mitzvah, I had sat next to a charming journalist from the *New York Times* who was now the paper's UN correspondent. I asked my friend to forward her my letter of resignation by e-mail.

I had forgotten how fast the news cycle moves. I hazily imagined I would have a day to prepare. Felicity Barringer's call woke me at 1:30 in the morning, when I was not ready for my moment in the spotlight. My resignation became a few incoherent remarks on page 13 plus the full text of my resignation letter on the *New York Times* website.

It was a well-written letter, and the Internet gave it wings. Within hours the embassy telephone was ringing off the hook with calls from journalists. The DCM had offered me a farewell lunch. He and the public affairs counselor, until that morning a close friend, struggled to remain decent in the teeth of the ambassador's fury at my going public. Inevitably, many of Miller's colleagues would leap to the conclusion that his leadership had prompted my defection. A natural defense would be to tell the world enough to let it conclude I was an embittered loser with delusions of grandeur.

Wiser heads prevailed in Washington, partly because the Privacy Act made it a crime to release information about me without my permission, partly because some senior people in the department thought I was a capable officer, partly because the substance of my letter supported the State Department and its basic policies, and mostly because criticism of my motives would make the media take more interest in my case (compare the storm of the Joe Wilson–Valerie Plame outing a few months later). So the State Department took the high road and made no public comment. I was entitled to my personal views. The White House maintained a disciplined silence, echoed by the true believers who controlled editorial policy at the *Washington Post*. And I was almost unreachable.

I was moved to an empty office outside the classified area. My phone calls were diverted to the Public Affairs Section. To the Athens-based journalists who knew my mobile phone number I explained that I was not in a position to say anything more until my resignation was effective on March 7. So I struggled to write efficiency reports that would help rather than harm my subordinates, cleaned out my office, and carried boxes of books around the corner to a friend's basement.

The night before I flew to New York, as parting gifts, I gave interviews to two Greek journalists I had known and respected for over a decade. Greek papers debated whether I was a token "good American" like the "good Germans" during the Nazi occupation of

Greece during World War II or whether I was another wheel within wheels in a U.S. plot against the planet. Happily, the Greeks reached the conclusion I had hoped for: that Americans of all kinds were exercising their freedom to protest an unnecessary, hence immoral, war.

## Some Afterthoughts

We never know our motives. In practice separating devotion to principle from other considerations is impossible. Working for a different ambassador, I might have kept my faith in American diplomacy and my career. Surrounded by friends and contacts less skeptical of the United States than Greeks are, I might have convinced myself that the damage to U.S. interests from invading Iraq would be less than it was. Had DS been honest, I might have accepted bureaucratic humiliation as deserved. Without some financial cushion, I would have fought harder to protect my livelihood. Circumstances combined to make doing the right thing possible.

My resignation from the State Department made me a hero because the U.S. antiwar camp needed heroes. Americans are remarkably forgiving of the human failings of their heroes—ours is a generation that even requires such failings. But I hoped to reach a few tough-minded conservative internationalists, men with a lifetime of public service who were uneasy with the choices of the younger Bush administration. Former National Security Adviser Brent Scowcroft had already gone public with his doubts about the war, and former Secretary of State James Baker hinted at his own. Because they prize personal loyalty so highly, conservatives would seize on any excuse to reject a messenger whose message was that their loyalty was misplaced. In writing this book, however, I wanted to leave an accurate account of how many stars aligned to make one diplomat act bravely.

## The End

Through two decades of diplomacy, I never forgot my archaeological past. To say farewell to my career, I invited embassy colleagues to join me the Sunday after my resignation at my favorite site, the temple of Nemesis in Rhamnous. The ruins crown an unspoiled green promontory looking out over the straits of Euboia. A comforting number of my colleagues accepted.

Nemesis is the goddess who punishes hubris, the arrogant transgression of the limits set by the gods on human ambition. I poured a plastic cup of red wine from Nemea on the ruins of the altar, a libation on behalf of America. My hope or prayer as a former archaeologist was that prudent respect for Nemesis would keep

America's statues of George Washington and Abraham Lincoln uncracked and out of the mud for a few more centuries.

# 2

# ★ *Understanding Foreign*

# *Nationalism* ★

*With the Hopes that our World is built on they were utterly out of*
*   touch.*
*They denied that the Moon was Stilton; they denied she was even*
*   Dutch.*
*They denied that Wishes were Horses; they denied that a Pig had*
*   Wings.*
*So we worshipped the Gods of the Market Who promised these*
*   beautiful things.*
                    *Rudyard Kipling,* The Gods of the Copybook
                                        Headings

Few diplomats have time to be theoreticians.[1] My career-ending
rebellion as a diplomat derived from the fact that I *knew* in September 2002 that Iraq would be an unprofitable mess for America if it
invaded. I believed, then and now, that accurate predictions about a
given government and people are possible, by analyzing the data
available to diplomats or indeed to anyone with the language skills
and curiosity. The certainty of failure in Iraq derived from Iraqi local politics and universal human nature, but not from any grand theory
of international relations a former classics major could point to.

This Iraq War prediction of mine was realistic in the sense that
it gave some basis for estimating correctly how many body bags the
United States would fill, how many hundreds of billions of dollars it
would spend, and how little Iraqi oil it would be able to export. The
competing version of reality seized upon by President Bush proved
nonsensical by that standard but not by a more self-interested political standard. The neoconservatives who advocated the war, like the
president they egged on, remain unapologetic, influential, and

35

gainfully employed. Their theories still strike a powerful chord because they flatter our narcissism, our faith in America's moral right to dominate the planet.

It seems elementary prudence to study potentially hostile foreigners abroad as carefully as we study our competitors at home. In practice, our leaders' eyes glaze over at the messy details of foreigners' behavior. To grab their attention in the marketplace of ideas, one must articulate a theoretical framework that serves their short-term self-interest while—ideally at least—offering some more humane and inclusive view of America's welfare as well. What follows are some commonsense lessons, mostly obvious since the Iraq debacle, about the relationship between human nature and American power.

Humans claim to be rational animals who make decisions based on predicted costs and benefits to their personal and group welfare. This is an exaggeration, as any real estate agent will confirm. "Legitimacy" is a diplomat's analytical tool for bridging the behavioral gap between us and our less-glib animal colleagues.

### *What Is Legitimacy?*

In the mountains of northern Portugal three friends and I hiked one August afternoon into a custom called in local dialect the Chega de Bois, the showdown of the village bulls. Northern Portugal is poor country. Until recently, mountain villages there could only afford to maintain one bull for shared breeding purposes. Villagers wanted a good one, and so the Chega de Bois began as a crude but entertaining way of choosing breeding stock, by having two bulls compete for dominance. Even in their new, European Union–subsidized prosperity, the mountaineers have not outgrown their fondness for Darwinian spectacle.

We followed behind the local champion, the black bull, as he shambled out of the village toward the Spanish border. He weighed about a ton and had nasty horns, but he let himself be switched along by a couple of boys with sticks. His out-of-town rival, red and eighty kilos heavier, had staked out his prior claim to the walled pasture a few hundred yards outside the village. As the range decreased, both of them sensed that their superpower status was about to be tested. They began to bellow and paw the ground.

When enough spectators had paid their five euros (six dollars), the black bull was let into the pasture. Implacable instinct took over. Red and black lowered their heads and locked horns. For the next twenty minutes the two bulls pushed each other back and forth across the pasture. It was an even match. Black was smaller, but more experienced with his horns and more aggressive. Red was simply determined not to lose. And the stalemate began to look danger-ous. Black was drooling and incontinent. Red was panting uncon-trollably. The flies gathered in swarms like defense contractors, div-ing in to suck blood from the flanks of the exhausted rivals.

Ideally, in the Chega de Bois one bull is smart enough to rec-ognize defeat and take to his heels. But bulls are not bred for brains. In the worst case the two bulls die on the field, an expensive re-minder to their owners that strength and aggression are not a guar-antee of reproductive success.[2] When the deadlock seemed abso-lute, the old rancher stepped forward. With a shout and a wave of his stick he told the two bulls the fight was over. With amazing docil-ity, indeed with obvious relief, they headed off in opposite direc-tions to brush their flies off on the hedge.

The other paying spectators seemed disappointed with the bloodless outcome. But I was relieved by this confirmation that some-thing more powerful than horns and dangling testicles is at work in the world. On the other hand, I had spent twenty years wracking my brains to help the State Department come up with ingenious solu-tions to disputes over territory—Palestine, Western Sahara, Cyprus and the Aegean, Kashmir, Nagorno Karabakh. A simple Portuguese farmer had authority over two warring bulls that the U.S. govern-ment, with all its wealth and power, could not manage to exercise over warring states.

Even in the grip of their most primal and deadly instincts, bulls will submit to outside control that needs be no more lethal than a stick and a shout. Human beings are no less brave and far more dangerous animals than bulls. They too, however, can be herded easily and gratefully, by a police officer with a stick or a priest with a book or a politician in a dark suit. That which makes us herdable is what political scientists call legitimacy.

Humans, like other animals, have various rules of behavior, some genetic and instinctive, some learned and specific to a tribe or individual. Whatever the rules are in any given set of circumstances, and however we come to learn and accept them, a working majority of us are conditioned to feel some dim biochemical pleasure when our rules are unambiguous and we obey them. We feel righteous anger at others who do not. Most Americans stop their cars at stop signs, even when the intersection is empty and no police are near. A stop sign enjoys strong legitimacy in American society. In Mediterra-nean countries a stop sign has more limited legitimacy. It is one factor, like gender, class, and vehicle size, in a permanently renego-tiated contest of dominance and submission between rival drivers.

There may be punishment for violating the stop sign, but there is no reward in obeying it.

Legitimacy is not a value judgment. Saddam Hussein was legitimate to a large number of Iraqis. His most callously self-seeking commands were obeyed willingly and energetically by subordinates, each for his own set of rational and irrational reasons. General Jay Garner and his successors running the U.S. military occupation of Iraq had similar legitimacy with their U.S. subordinates. Moral and rational Iraqis would have done far better to obey Garner than Saddam. They didn't.

Humans killed off their last nonhuman competitors thousands of years ago, and our social evolution since then has been driven by competition against other humans. Were that competition always regulated through violence, humankind would have died out as soon as it began. Violence is too inefficient for everyday use. It uses up too much energy, is unpredictable, and often leaves the survivors too weak to resist disease and predators.

Humans multiplied to overrun the planet through social evolution that rewarded habits of cooperation within an expanding circle of distant kin and finally even strangers. The turning point in human civilization was the development of groups large and cooperative enough to reshape their environment on a large scale, through agriculture, trade, tool use, and the elimination of nearby rivals. Social evolution, in turn, included the evolution of religion, politics, and law as new and powerful sources of legitimacy for collective action toward the common good. Social evolution has not yet made humans dramatically less territorial and tribal than their baboon cousins.

Growing population density and the competition for scarce resources puts internal stress on any political system. Diplomats and politicians discover that collective defense against outside threats remains the most powerful source of legitimacy humans have. There are complex, mostly instinctive rules for identifying insiders and outsiders in any given situation. The rules governing our behavior, the kinds of legitimacy available to us, change radically depending on whether insiders or outsiders are involved.

## Nations and States

Once a week "Kostas" arrived at my friends' restaurant in Athens to pick up his agreed share of the proceeds. In exchange, my friends did not need to worry about mysterious fires or accidental hand grenade detonations. Human beings are prudently resigned to paying protection money to others more violent and disciplined than themselves. Empires cloak their much larger extortions in fine language and sometimes provide useful services beyond mere continued survival: parts of India were better protected against the predations of local rulers under the British than they are now under India's democratic system. Empires, however, create a steady, resented outflow of the subject peoples' wealth. Washington is full of marble monuments paid for by the spoils of America's short-lived geographic empire and ongoing financial empire.

Empires depend on their subjects' willingness to acquiesce to rational economic calculation. Five or ten Athens restaurant owners could easily band together to shut down Kostas's extortion racket, but at least one of them would lose his business or his life before the Greek police renounced their kickbacks and arrested the gang. Then, a new gang would move in, and the same sacrifice would need to be repeated.

The British could never have shipped enough troops to India to hold that enormous country militarily, had India mobilized a unified interest in resisting occupation. The British subverted that unity by offering the rulers of each constituent village or principality compelling benefits of security and stability at a price no higher than previous empires had demanded.

The British Empire was killed off by the triumph of an eighteenth-century fad called nationalism, a set of rhetorical strategies that reshaped the way we identify insiders and outsiders. Once a group can reach a certain size and inculcate in enough of its members the willingness to resist outsiders with irrational persistence and intensity, the protection racket ceases to be a viable economic strategy. Armies are expensive. Mass communications and improved technology make resistance movements larger and deadlier. If even a tiny percentage of the population (e.g., "a few Baathist dead-enders" in Iraq) is willing to die to expel the outsiders, then the cost of keeping an empire mushrooms beyond any hope of offsetting revenue.

Cold economic calculation by former imperial powers, not any improvement in human morality over the past three thousand years, is the reason the UN is now composed of almost two hundred sovereign member states, mostly ex-colonies of vanished empires. Multinational empires, including Russia, China, India, Pakistan, and Indonesia, still exist, but they strenuously insist that they are nations instead. Russia is bleeding itself white in its zeal to prove that Chechnya (if not the Chechens) is an integral part of the Russian nation.

Americans confuse themselves and everyone else by misusing the term "nation." For Americans, "nation" is simply the more sentimental word for "country," which is in turn a less legalistic word for "state." Membership in the American nation is obtained together with the formal legal tie of U.S. citizenship. For Americans, "nation-state" is a harmless redundancy, like "irregardless."

Greeks guard membership in their sacred in-group far more jealously. Their nation is an ethnic group, a people, a community linked by mystical ties of blood-kinship and reinforced by a common language, history, and culture. Members of the Greek nation are spread across the globe. Many of them hold a non-Greek passport and never learn Greek. Citizenship in the Greek state, Hellas, whose capital is Athens, can be acquired by people of any nationality. Only a tiny handful of outsiders are accepted into the Greek nation, by assuming all the trappings of "Hellenism," including language, religion, politics, and worry beads, in an extreme and ostentatious form.

During World War I President Woodrow Wilson helped reinforce the notion that each nation should be institutionalized as a state, with each state living peacefully behind borders recognized and enforced by the whole "international community" of states. This international system would replace once and for all the repressive multiethnic empires whose struggles against national movements and one another had led to World War I.

Nationalism would be a more attractive cure for imperial extortion if human society divided itself naturally into nations. Before the eighteenth century, people shared an identical dialect and set of customs only at the level of a group of villages within a single watershed. Ethnic groups are still as likely to be characterized by the distinctive ecological niches they occupy—Kurdish sheepherders, Korean grocers—as by geographic location. Even the most inbred communities, those set apart by high mountains, wide seas, and deep deserts, are rife with internal divisions when viewed through the diplomatic microscope. Each national state begins its existence as an embattled fiction.

Evolution toward unity as a "nation" is an ongoing process of promoting internal cooperation by channeling competitive violence outward against real or imagined external foes while suppressing internal differences. Successful nationalism sanitizes its history, homogenizes its culture, and purifies its language to create a group whose attachment to a given territory is strengthened by exaggerating the differences with the tribe across the border.

The French "nation-state" was formed by centuries of horrific warfare. Despite two centuries of centralized education and administration, France has not yet fully imposed a single dialect onto linguistic and cultural populations as distinct as Basques and Corsicans, many of whose members are far from reconciled to the submergence of their ethnic identity into the French nation. Superficially greater Greek homogeneity is the result of a massive exchange of Muslim and Christian populations with Turkey in 1923, combined with less systematic assimilation, expulsion, or marginalization of Slavs and other minorities. Greek or any other national uniformity is a patriotic convention, not an objective description.

No state in the world consists of a single ethnic group living within a border that embraces, protects, and satisfies the whole nation. When two nationalisms collide over territory each claims, as France and German repeatedly collided over Alsace-Lorraine, their wars are bloody and inconclusive, and the grudges they leave behind distort the political environment. Civilized and orderly Danes, with a perfectly fine state called Denmark, still pine for the duchy of Schleswig, wrested from them by Germany in 1864. My Hungarian cousins still gaze across the Romanian border at Transylvania, lost through the Treaty of Trianon in 1920. Greeks think wistfully of Constantinople, notional capital of Hellenism, entombed since 1453 somewhere in the Turkish city of Istanbul.

The costs of nation building, both military expenses and foregone economic efficiencies from transnational cooperation, are very high. When nationalism is pushed too far toward its logical conclusions, as Hitler tried, the results are catastrophic. Only a state as wealthy as the United States could sustain its huge military mobilization over decades without direct threats to justify to its citizens the distorted allocation of resources nationalism provokes.

After 1945 the United States and its allies found ways to limit the costs of nationalism by imposing a legalistic, almost religious, respect for the national boundaries that emerged at the end of World War II. The milestones of this process were the creation of the UN, the European Economic Community (now the European Union), and the Helsinki Final Act, which in 1975 traded agreement with the Soviet Union on the existing national borders of Europe for guaranteed rights for minorities stranded on the wrong side of those borders. Less ambitious security arrangements elsewhere in the world helped lock in borders that the international community has allowed to change remarkably little in sixty years.

## Nationalism as Domestic Politics

The advantage practicing diplomats have over their academic rivals is the daily reminder that the bitter 51-to-49 domestic political division in U.S. society in 2004 is replicated in most countries around the world. The competition that absorbs the attention of national leaders is not state-against-state but rather the highly personalized competition for local dominance with their political peers at home.

Only in rare circumstances can a politician be lured into chest-beating displays of dominance against a foreigner. Officially, Greece and Turkey are competitors in the Aegean Sea, but Greek prime minister Kostas Karamanlis treats Turkish prime minister Recep Tayyip Erdogan (at whose daughter's wedding he served as witness) as a colleague. The rivals he must dominate or humiliate are George Papandreou, the leader of the Greek opposition party, the Panhellenic Socialist Movement (PASOK), and a handful of ambitious politicians within his own New Democracy Party. President Bush's chief preoccupation is to dominate his own cabinet and congressional leadership, not President Vladimir Putin or Chairman Hu Jintao.

Governments in a few well-developed states, Singapore perhaps, enjoy a mandate built on proven success in meeting the needs of their people over time. Most states are less fortunate. Humans are little more able than chimpanzees to agree on how well the long-term collective interests of their group are advanced by its leaders. Sociologists inform us gloomily that voters still tend to rely on crude estimates of leadership based on height, facial shape, and perceived self-confidence. A key index of any human leader's legitimacy is his perceived determination to protect and expand the group's territory and keep foreigners from meddling in it.

That is why Greek politicians and journalists routinely become hysterical at real or purported challenges to Greece's territorial integrity. When the U.S. government disrespected Greek sovereignty by mistakenly printing a map that implied that northern Greece was part of the neighboring Republic of Macedonia, the entire Greek political universe swung into frenetic activity, not against the United States but rather against the reigning Greek prime minister. Opposition politicians blasted him in Parliament and on television, seeking to score maximum political points from the politician's prima facie failure to have done his utmost to protect national dignity.

The compensation for this unjust domestic criticism is the ability of leaders to exploit the instinct that in time of crisis drives the members of a herd to form a circle and point their horns outward. Even in the civilized heart of Old Europe, after fifty years of generally successful experiments in transnational cooperation through the EU, anyone who reads a mass-circulation local newspaper will recognize that the easiest way for a politician to weather a challenge to his legitimacy is to create an atmosphere of crisis. Stymied by domestic political opposition in 1991, Greek government politicians rallied the public around an imaginary threat from the fledgling, bankrupt Republic of Macedonia. Chancellor Gerhard Schroeder of Germany regrouped wavering voters in a close-fought election by claiming that he and his party were Germany's best protection against U.S. hegemony. President Bush patched together from shreds of evidence a global terrorist menace and won reelection in 2004 despite mounting public concern over his conduct of the war in Iraq.

## *Looking for Transnational Legitimacy*

Through 230 years of independent political life Americans evolved their own Chega de Bois, a complex and highly competitive electoral system that requires the successful presidential candidate to demonstrate enormous strength of will, persistence, and ability to persuade others to contribute financially to his cause. The winner is rewarded with enormous legitimacy, no matter how small the margin of victory. A large, opinionated, and heavily armed American population willingly follows its elected leaders, obeying most of the laws imposed on it and paying enough taxes to support a huge state mechanism with a bare minimum of coercive violence. But even a democratically elected U.S. president, half-deified by the institutions that surround him, on a continent mercifully remote from deadly threats to U.S. security, still uses nationalism and perceptions of outside threat as a fundamental source of his legitimacy.

Even with its strong, legitimate political system, America recoils from painful decisions like health care reform. One of the most painful decisions a leader can make is to yield any part of the national dignity to an outside power. America routinely requires much weaker and more divided foreign governments to take decisions, such as handing over war criminals to an international tribunal, that the U.S. Congress would reject with horror and contempt as an insult to America's national sovereignty. A key aim of U.S. foreign policy is to reinforce the legitimacy of foreign politicians so that they will be secure enough domestically to ignore the political costs of doing what America demands.

Legitimacy would be a miraculous gift if America had it to bestow. If the president's standing with foreigners was like the rancher's with his bulls, or even his own with the U.S. public, he would wave his stick and shout and the Iraqi government would have sent Saddam Hussein under guard to The Hague for trial with no need for invasion. The Israelis would have heeded the U.S. request not to colonize the West Bank and Gaza, putting a viable Palestinian state within reach and saving billions of dollars. The leaders of India and Pakistan would have gratefully accepted a solution for Kashmir that put the welfare of the people of that unhappy principality ahead of murderous Indian and Pakistani domestic politics. Asia's lust for nuclear weapons would evaporate, and Pakistan would busy itself civilizing its Taliban-infested frontier with Afghanistan by building schools for girls.

Unfortunately, there is no such source of American transnational legitimacy. Each society divides the world into members and outsiders. No society accepts outside sources of legitimacy, even when they are beautiful, democratic ones identical to its own. The processes and characteristics that make the U.S. president legitimate as America's leader make him unacceptable as anyone else's.

### The Smoke-Filled Room

A crucial insight into human nature is that humans evolved to function in small groups, and the small group remains the basic environment in which legitimacy is generated. Groupthink is the basic mode of human thought. Group conformity and loyalty are survival traits of proven utility, when rational calculation is not even something we know how to define. Every human decision of cost and benefit is clouded by the disproportionate weight we give to the likely effect of our behavior on our standing within our group.

The approval of the peer group is a powerful source of legitimacy, not only for five-year-olds about to embark on some ill-advised bonding experience on the playground, but also for balding senior officials sitting around a conference table in the White House or Islamic militants hiding in a bunker in Fallujah. Surrounded by a small group of peers, human beings can find legitimation for behaviors that overrule even the most vital and elementary calculation of self-interest, their own survival.

One way to break the deadlock nationalism imposes on international relations, therefore, is to create scenarios in which small groups of decision makers come together as peers outside their normal circle of yes-men and outside the normal confines of narrow group self-interest. The Camp David Accords in 1978 were a famous example of how the group dynamics of a small team of players can sometimes generate results that no politician could match in his cabinet room back home. Egyptian president Anwar Sadat was later murdered for having struck a deal with Israeli prime minister Menachem Begin, of course, and so later was Israeli prime minister Yitzhak Rabin for a similar breakthrough with the Palestinians at Oslo. It takes a deft and legitimate politician indeed to transform the chemistry of a small group into viable domestic politics.

The EU is the rare example of a peer group that generates transnational legitimacy among its members and particularly among countries that wish to become members. One of its most powerful tools is the European Council, the twice-yearly summit of EU heads of government. Fifteen or (now) twenty-five prime ministers gathered in a room can produce better consensus outcomes than their separate national processes could ever achieve. Locked in a room with scoffing European peers at 2:00 AM, even the most tough-minded national politician will occasionally tiptoe away from the sacred principles of his tribal group. On returning to the national capital, he or she will generally survive the storm. And Europe is richer and more peaceful as a result.

The nation-state may turn out to have been a passing fad, to be replaced by some more efficient and humane way of mobilizing people and their resources around the collective long-term goal of human survival. If so, the change will not be made during this generation, nor will America lead the process. Our own politicians are too insular, too content to make cheap use of Americans' own powerful nationalist instincts. Nor is restored imperialism an option. Americans are correctly skeptical of using military might to maintain an empire, even the benevolent one proposed by imperial dreamers such as Max Boot and Niall Ferguson.[3] The intervention of foreigners in the inner workings of a struggling state hands the most violent faction in that state, Hamas for example, a source of legitimacy—violent resistance to outsiders—more powerful than any its more humane competitors can generate to compete with it. The superpower soon discovers that in resisting such violence it has forfeited any credibility of its aspirations to impose government by the consent of the governed. Benevolent empire becomes a prohibitively expensive exercise in national vanity.

The transnational model of the EU has been successful as a force for democratic state building. Perhaps the EU and the United States can help something similar evolve in Africa, where states composed of multiple, competing tribes otherwise face the dreary prospect of decades of European-style bloodshed to turn them into nations as well. In the short term, however, America has no choice but to recognize the dominance of nationalist reflexes in shaping the domestic politics and thus the international behavior of most of its foreign partners. As it prepares its arsenal of effective diplomatic strategies, the United States must keep the implications of nationalism, others' as well as its own, firmly fixed in mind.

# 3

# ★ *The Sources of U.S. Legitimacy* ★

*When, however, Themistocles gave them to understand that the Athenians had come with two great gods to aid them, Persuasion and Necessity, and that the Andrians must therefore certainly give money, they said in response, "It is then but reasonable that Athens is great and prosperous, being blessed with serviceable gods. As for us Andrians, we are but blessed with a plentiful lack of land, and we have two unserviceable gods who never quit our island but want to dwell there forever, namely Poverty and Help-lessness. Since we are in the hands of these gods, we will give no money; the power of Athens can never be stronger than our in-ability."*

*Herodotus*, Histories, *Book 8.111, tr. Godley*

Nationalism makes the domestic politics of foreign states a difficult environment for the exercise of U.S. power. This is hardly a confession of helplessness. A 1996 Greek-Turkish episode in the Aegean is one of countless examples of how a reasonably benevolent superpower has helped two governments find a way for the interests of their citizens to prevail over the cruel logic of domestic politics.

Sensible politicians know that war will bankrupt their country, even if they win. Occupied territory has little value in the international economy, even for states so far from a CNN satellite uplink that they are allowed to keep their winnings. Greedy officers extort a percentage from the plundered television sets, carpets, and window frames carried home by their soldiers. Otherwise, the profits of war boil down to revenue for defense contractors and military glory for generals, who then become rivals to the politicians who made their glory possible.

The trigger for conflict between Greece and Turkey was two rocky islets the size of a few football fields that protruded from the

47

Aegean Sea between the Greek island of Kalymnos and the Turkish mainland. In the spring the rocks sprouted enough grass to support a small herd of goats, allegedly kept there by a Greek shepherd when the sea was calm enough. Greece claimed Imia, or Kardak, as the Turks called it, on the basis of a 1932 joint protocol with Italy, then a colonial power, that Turkey had initialed but never ratified. Turkey insisted that no valid international agreement had ever ceded Turkey's ownership of the islets. Therefore, Turkey claimed, it owned Kardak unless and until the International Court of Justice at The Hague ruled otherwise.

In January 1996 Kostas Simitis, a wizened, warty economics professor nicknamed "the Chinaman," took over as prime minister of Greece when the more charismatic Andreas Papandreou resigned because of his failing health. Simitis had an accountant's eye for Greece's national interests. The prospect of locking horns with neighboring Turkey, which had five times Greece's population and a substantially larger military, inspired in him no martial enthusiasm.

Taking advantage of the power vacuum caused by Papandreou's resignation, politically ambitious Greek and Turkish local mayors engaged in an impromptu contest of flag-raising on Imia, each bringing journalists to record the event. The respective coast guards came out, backed by the respective navies. A Greek helicopter crashed and three men died. Greek pilots caressed their firing buttons, ready to launch antiship missiles into the Turkish fleet. Turkish fingers twitched reciprocally.

War would have been idiotic, but the logic of nationalism is implacable. To safeguard itself from predators the nation must demonstrate that it will go to war for even the most worthless square centimeter of the sacred soil. Both the Greek and Turkish prime ministers were new and untested, with poor nationalist credentials. Their rivals, some in the opposition but many in Simitis's own party, were poised to pounce. By yielding to common sense and pulling the Greek military back from the island, Simitis would prove himself unfit to lead the nation. But by accepting war, Simitis would wrap himself in the legitimacy that makes the leader of a national struggle politically untouchable—until his country is humiliated.

Simitis was a patriot, looking for a sensible way out for his country as well as himself. At times like this diplomacy comes into its own. The UN secretary general could have intervened, but the United States had a louder shout and a faster stick. Greeks and Turks accepted President Clinton as the legitimate leader of a North Atlantic Treaty Organization (NATO) alliance both countries saw as vital to their security. With a series of phone calls to Prime Minister Simitis and Turkish Prime Minister Tansu Ciller, Clinton and his aides brokered an agreement by which both sides withdrew their military forces in the interests of NATO solidarity, rather than by the unacceptable demand of either side. Both sides pledged to preserve the previous status quo in the Aegean. Neither side made any concession except to common sense, and both could claim to have preserved their country's sacred dignity and national interests.

Simitis then made a political mistake by publicly thanking the United States and President Clinton for their assistance. Nationalists considered this an insult to Greek sovereignty—the United States should have thanked Simitis instead, for his superhuman restraint in the face of Turkish provocation—and he was slammed by all parties in Parliament. It took a year for Simitis to earn enough political legitimacy to be able to head off future manufactured crises before they developed. He did it the democratic way, by winning an election and by convincing skeptical Greeks that his careful management of the Greek economy served their rational self-interest.

Just like the rancher with his exhausted bulls in chapter 2, the United States can be quite persuasive when it asks countries to do things that are clearly in their own interests. That clarity about the national interest is hard to find in practice. Information about short-term domestic political costs and benefits was screaming at Simitis from the front page of every Greek newspaper, but reliable military assessments are impossible to achieve. Greek military officers swore to their political leadership that they could bloody Turkey's nose and demonstrate Greek dominance of the Aegean without full-scale war. Turks presumably claimed the opposite. Part of America's diplomatic effort was to remind each side not to underestimate the other's military capabilities. Good diplomacy finds a compelling excuse not to put competing versions of reality to the test.

### *The Art of Friendship*

Humans believe in leadership and leaders. They also believe in character and personal relationships. There is thus one small but useful way that a U.S. president's legitimacy can translate into power to affect foreign domestic politics: the art of friendship. A politician who obeys the dictates of a hostile superpower is toast. A politician involved in a reciprocal friendship perceived by his own population as genuine can offer generous gestures to a superpower president and be praised for it.

One of the arts of diplomacy is creating the conditions in which useful friendships can spring up rapidly between two large egos with no common language but the shared experience of power. For diplomatic friendships to have any legitimizing effect, however, they cannot be instant. The U.S. president must be seen publicly to have invested time and commitment in a relationship. When he does so, a gesture by his foreign counterpart will be read not as capitulation but as a brave diplomatic act of faith. This was one of the advantages of President Bush's second term: he had a second opportunity to build credible personal friendships with foreign counterparts he neglected during his first four years in office.

## *The Limits of Violence*

Patience is a virtue, but all of us prefer strategies that do not require it. In the run-up to the Iraq War, the neoconservatives failed to recognize how little legitimacy America wielded outside its borders because legitimacy for them was not an issue. They pointed to World War II and the postwar transformation of Japan and Germany as examples of how overwhelming U.S. military power gave the United States the legitimacy it needed with outsiders to reshape the world in its own interests. Fear of death—"shock and awe"—would generate the legitimacy to govern Iraq in accordance with American priorities.

In Iraq, this notion of U.S. legitimacy through violence was an immediate failure. The United States could install a government, but it could not make ordinary Iraqis feel virtuous or secure in obeying its orders. Where the occupying authorities succeeded in persuading Iraqis to promote a shared democratic agenda, it was not through any legitimacy created by overwhelming violence, such as by destroying the city of Fallujah, but rather through preexisting sources of local legitimacy, such as religion, tribal authority, and Kurdish nationalism.

President Bush learned his conservative strategy for success in Washington by watching the struggle for dominance in a Texas schoolyard. Bullying someone weak and helpless indeed sends a clear, convincing message of dominance—to peers in one's own schoolyard. But pounding some weakling in the schoolyard down the road sends a much less useful message. Indeed, that schoolyard's resident bullies, though they happily pound their own weakling, are honor-bound to preserve their dominance hierarchy by rallying to his defense against an outsider.

A close look at World War II, the neoconservatives' guiding memory, confirms that successful violence is valid primarily as a source of legitimacy at home. The deadliness of the two atomic bombs dropped on Japan was different in kind but not in degree from that of previous air raids, which had only hardened the Japanese sense of moral superiority over the Western barbarians. The bombs' decisive effect was instead on American politics. President Harry Truman had lacked the political stature to overrule the late President Franklin Roosevelt's popular slogan of unconditional surrender. The horror of Hiroshima and Nagasaki gave Truman the legitimacy on the home front to redefine American views of unconditional surrender in terms the defeated Japanese could at last accept. The emperor could stay on his throne. America's ability to enlist the legitimacy of an existing emperor and government, not "shock and awe" or General Douglas MacArthur's bureaucratic genius, allowed the bloodless, highly successful, U.S.-led transformation of Japanese society.[1]

War is at the best of times an ugly last resort. Under the threat of violence, foreigners can make concessions that become politically impossible once violence actually begins. But threats are difficult to calibrate. A state that cannot defend its territory from outsiders loses its legitimacy. A typical response to the threat of overwhelming force is simply to go limp. As failed states like Haiti and Iraq illustrate, the legitimacy vacuum will be filled by the successful violence of local thugs, not international peacekeepers. This collapse into anarchy and looting does not serve U.S. interests. Failed states lead to starvation, environmental destruction, rampant disease, crime, and mass migration. All these one day wash up on America's shores.[2]

Foreigners will actively and competently carry out what Americans ask without a threat of violence to back up the request, once the United States finds a way to make that request legitimate in the foreign country's own national terms. The term coined by international relations scholar Joseph Nye to apply to legitimacy in international relations is "soft power."[3] America indeed has soft power, the ability to use its image and values to convince others that its requests and even demands must be respected. It often, however, confuses soft power with its ideological fad of the moment, or else with self-congratulatory moralizing. This is a deadly error.

## *The Limits of Ideology*

The neoconservatives distort the history of the Cold War to exaggerate American predominance in the battle of ideas. Misrepresenting the Cold War as the victory of one people mobilized by democracy over another mobilized by totalitarianism, they conclude that Ronald Reagan's stirring appeals to mankind's shared love of liberty gave America the legitimacy it needed to win the Cold War. According to American ideologues, this same American ideology of liberty provides whatever soft power the United States needs to overcome the nationalist paranoia of smaller states and persuade them to follow America's lead.

Dividing the world into people who love freedom and those who hate it is easy if you have never dealt personally with the scarred victims of such fictions. From my archaeology days, I knew Greek villagers whose relatives had been denounced as communists and executed by the Nazis or denounced as German collaborators and executed by the Resistance, in furtherance of village feuds that long predated World War II. Then I had the educational experience of dealing with Romanians as the desk officer at the State Department from 1992 to 1994, two years after the December 1989 ouster and execution of Nicolae Ceausescu and his repellent wife Elena.

Sandwiched between the Russian, Ottoman, and Austro-Hungarian empires, the Romanians have seldom had the luxury of being straightforward in expressing their opinions to powerful strangers. "Kiss the hand you cannot bite" is a rueful bit of Romanian folk wisdom. Ceausescu kissed a lot of hands abroad so that he could bite hands at home. He ingratiated himself with Moscow by keeping Romania a docile, single-party state in Russia's economic orbit and with Washington by breaking ranks with the Russians on foreign policy issues of secondary importance. He was left free to fund his nationalist megalomania by exporting for hard currency almost everything Romania had worth selling, including some three hundred thousand Romanian Jews and the trapeze artists at the Romanian State Circus. Romania finally became democratic *not* because President Reagan or Pope John Paul II had made a detectable effort to overthrow Ceausescu.

Every Romanian in Romania was a loyal communist, apart from a handful of dissidents preserved to trot out for visiting U.S. congressmen. But late in 1989 Mikhail Gorbachev signaled that the Red Army would not intervene in the domestic political decisions of Russia's Warsaw Pact allies. Overnight, a huge crowd of freedom lovers filled the square, and the Ceausescus were decamping. Vicious gun battles flared around the state television building. Neither then nor afterward did the opponents of Ceausescu have any idea at whom they were firing. Because no one was a communist. They had evaporated like the dew on the grass. What they left behind was Romanian nationalism, reawakened religious sentiment, and the desire to feed their families. Those ideas are indeed powerful.

For Romanians, I soon discovered, liberty first meant liberty from Russian domination, a goal shared by essentially the whole population. Next, liberty meant deliverance from a crass dictator tainted by foreign support and unable to maintain the population's basic standard of living. Third, it meant keeping a close national eye on Romania's Hungarian and German minorities. Other meanings of "liberty" could be introduced but only by finding and rewarding Romanian politicians and intellectuals willing to promote them.

Looked at from the viewpoint of most of the protagonists, Cold War conflicts were brutal civil wars. Abstract ideology played little role in moderating each state's cruelty. Predictably, neither capitalism nor communism had a clear advantage in winning hearts and minds. Instead, the domestic faction that most successfully identified itself with the forces of nationalism prevailed, while the side that was most tainted by association with alien intervention lost. "We" won in Greece in 1949 and Afghanistan in 1989, but "they" won in Vietnam. In Korea, where both sides depended on massive intervention by outsiders of roughly equivalent legitimacy to the locals,[4] the result was stalemate and partition.

The most measurable role ideology plays is in relabeling pre-existing feuds in terms that entice outside support. Both the United States and the USSR systematically exaggerated to their own populations for domestic political purposes the role of ideology among their Cold War proxies. Shared devotion to liberty, like socialist solidarity with the struggling workers and peasants, masked unappealing alien nationalisms, heroized unlikely allies, demonized their all-too-similar opponents, and created the illusion of shared vital interests that justified sending soldiers to fight and die far from home.

When the Soviet empire collapsed, democracy and the free market became Romania's ticket to joining NATO and the European Union (EU) and hence to ensuring national security and individual prosperity. Every Romanian, from President Ion Iliescu down, would bend over backward to win America's pledge that the Russians would never return and that Romanians could hope to live decently some day as part of Western Europe. And those narrower, more selfish, completely natural motives were perfectly sufficient, because of the democratic rules that NATO and the EU imposed, to drive Romania's successful transition to democracy.

Over a twenty-year diplomatic career, I encountered a handful of Greeks, Armenians, Romanians, Indians, and Americans who put abstract ideas like liberty, justice, honor, reason, or God ahead of the ordinary social virtues of conformity and reciprocity. Such idealism makes it possible to justify fraud and murder when ordinary social instincts do not. Still, none of them managed to recruit more than a handful of followers willing to murder on their behalf. For the rest of us, group loyalty and conformity feel instinctively right and offer compelling benefits. The commitment to ideology or religion professed as part of social solidarity does not include the promise to kill and die for an idea.

Americans have recently embraced an exaggerated fear of the power of Islam. In the hierarchy of values determining who will fight steadily and effectively alongside whom against what opposition, local nationalism and resistance to outsiders trumps the call of ideology or religion. Iranian mullahs were distressed to discover in the years following 1979 that, despite centuries-old religious ties, they could not export their uniquely Persian Islamic revolution. Arab Iraqi Shiites fought loyally for the Sunni-dominated Iraqi army of the hated Saddam Hussein and died in the hundreds of thousands in an unjust war against ethnic Persian fellow Shiites in Iran. Col. Muammar al Qaddafi of Libya sent millions of free copies of his little green book around the world. I was in Morocco, watching carefully. Qaddafi recruited an insignificant number of followers outside Libya, and he had to pay them for their trouble.

It is a remarkable tribute to America's Founding Fathers how many foreigners have embraced their stirring ideals of civic responsibility and checks and balances. To most people, however, most of the time—in the 1821 Greek War of Independence, as in the U.S. War of Independence—the complex web of values and rights philosophers lump together as "liberty" is brutally simplified to mean freedom from domination by outsiders. As long as the United States is perceived as the world's dominant predator, America's war cry of liberty is almost worthless for persuading foreigners of the benevolence and sincerity of U.S. intentions.

"Democracy" is a more effective battle cry, at least with foreigners who have practical, personal reasons to share America's goal of overthrowing a government in power. To a depressingly large number of ambitious foreigners, "democracy" means merely "regime change." Once the tyrant (and tyranny, like beauty, is sometimes in the eye of the beholder) is overthrown, democracy's local meaning will be renegotiated in ways outsiders cannot control.

Even the persuasiveness of America's virtuous rallying cry of "human rights" needs to be weighed within its local context. As a human rights officer in Greece I learned through repeated mutual misunderstandings that nationalism inoculates its adherents against most outside moral pressure. The main Greek human rights organizations in 1988 were in the business of protecting Greeks, not human rights. Those rights applied to Greek irredentists in Albania but not their Albanian counterparts in Greece. Only after Greek nationalism softened under the benign influence of the EU did activists begin to find local sympathy when they applied human rights principles to Greece's minority populations.[5]

## *The Limits of Justice*

In two decades as a diplomat I never met a politician I could write off as "evil" or "a madman" as a legitimate excuse for my inability to understand his behavior. I met nationalist zealots who had led wars, orchestrated ethnic cleansings, and supervised secret police, who in turn tortured some unknown number of people to death. I met colorless bureaucrats in gray suits to match their gray personalities. I met idealists who had spent years in jail for political views that in some cases almost merited jail. But successful politicians have the ability to cater to moral and social sensibilities. They have decent handshakes and a sense of humor. They prove their sanity by being able to tell plausible half-truths that put their calculations of political self-interest in terms an American might find morally palatable. They all claim truth and righteousness as a source of their political legitimacy. They all are on the side of justice.

By happy coincidence, America is also on the side of justice. Dick Cheney, that most inscrutable and frightening of American vice presidents, believes in democracy and tolerance and justice so long as they do not conflict with U.S. security and the private pursuit of wealth. But does this brotherhood of virtue help us persuade foreigners that it is fitting and proper to cooperate with us? It ought to, of course. Alas, the cognitive process by which justice and injustice are calculated is a product of the same social evolution that produces nationalism.

A formative moment in my diplomatic understanding was the morning back in 1990 or 1991 when a very senior professional diplomat of the Greek Foreign Ministry told me sternly that adherents of the Macedonian Orthodox Church (Greece's neighbors across the border) were schismatics and that it was therefore a sin even to talk to them. He was not joking.

The universal God of Christians, Muslims, and Jews is for foreign policy purposes a narrowly tribal god of Southern Baptist farmers or Serbian Orthodox dentists or Saudi Wahhabi policemen or militant Jewish settlers from Brooklyn. A few enlightened philosophers and liberal theologians in every society will insist otherwise, as will any competent diplomat, but the understanding of ordinary Iraqis and Americans is that God speaks their language, shares their prejudices, and will smile on them if they destroy the Amalekites "root and branch." America's moral or godly course of action will not automatically be recognized as such by foreigners. On the contrary, any proud nation has the patriotic duty to scoff at America's superior access to divine truth, just as Americans scoff at the French for their pretension to superior culture.

Some gestures, however, are so unambiguously decent that they penetrate our nationalist filters. Altruism and self-sacrifice command such deep and universal respect that they must have been wired into our brains very early in our evolution. When Greeks instantly sent rescue teams to Turkey after a catastrophic 1999 earthquake and Turkey then responded in kind when an earthquake shook Athens soon afterward, the political impact was disproportionately positive. A remarkable number of ordinary people are hungry for proof of their moral intuition that their neighbors are not the savages advertised by nationalist politicians. American tsunami relief to Indonesia had a similar impact there on perceptions of the United States. Altruism is thus a fundamental legitimizing source for American or any other leadership.

### Brotherhood in Arms

America is still the beneficiary of a source of international legitimacy powerful enough, when the government looks after it, to compensate for all the frictions U.S. power generates. The United States is brother in arms with national armies all around the world.

Humans bristle at the presence of armed strangers—with their alien gods and suspect sexual appetites—on the sacred soil of their country. America has military installations in at least forty countries around the world and uniformed military personnel in many others. The U.S. military tries hard to be a good and unobtrusive neighbor. Still, U.S. soldiers are supposed to look frightening, and they do. A girl is raped on Okinawa. A skylarking U.S. jet cuts a cable car line in Italy, and nineteen people die. The brilliant Greek populist prime minister Andreas Papandreou won thunderous applause at every campaign rally by promising to evict the four U.S. military bases in Greece, but the bases stayed and his voters did not punish him. Shared military mobilization against a common threat exploits the nationalist instinct that would otherwise make us unwelcome.

During the Cold War, German fear of the Soviet Union made American soldiers and nuclear weapon delivery vehicles welcome on German soil. Saudi fear of Saddam Hussein made our military presence in Saudi Arabia tolerable. Uncertainty about North Korea makes South Korea happy to host a large U.S. presence. Americans are loved as liberators in Kuwait and Kosovo. And fighting shoulder to shoulder with the British army gives the U.S.-UK "special relationship" enough warmth to allow Prime Minister Blair to do the

United States favors that would ordinarily outrage his prickly nationalist electorate.

Greeks would embrace any number of U.S. bases if Turkey were the threat those bases countered. Pakistanis would tolerate a U.S. military presence to fight al Qaeda on its soil if America took its side against India. But as a superpower with important interests on both sides of any international conflict, the U.S. government cannot afford to indulge the Pentagon's appetite for overseas real estate when taking sides with one partner against another is the price demanded.[6] Fortunately, few foreign governments insist that America be "either with us or against us."

One of the key goals of U.S. diplomacy is to find affordable ways to persuade our foreign partners to adopt a threat perception that legitimizes America's privileged role in the world. Robert Kagan's valuable book *Of Paradise and Power* conveys how contemptuous U.S. officials and scholars are of their European counterparts' perception of a low-threat environment. Americans are from Mars, and Europeans are from Venus. Every senior U.S. official who comes to NATO finds his European partners are talking about a different planet from his own.

Factually the Europeans have it right and Americans have it wrong. From a military point of view, most of planet Earth resembles peaceful Venus more than belligerent Mars. The Soviets are gone, and the Russian military is a hollow shell ringed with empty vodka bottles. Even Greece's national shadowboxing with itself over Turkey has yielded since 1999 to cooperation on Turkish EU membership. No country but the United States retains the force structure and huge logistical capacity to undertake the conquest of any developed-world country, and no one feels the lack.

America's continued dominance in NATO is legitimized by history but not by any immediate threat. "The global war on terror" against a secret army of Islamist terrorists armed by a suicidal nuclear Iran or North Korea is a scenario that serves a number of U.S. domestic bureaucratic and political interests. It is less effective at promoting U.S. brotherhood in arms with foreign partners. This is a problem for a U.S. military that instinctively seeks to hold onto every base and privilege foreigners have ever granted it.

The Islamic terrorist threat does not legitimize the U.S. military partly because many foreign partners believe current U.S. policies heighten the threat rather than reduce it. More problematic for American security purposes, terrorism is not a threat that America's overseas military presence deters, nor are U.S. tanks and missiles required to fight it. The European members of NATO have embraced the small number of military roles that reduce even fractionally the likelihood of successful terrorist attacks. Our allies accept broader roles, such as helping secure reconstruction efforts in Afghanistan, only when convinced that they are making a practical contribution to the agreed defensive purposes of NATO rather than simply supporting the domestic political agenda of an unpopular U.S. president.

For the moment, inertia and economic self-interest substitute for the absence of common threat perceptions to legitimize the U.S. military presence overseas. Reenlisting the European members of NATO for more muscular tasks than hospitality and light peacekeeping, however, requires rebuilding a frayed brotherhood in arms around some shared legitimizing crisis, preferably not a crisis of America's own making.

## *The Legitimacy of International Law and the United Nations*

The diplomat-scholar E. H. Carr brilliantly dissected international law and treaties from a weary realist perspective back in 1939.[7] He noticed that states bind themselves by treaties only when they wish to bind a dangerous rival as well. When the international balance of power changes in their favor, they violate treaties or redefine them. When the balance shifts against them, they insist desperately on the sanctity of treaties as an instrument for preserving the status quo.

America's unilateral sources of international legitimacy, its military alliances, are fully adequate to protect Americans against the tiny conventional threats we currently face. They are painfully inadequate to update in America's interests, particularly its economic interests, the rules of a weak and flawed international system full of prickly, competitive not-quite nation-states. Are there multilateral alternatives? Is international law a source of legitimacy that will help foreign politicians do what America wants and survive politically? The answer is yes, usually, but at the price of binding the United States by the same legal and institutional constraints it imposes on others.

Carr's cynicism was made credible by the failure of the League of Nations and by Hitler's success in unilaterally rectifying the injustices of the Versailles Treaty. Notwithstanding these ugly precedents, the Bush administration set about abrogating or ignoring treaties that constrained U.S. behavior—the Anti-Ballistic Missile Treaty, the Comprehensive Test Ban Treaty, the Geneva Conventions, the Kyoto Protocol, and the International Criminal Court. Only on the economic front was the Bush administration willing to uphold its international commitments—and only where the risk of retaliation by trading partners was immediate and credible.

The problem with denying the application of international law to the United States is it makes international law less compelling as a political excuse for foreigners to behave decently. The United States does not have to depend on the Geneva Conventions to protect captured U.S. service members. It can threaten massive military retaliation and often that threat will succeed. By doing so, however, the United States incurs substantial foreign policy costs. Appealing to the Geneva Conventions, by contrast, is free and even admirable, provided America pays the negligible extra cost of having to abide by them itself.

Today, the world's main source of transnational legitimacy is the UN, a large, unwieldy, inconsistent body that Americans are taught by their nationalist politicians to despise. At any given moment, a tiny but well-publicized percentage of poorly supervised UN officials are gossiping over coffee, groping their subordinates, procuring underage prostitutes, diverting funds, committing espionage, parking illegally in fire lanes, or drafting speeches grossly inimical to U.S. national interests. We should remember, however, that a roughly proportionate number of U.S. officials is doing the same.

A much larger UN group, less well publicized, is inoculating children against deadly diseases, feeding starving refugees, intervening between two groups of heavily armed Sudanese tribesmen, shaming governments into cleaning up cross-border pollution, or policing the Nuclear Nonproliferation Treaty's ban on producing nuclear weapons. The largest group, thousands of mild-mannered bureaucrats, is condemned by the internal politics of 191 member governments, often led by the United States, to move paper from one pile to another as a substitute for bold initiatives to promote the peace and prosperity of the planet.

UN employees perform many necessary and praiseworthy tasks around the world, tasks the U.S. government has no desire or standing to perform itself. It was not for that reason, however, that the United States created the UN during World War II. Even if the UN stopped performing those good tasks and was ten times more corrupt than America believes, its existence would still be justified by U.S. national interests. America is indebted to the UN as the one institution that can legitimize American leadership in policing the planet.

The UN has no standing army, no fleet of mysterious black helicopters, not even its own transport aircraft to deliver tsunami relief. For most practical purposes, the UN is simply a coordinating mechanism for international cooperation and a loose set of rules governing international behavior. Those rules are enforced by a small group of member states, frequently led by the United States, operating under a UN flag and a protective UN aura.

The virtue of the UN is that it can speak to an unruly member state as an elite club of which that state is a member and beneficiary, enforcing a set of rules to which that state has formally and legally agreed. When the UN speaks, a politician who obeys can shield himself from domestic criticism by pointing to international and domestic law to legitimize his obedience. Normally the UN's voice will harmonize closely with America's. When the United States alone does the talking, it offers less political cover to the foreign politician who listens. The UN is never as large a fig leaf as a prudent politician would like, but American unilateralism is heroic nudity by comparison.

If the domestic political balance between peace and war is close enough, as it often is, the UN's tiny bit of extra legitimacy can tip the balance in favor of peace. When it fails, the UN provides a huge pool of peacekeepers, almost none of them American. In 2005 UN peacekeeping missions kept combatants apart in sixteen countries, some of them tropical hellholes like Liberia, where tough, well-trained American marines lasted only a few weeks before malaria drove them back onto their ships. Troops donated by Norway and Sweden or rented from Bangladesh and Fiji are far cheaper to field than America's own. Many countries believe strongly enough in the UN that they provide troops without a whimper, while donating them to an American "coalition of the willing" would cause massive domestic protests. The UN blue helmet makes its wearer's presence on foreign soil less illegitimate and thus a marginally less valid target for local resentment than Americans in green helmets.

The voice of the UN, even the voice of the Security Council (UNSC), is of course not always obeyed. Israel, for example, disregards UNSC resolutions. Its politicians claim that the UN is biased in favor of the Palestinians and ignores Israel's inalienable right to self-defense. For domestic political purposes, America agrees. Despite UNSC demands, Armenia has never given back the territory it seized from Azerbaijan. Both these countries can count on U.S. and Russian benign neglect or better. But no country ignores the UN when the United States throws its weight behind a resolution. Massive diplomatic battles are fought to soften the wording of those resolutions because the states involved see their success or failure in the UNSC as reflecting the real international odds for or against them.

After his military defeat in the Gulf War in 1991, Saddam Hussein complied grudgingly with the UNSC resolutions passed against Iraq, including (to the CIA's subsequent embarrassment) on weapons of mass destruction. He thus allowed American, British, and Russian inspectors to climb all over his country and poke into his most secret installations. This national humiliation was tolerable to Iraqis, barely, as long as the UN fig leaf covered the brute force behind it. Saddam made a point, however, of proving to his own people that he respected only the UN, not the threat of force. The U.S.-British no-fly zone to protect the Kurds was a unilateral extension of UNSC resolutions, not formally enshrined in international law. Saddam's air defense commanders routinely offered suicidal challenges to U.S. Navy fliers because Iraqi nationalism required a response to unilateral aggression. The United States portrayed those gestures as a challenge to the authority of the UN, but Iraqis saw them otherwise.

Americans moan about paying UN dues that fall well short of the U.S. share of the world's resource consumption. For fiscal year 2006, the U.S. government budgeted just under $2 billion dollars for UN dues and peacekeeping assessments, including a major new peacekeeping operation the American public wanted to see in Darfur. This amount is trivial given the right it buys American officials and select foreign partners to intervene collectively in the public health of the planet. The U.S. taxpayer sacrifices twice that amount every year to support the lifestyle of twenty-five thousand U.S. cotton farmers and vastly more on intelligence gathering that often proves, as in the case of the Iraqi nuclear program, significantly less accurate than the publicly available reports of UN bureaucrats.

The price of UN membership ordinary Americans seem to resent most is an affordable and necessary one: the criticism of its behavior America hears in the General Assembly and some of the specialized committees. The General Assembly gives every state in the world the right to make speeches no one will listen to and vote for resolutions no one will implement. America buys the necessary cooperation of small countries by giving their leaders a token fifteen minutes on the world stage and by giving their senior bureaucrats and politicians or their spouses a well-paid UN job in New York. If the small nations of the world did not have a guaranteed seat and voice, a guaranteed right to prove their sovereignty by trash-talking the superpower, the UN would lose the precious domestic constituencies that make its universality possible. Without universality, the UN could not serve U.S. national interests.

The nontrivial price America pays for the blessings of UN

legitimacy is giving up some of its freedom of action on foreign affairs to the UNSC and the UN Charter. Some worthy initiatives of importance to the United States have died or been emasculated because each of the UNSC Permanent Five—China, France, Russia, the United Kingdom, and the United States—has the right to veto any resolution. The United States vetoes far more resolutions, mostly regarding Israel, than anyone else, but a significant number die before a vote is taken because China and Russia do not believe the UN should meddle in the internal affairs of any but the most bloodily dysfunctional dictatorships. The United States can and does go it alone when the UNSC cannot be convinced, but exercising that freedom is expensive.

When the United States invaded Iraq, the world's anger focused not on Saddam's guilt or innocence but on the U.S. assertion that its military power was subject to no outside law or institution. This assertion weakened the UN, marginally destabilized the planet, and caused additional foreigners to hate or fear America. Every time the United States undermines the UN, it loses a little more access to the legitimacy a strong UN could give it when it needs it, such as when the UN made Desert Storm legitimate and practically cost free for the United States as the world's collective response to the Iraqi seizure of Kuwait in 1990.

America's long-term national interest lies in strengthening respect for the UNSC as a compelling excuse for countries to obey international law. Locked in their desperate internal power struggles, competing warlords hesitate to irritate their followers by requiring them to respect human rights, environmental sustainability, or any other cherished interest of the planet as a whole. When the united international community is visibly poised to reward good behavior and punish bad behavior, a failing state may pull itself back from the brink.

No individual democracy can justify to its own citizens the huge costs of humanitarian intervention outside its borders. That responsibility must be seen by all as collective and shared. Only the UNSC is credible enough, and barely at that. In its current form the UNSC is generally unwilling to intervene—one or two permanent members often find some ideological or selfish reason to block international intervention in even the bloodiest internal disputes of their Third World friends.

To better harness the UN's limited but useful legitimacy, the U.S. would do well to ask that the five permanent members yield two-thirds of their right of veto as part of the process of expanding the UNSC. If three negative votes of nine permanent members were required to veto a resolution, America and its UN allies would gain the ability to overrule Russia's and China's allergy to international intervention. By weakening the veto, U.S. politicians would also gain the excuse available to most of their foreign counterparts when justifying to their publics why they did not insist on some stupid, immoral national position: "the UN made me do it." No U.S. leader is brave enough to admit that when the United States cannot muster the support of two great-power allies on a given issue, it is because the United States is advocating something that will harm its own interests as well as the world's. But this is true.

### *Lesser Breeds of Multilateralism*

Out of frustration at its inability to make the UN or even NATO a docile instrument of U.S. unilateralism, the Bush administration took refuge in the claim that "ad hoc coalitions" should be assembled from a different cast of characters for each specific crisis. The political problem with ad hoc coalitions is that they do not generate legitimacy.

Any international organization conveys measurable legitimacy only for its members and aspiring members. When the United States bombed Serbia over Kosovo in 1999, the political cover of Greece's obligation as a NATO ally made it possible for the Greek government to let U.S. forces use Greek territory, despite the universal outrage of Greek citizens. Americans felt better invading Iraq in the company of Honduras and Poland, but the existence of that ad hoc coalition offered allied governments no protection from domestic criticism. NATO sponsorship, had it been available, would have protected Spanish prime minister José María Aznar from much of the damage Spanish participation in the Iraq War did to his party's popularity.

NATO sponsorship of Operation Iraqi Freedom would have added nothing to America's legal or political standing with the Iraqis. If the United States had democratized Iraq under the auspices of the Arab League or the Organization of the Islamic Conference, marginally more Iraqis would have rallied around the banner of the provisional government. But the Arab League, a creature of tenuous legitimacy itself, could never have placed that legitimacy at U.S. disposal for a war without blowing itself apart. The UN, for all its faults, is the broadest and best multilateral source of legitimacy on the planet, and the United States pays in American blood when it fails to make good use of it.

## Withholding Legitimacy

The U.S. government believes, apparently genuinely, that it can withhold legitimacy from hostile foreign politicians. U.S. officials explained in February 2005 that the United States would not take part in nuclear nonproliferation negotiations with the government of Iran because U.S. presence at the talks would "legitimize the mullahs." But this is wishful thinking. The mullahs' legitimacy, a product of Iranian domestic political processes, is safe from America's power to add or detract. Just as the United States has no magic supply of cross-border legitimacy, neither can it snatch it away.

Breaking diplomatic relations, banning trade, and other international means of showing U.S. displeasure serve clear and understandable domestic political aims in the United States. Those domestic aims are in conflict with U.S. foreign policy interests. Foreign leaders do not derive their authority from the Letters of Credence handed to them by a U.S. ambassador with a dignified semibow in front of television cameras. When the United States withdraws its diplomatic presence from a country, it makes itself half-blind, deaf, and dumb with regard to the internal politics that are the arena within which the superpower must exert its influence. A leader who cannot travel to Washington is not visibly disfigured by a U.S. visa ban. On the contrary, Fidel Castro glories in being detested and disparaged by the sole superpower.

America has substantial power to create economic conditions in which the continued rule of a hostile foreign leader does not serve the rational self-interest of the people he governs. But rational self-interest has limited impact on local politics. Moreover, by harming the local population through sanctions, America delegitimizes itself as a spokesperson for that population's self-interest. The threat of sanctions is a powerful tool in diplomacy. Actual use of sanctions, especially ineffective bilateral ones, underscores America's inability to generate alternate sources of local legitimacy for some rival to supplant even the most depraved local ruler.

The credible threat of violence is a necessary component of defending the interests of the American people. American violence is most effective as a legitimizing or delegitimizing force when foreigners perceive themselves part of the same dominance hierarchy as Americans. Incorporating them into our dominance system through imperial conquest and occupation is impossibly expensive as well as wicked. The affordable alternative is to broaden and deepen the "international community" the neoconservatives so despise. Under the flag of a strengthened, respected UN, America's formidable military competence has some hope of one day achieving more of the ambitious political goals American idealism sets for it.

In the short term, the United States wields its influence affordably by building up its political and military friendships with the widest possible range of foreign partners. The nationalism of others is not in conflict with America's own, provided the super-power has the patience and curiosity to navigate the shifting shoals of local politics in 190 alien countries. This is the art of diplomacy.

# 4

# ★ *Some Rules of the Game* ★

*"Among virtuous friends a slight inclination of the head is as efficacious as the more painful admonition from an iron-shod foot."*

*Ernest Bramah Smith,* Kai Lung's Golden Hours

Avalon Hill makes a board game called Diplomacy, a map of Europe on which the players pretend to be statesmen, or rather Henry Kissinger. They move their armies around in accordance with a set of arbitrary rules and make and break alliances with other players in a bid for world domination. I played it once when I was about thirteen and stomped off in a rage. My weaker ally had betrayed me to a rival empire. Like Kissinger, he was confident that nothing in the rules of Diplomacy required him to fear outraged public opinion or avenging Nemesis. He fooled me so easily, however, only because his treachery was a betrayal of his own self-interest as well as mine. The empire he sold me to would devour him next.

Real-world diplomacy is a much more excellent game, as I discovered by a happy accident in the spring of 1980. I was studying archaeology in Greece. A college friend passed through Athens to visit her parents at the U.S. embassy in Bucharest. Smitten, I tagged along. We descended from the plane and found ourselves in Nicolae Ceausescu's Romania, then a ghastly hybrid of Third World efficiency and Soviet charm. As we stared in despair at the chaos ahead of us at passport control, a distinguished figure in a dark suit parted the confusion, scooped us up, and murmured a few words in a mysterious language to the passport and customs officers. We were wafted to a waiting car. I had met, at last, a man fluent in the rules of a game absorbing enough to play for a whole lifetime. I took the Foreign Service exam a few months later.

In the car from Bucharest airport, Clint briefed us on an unusual diplomatic challenge. The local currency would buy nothing worth having. Resilient Romanians had worked out a substitute for cash. An unopened pack of Kent cigarettes would get you a good restaurant table, and two would buy you a date with a beautiful woman or, more usefully for the embassy, expeditious processing of requests for diplomatic visas and customs clearance. The choice of currency, peculiar though it was, suited U.S. interests very well—the embassy had access to an infinite supply of Kents, tax-free, via diplomatic pouch. By mistake, however, the embassy had received a huge shipment of Kent Gold 100s. As the economic counselor, Clint was reaching out to the invisible arbiters of such things to tweak the rules of Romanian society so that this unfamiliar package would be as negotiable as ordinary Kents.

Romania, like most countries in the world, gives a confident foreigner in a good suit the right to stroll past the Authorized Personnel Only signs. Once past, a trained diplomat has a reasonable chance of persuading people that it is legitimate by their own rules to do something that also happens to advance U.S. interests. Even a superpower, however, cannot easily change another country's internal rules to its benefit. Too many people have too much at stake in each society's precarious but functional balance of wealth and power. The embassy staff ended up having to smoke the alien Kents.

Diplomats discover that recognizable, even logical, rules have evolved in every country to solve the universal problems of allocating scarce resources and generating scarce legitimacy. President Bush assumed when he invaded Iraq that the local rules were so arbitrary and evil that the Iraqi people would be grateful when U.S. power rewrote them. Military power indeed allowed him to tear up the Iraqi rule book, but few Iraqis would obey an alien replacement. The result was chaos. Not every country is as murderously complex as Iraq, but there is no country in the world where America can play God, or even Avalon Hill, at a cost it can afford. Diplomacy, when the United States uses it properly, keeps it from needing to.

The task of diplomacy is to find ways the U.S. government can advance its national interests without requiring a foreign society to violate its rules. Diplomats spend their working hours—typically very long hours—discovering what those rules are, who polices them, and which local personalities are willing and able, operating inside them, to help the U.S. government effectively. Ideally, a country's local rules include respect for international law and some willingness to put the collective national welfare ahead of personal or tribal benefit. In such cases, a reasonably virtuous superpower can conduct much of its diplomatic business via fax machine. More often, however, diplomats must cope with societies whose most important rules are primitive and personal. They learn those rules practically one personality at a time.

## *Conflict Resolution*

In the popular mind, diplomacy is the art of negotiating treaties and resolving international conflicts. I have never seen a real international conflict resolved. Strictly speaking, the task is probably impossible. The most primitive and basic rule of every society, a rule diplomats can bend but not break, is that what is ours must remain ours. Instead of solving conflicts, therefore, diplomats find themselves managing them. Diplomacy redefines bloody battles over disputed tracts of ground as vague, open-ended political processes. It is remarkable how well and peacefully two peoples can live almost side by side, in Cyprus for example, while the harsh frontier justice they yearn for recedes imperceptibly down some endless diplomatic corridor.

I thought for a few weeks once that I would witness the impossible. In October 1999 President Haidar Aliyev of Azerbaijan and President Robert Kocharian of Armenia decided that enough was enough. Aliyev was getting old and did not trust his playboy son Ilham with an unfinished war. Kocharian was glumly convinced that he would never turn the Armenian economy around without peace and open borders. Time was making Azerbaijan richer and giving it dangerously powerful friends because it had oil and gas deposits just offshore in the Caspian Sea. Meanwhile, impoverished Armenians were beginning to colonize the Azerbaijani territory they had captured in 1992–94 in the process of liberating the Armenian-inhabited enclave of Nagorno Karabakh. Soon they would refuse to give up the territory as part of a peace deal. So the two leaders met on the border and secretly agreed to resolve their dispute through an exchange of territories.

When the good news reached it, the State Department swung instantly into action. Solving the Nagorno Karabakh dispute would be an important step toward regional stability, which would help persuade U.S. energy companies that it was safe to invest in Caspian Basin oil and pipelines. It was a rare opportunity for Deputy Secretary of State Strobe Talbott to earn the heavenly blessing promised the peacemakers. A peace deal would also be a splendid political gift for President Clinton at the upcoming November 1999 summit meeting of the Organization for Security and Cooperation in Europe (OSCE) in Istanbul.

As the former political counselor at U.S. Embassy Yerevan, now the U.S. deputy special negotiator for Nagorno Karabakh, I was the delegation note-taker and fount of geographical and historical minutiae. I packed my maps and suitcase and presented myself at Andrews Air Force Base to accompany Talbott and a select interagency team to Baku and Yerevan to seal the deal. It was a heady feeling. Caught up in the enthusiasm, I didn't ask my boss, the cherubically self-confident Carey Cavanaugh, why we were sprinting off without consulting our French and Russian partners. The U.S. was one of three equal cochairs in the so-called Minsk Group set up by the OSCE to guide the Nagorno Karabakh conflict toward resolution. Since the Armenians had told the United States first, the ball was in our court.

VIP travel is bumpier than advertised. The D.C. National Guard Gulfstream jet broke down in Zurich airport, so we hitchhiked to Baku and Yerevan on a hastily chartered replacement, then a KC-135 aerial refueling tanker, and finally an old DC-9 scrounged from U.S. European Command. More uncomfortably, we had not brought in our diplomatic baggage what our hosts were looking for. Aliyev and Kocharian were hard, practical men aiming at a solution that suited them both as individuals. Kocharian's home territory, Nagorno Karabakh, would be free and linked to Armenia. Aliyev's home territory, a similarly isolated enclave called Nakhichevan, would get a land bridge to Azerbaijan. We showed them the draft agreement we had prepared, with timetables, security guarantees, and ingenious transitional arrangements. Kocharian and Aliyev scanned the text in vain, however, for the magic formula that would allow them to reveal the terms of their agreement to their people without being lynched.

Aliyev's foreign minister resigned in protest before we arrived in Baku. An hour after we took off from Yerevan to brief the Turkish government in Ankara, a little group of gunmen stormed into the Armenian parliament and murdered the prime minister, Kocharian's key political ally, and the speaker, the most popular politician in the country. We are reasonably certain that the timing was coincidental and that the plot was driven by a personal grievance, not by our mission. Still, at one blow Kocharian was deprived of most of Armenia's accumulated store of political legitimacy. The peace deal went into hibernation because Kocharian, now on his own, lacked the standing to survive signing away even a single inch of Armenian soil.

Our little office spent the next month rebuilding frayed cochair unity. Our Russian colleagues endorsed the deal, sincerely I was sure, but we secretly doubted they (or anyone) spoke for the Russian state apparatus as a whole. They harbored similar suspicions of us. With the optimism that distinguishes successful U.S. bureaucrats, we plunged ahead. We mobilized President Clinton to cajole and congratulate Aliyev and Kocharian. We worked with the World Bank and UN to assemble an enormous Potemkin village of international assistance promises. Ultimately, in April 2001, nine months after I returned to U.S. Embassy Athens, a grand negotiating session was held in Key West, Florida. Air Force One was standing by to fly Clinton to Florida for a three-way handshake. This time Aliyev blinked. He knew his dynasty would not survive the wrath of unrequited Azerbaijani nationalism should he accept even the much modified deal now on the table.

While the diplomats struggled for ten years to find magic words that would allow both sides to sign a deal, the victorious but cold and hungry Armenians were scavenging everything worth scavenging in the territories they had captured. Azerbaijani forests and fruit trees became firewood in Yerevan. Across the cease-fire line, hundreds of thousands of Azeri refugees shivered in railroad boxcars and cargo containers, surviving off international charity. They agitated for the day the victorious Azerbaijani army would lead them back to their houses and farms. As our little group of Minsk Group negotiators toured the rubble of no-man's-land, we knew that redeeming this wasteland and its people would take more political courage than most politicians have.

## *Negotiating*

Washington is full of expert negotiators. I was never in the right place to watch one at work. My own cautious conclusions about the negotiating process are influenced perhaps too heavily by my experience buying rugs in Morocco. No sensible rug merchant will contradict the customer who congratulates himself on his eye for quality and negotiating prowess. At dinner parties my diplomatic colleagues would routinely trot out some unique treasure for which they had paid a fraction of its true value. I never paid much less for a rug I wanted than I would have for a similar one in a Bethesda antique shop. I scored an occasional amazing bargain, for a rug I did not particularly want, a rug I would drag around for a decade and then give to the Salvation Army.

My one display of diplomatic negotiating brilliance belongs atop the pile of rugs I bought cheaply because I did not really want what I was buying. With the country director for Save the Children looking on admiringly, I interrupted the "prime minister of Nagorno Karabakh" (quotation marks are our polite signal of diplomatic nonrecognition) in mid-harangue and told him to drop his claim to collect value-added tax on the humanitarian assistance the United

States was about to give his little entity. Diplomats do not interrupt prime ministers very often, but I could afford to be rude. America did not recognize the government of Nagorno Karabakh or approve of the ethnic cleansing involved in that government's creation. Against the State Department's advice, Armenia's friends in Congress had written an earmark into the foreign assistance budget for $15 million to help Armenian refugees in Nagorno Karabakh. I was deadly sincere in telling the "prime minister" that the U.S. government would cancel the assistance instantly if he sent his tax collectors after our program. The "prime minister" had no option but to agree. My satisfaction was tempered by the certainty that Karabakh's local authorities would squeeze the aid recipients if they could not squeeze the donors.

The chance to say "take it or leave it" and truly mean it is discouragingly rare in diplomacy. International negotiations seldom resemble matching wits on a Moroccan sand dune near Merzouga with a rug merchant who will never see you again. An international agreement takes place between states condemned to stare at one another across the breakfast table every morning until the end of time. Unlike rug merchants, diplomats have to tell the truth because lies come back to haunt them. The deal must make winners of the politicians on both sides. No parliament ratifies a losing agreement. If it does by mistake or under coercion, politicians will find a way to get around the deal because otherwise their domestic opponents will crucify them. An unequal agreement thus becomes a source of permanent discord, worse for U.S. interests than no agreement at all.

My second tour in Athens coincided with the successful completion of two decadelong negotiations. The more satisfactory one concerned the embassy parking lot. Back in the mists of time, the U.S. government bought for a negligible price a parcel of land at the unfashionable end of a major Athens boulevard on which to build an embassy. Parking was not a problem in 1960, but in making the purchase, the government forgot a crucial point: in forty years America would still be a superpower. Thus the government did not buy the empty lot behind the embassy, preferring to rent it for a nominal price.

A generation later, Athens was much larger and the land had become obscenely valuable. Security reasons, including a failed car bomb in the 1970s and a failed antitank rocket attack in 1996, reinforced the embassy's determination to hold tight to its parking lot. Meanwhile the U.S. government had gradually improved the property with impermanent structures that reflected the embassy's precarious legal tenure. The Greek state did not dare evict the U.S. embassy, but the state employee pension fund that owned the land was going broke.

There was a strong shared interest in a deal. The United States needed clear title so it could consolidate scattered embassy operations, including a house for the Marine Security Guards and a warehouse jutting illegally into a flood-prone streambed, into a single defensible compound. The Greek state was embarrassed by the complaints that leaked into the newspapers over the pitiful rent the United States paid. Negotiations stalled, however, from the 1980s through the 1990s. The United States would not pay full market price, since the low-density structures the embassy needed would be worth far less than what a builder could get from high-rise offices, but the pension fund could not accept a derisory countervaluation based on the inability of any alternative purchaser to evict the current tenant.

Finally both sides got serious. Clever Greek lawyers discovered that with a minor amendment to legislation the unused building density could be transferred to another plot of land and sold to a developer for enough to make the deal affordable to all sides. On this win-win basis, developed in negotiations conducted with enormous secrecy and patience right up to the day our authorization to spend the money would expire, the Greek side agreed to a price that matched with remarkable precision the maximum amount of money the State Department had secretly allocated for the land. A secure new Marine house, warehouse, and consular offices were built, and all ended happily except for the embassy employees who discovered the U.S. Office of Management and Budget did not permit government funds to be used for their parking.

The second negotiation I witnessed was for the Comprehensive Technical Agreement (CTA). This was a grand status-of-forces agreement designed to consolidate all the legal arrangements governing the U.S. military presence in Greece into one tidy document. The CTA would, in theory at least, replace dozens of ad hoc agreements, some secret and some long forgotten, signed between the U.S. and Greece since the U.S. military arrived in Greece in 1947.

Constant access by the U.S. Navy to the protected deepwater harbor and nearby airport at Souda Bay in Crete is necessary for any significant U.S. military operation in the Middle East. Opposition politicians charged that the old base agreements, a relic of shared Cold War threat perceptions, violated Greek national sovereignty. They pressed the Greek state to make America live up to an old promise to negotiate a more equal CTA. The U.S. military was reasonably happy with the old rules but finally was lured into negotiations by the prospect of a commitment from the Greek state that U.S. service members accused of crimes in Greece would be prosecuted only by U.S. military courts.

The State Department retained control of the CTA negotiations through a special negotiator, knowing from years of experience that the Department of Defense would be completely inflexible if it took the lead. The negotiating process was agonizing. Each new deadlock took the pressure of a high-level visit to unblock it. America's major concession was a symbolic one designed to make the agreement politically more palatable in Greece: the handful of Greek military personnel in the United States at any given time would enjoy the same CTA protections as Americans in Greece, though only to the extent this did not conflict with rights of the various U.S. states. Greece accepted legal language that almost fully waived local criminal jurisdiction when the accused were U.S. military personnel.

After the agreement was initialed by the negotiators, it went into the deep freeze for a year. Neither the Greek government nor the Pentagon was eager to take political responsibility for it. My colleagues and I explained to every Greek politician we could find why the CTA, by absolving them of involvement in each little misdemeanor, genuinely served Greek political interests. Our arguments were true enough but had no impact. The CTA had become a pawn in an internal competition between political supporters of the defense minister and the foreign minister. Foreign Minister Papandreou unfroze the CTA to have something to sign with Secretary Powell during a July 2001 visit to Washington. Parliament ratified the CTA in January 2003, amid charges by Papandreou's rivals in his own party that the new language on criminal jurisdiction was a betrayal of Greece's national dignity. CTA opponents missed forcing a roll-call vote only because one deputy mysteriously left the hall. If he had been present, the CTA would have died that night.

We embassy diplomats worked with the Americas Desk at the Greek Foreign Ministry all through the long process. We had a shared interest in knowing exactly where the practical problem lay at each moment of bureaucratic blockage. Then together we could orchestrate the cheapest possible solution. Mostly this meant knowing whom to cajole and when. Six ministerial signatures were required before the agreement could be submitted to Parliament. One minister, before putting his signature on what he feared might turn out to have been a suicide note, wanted the U.S. ambassador to be aware that he was doing so. A friendly phone call moved the CTA into the ministerial out-box, but also into his little black book as a favor to the U.S. government.

The CTA negotiations were a bureaucratic victory for the U.S. military—at least resentful Greek diplomats thought so—but in practice a meaningless one. The process by which Greece waived its criminal jurisdiction over American military personnel who committed crimes in Greece had an escape clause for crimes of exceptional political importance. Normally, the crimes committed by drunken sailors do not fall into that category.

There was a small but vocal anti-base lobby on Crete, backed by local leftist politicians who would normally be ignored. The Greek Ministry of Foreign Affairs Legal Division was furious at the Bush administration for its attempts to destroy the International Criminal Court (ICC) and then for the war on Iraq. As the political climate grew tense, all crimes committed by U.S. military personnel suddenly took on exceptional political importance. Jurisdiction stopped being waived. Tried in Greek courts by Greek judges angry at the Iraq War, American soldiers ended up sentenced to lengthy terms in Greek prisons, exactly what the CTA (and U.S. opposition to the ICC) was supposed to prevent. And Greek politicians knew better than to intervene in the workings of the independent Greek judiciary when the U.S. bases were involved.

The first moral I draw from my Greek negotiating experiences is that local politicians and lawyers are a better guide than visiting American officials to the shoals lurking in local law and politics. Greek ministers took a political risk on our behalf to pass a CTA with language we thought we wanted. In the end it did not help us. We would have wasted less time if we had seen our discussions not as an exercise in proving the State Department's negotiating prowess to the Defense Department but rather as a cooperative exercise in how to limit the political problems caused by the presence of U.S. troops on Greek territory.

Second, strong personal relationships with key politicians are more useful than tough negotiators in protecting our interests, at least in a country like Greece where the rule of law is highly personalized. No piece of paper will protect offending Americans against an outraged populace. Outrage can be prevented, deflected, or managed only if the right American can ask the right Greek for the right favor with the right degree of friendship and respect.

### Relationship Building

In America I deluded myself well into adulthood that personal relationships were a luxury, not a necessity. Getting a job as a U.S.

foreign service officer, a fine and prestigious profession, simply requires filling out an application form, passing a tough but reasonably objective set of exams, and answering more straightforwardly than President Bush the security clearance question on youthful marijuana use.

Acquiring a U.S. passport or driver's license or business permit takes a few hours or days with no need for a friend who has a friend. Only when the stakes get higher, for high-paid jobs and major contracts, does one discover how much America resembles everywhere else. Evolution creates a food chain headed by politicians, corporate managers, and senior bureaucrats who see difficult decisions as not worth making unless the decision can be portrayed as a favor to someone powerful enough to reciprocate it.

The United States is a mobile society. Working relationships with doctors, plumbers, or senators can be cultivated quickly with ordinary politeness and a standard price list. Lawyers and consultants step in as relationship brokers where necessary. In Greece and other close-knit societies, key relationships are less straightforwardly mercenary. Public health services, for example are ostensibly free. Overloaded and dysfunctional, the health system perks up at an envelope full of cash. It responds even better to the use of social capital, to a good word from a friendly doctor or politician.

Over a career I wasted hundreds of hours in four countries being American and self-reliant, leafing through government directories, making cold telephone calls, and laying out lovely but useless diplomatic arguments before skeptical strangers. Diplomatic business can be managed with a single phone call, once the right person has placed the diplomat and the errand in the right local process of social capital formation.

In Greece a bureaucrat's signature on a piece of paper is a personal favor, with an unstated understanding that the favor might some day need to be returned. No judicial system can enforce such implied contracts, particularly not the slow, corrupt courts in the developing world. This makes personal trust vital. Ordinary folk tend to establish by the time they graduate from university or finish the army most of the trusting relationships they are ever going to have. Investing trust in a U.S. diplomat, parked in a country for three or four years at most, is a leap of faith indeed.

By the end of six years in Athens over two postings, in my diffident way I had built a network of enough politicians, Greek and foreign diplomats, academics, and journalists to accomplish the basic chores of my Political Section reasonably fast and reasonably well. I had done a few modest favors, bought a few lunches, hosted the occasional dinner, sped up a visa or two. Mostly, I had simply been a well informed, honest, occasionally witty window into what a prestigious superpower was thinking. Knowing me offered some slight additional cachet to people in their social competition, and that was often enough of a basis on which to develop a working relationship over time.

These relationships of trust and mutual interest, multiplied by thousands of foreign service officers in 165 or so countries, are a vital part of America's accumulated national security capital. One simple example is the hundreds of Americans who every year avoid a ghastly interlude in a foreign jail because the police chief has drunk imported whiskey at the home of the U.S. consul general. This is a crucial reason the United States needs some number of diplomats with long, repeated experience of a given country. It is also a reason to train diplomats in the relationship-management tools and techniques that any international corporation uses routinely.

Better-funded U.S. government agencies arrange a period of overlap when one of their officers leaves, to ensure key relationships are handed over intact to the replacement. Because of staffing shortages, State Department officers usually arrive at their embassy a month after their predecessor has left. Once I found a neat memo waiting for me, listing key contacts to call on early. More often I found a jumble of business cards in a desk drawer, with a few cryptic notes. With more careful supervision, the U.S. government would not lose so much local influence every time a diplomat transfers.

U.S. ambassadors have an easier time building personal relationships than their subordinates. They need no introduction, and only the prime minister is ever too busy to see them. The relationships with the foreign minister and the prime minister are key elements in America's diplomatic arsenal, provided trust is built and not betrayed. Diplomats cannot, however, presume too much on these relationships. U.S. ambassadors are lightning rods for the bitter political jealousies that dominate the day-to-day struggle of politicians for public attention and approval. Politicians put survival in their domestic political competition above even the warmest personal feelings toward the U.S. ambassador.

George Papandreou, Greece's Greek-American foreign minister from late 1999 to early 2004, did a superb job of keeping U.S.-Greek relations on an even keel. When elections rolled around, his political foes plastered his home district with photographs of him standing next to the U.S. ambassador. What saved the U.S.-born Papandreou from major political damage was not his likeability or even his status as the son and heir of a deified prime minister.

Papandreou headed a foreign ministry loaded with political supporters of the other political party. Over four years no rival could point to a damning instance of Papandreou's championing a U.S. request that his ministry had strongly opposed. Papandreou always found time for the U.S. ambassador and listened respectfully, sometimes for an hour or more. At the end of the day, however, the telegram I drafted as the ambassador's note-taker was generally an artful embellishment of Papandreou's dutiful promise to look into it.

Prudent ministers delegate the day-to-day business of relations with the United States to their professional diplomats, and prudent U.S. embassies make the best of it. By finding and working closely with the one or two people in any given office who do the work, American diplomats can often ensure that the recommendations they make to their minister will protect U.S. interests. High-level political intervention is not a substitute for relations with the people at the working level who write the talking points.

The natural partner of every U.S. embassy is the Americas desk officer at the Foreign Ministry. Given the job of keeping the bilateral relationship running smoothly and out of the headlines, the desk officer is the embassy's natural interface with foreign bureaucracies that, from outside, are as faceless and confusing as America's own. A good desk officer will lift the veil, making a good deal of espionage unnecessary.

Next most valuable is the America expert any prudent foreign minister will keep on the private payroll. To keep close track of the superpower, these experts create multiple channels to U.S. officials both in Washington and at the U.S. embassy. They therefore need to be watched carefully, but their bureaucratic insights are precious. When they are honest and intelligent, they perform an invaluable service in confirming the integrity of the system to mutually suspicious officials. Occasionally they will perform a risky end-run to the minister, bypassing a diplomatic hierarchy that has locked up for some reason.

The embassy's support group includes similar advisers in the Defense Ministry, a handful of specialized journalists, a few ambitious opposition politicians, and a scattering of think-tankers and academics with intellectual or sentimental reasons to endorse America's policy positions. Beyond this tiny institutional constituency, on any specific issue certain local constituencies will support something close to the U.S. position, even in a country that is generally hostile to the United States.

Normally the local business community is America's good friend. Greek, Armenian, Indian, and Moroccan business people believe in wealth and security as fervently as any Republican. Provided U.S. diplomats do not look too closely at how they make their money, local business people are crucial allies. The union of Greek ship owners, which has enormous clout with the Greek government and parliament, depends for its prosperity on America's import-driven economy. Greek tour operators share the U.S. interest in improving the security reputation of Greek airports. Greek technology companies share an interest in fighting intellectual property piracy. The Greek Communist Party shares an interest in minority rights. There is always an underexposed deputy minister of something willing to cooperate if favorable headlines will result.

As human rights officer, I learned that most nongovernmental organizations consist of one megalomaniac and a few sheets of printed letterhead. The real ones, however, are the best allies a superpower can have on issues it cares about, such as minority rights, public health, environmental protection, or halting international trafficking in persons. The investment in cultivating such organizations is worth it. A local group has far more legitimacy than any foreign embassy to champion a shared issue.

The United States has wonderful diplomatic constituencies in the form of thousands of former students at U.S. universities and hyphenated Americans who return to the motherland. The care and feeding of rich Greek-Americans is a necessary diplomatic exercise. The U.S. embassy gives them entry to a snobbish Greek upper crust. They reciprocate by lobbying the U.S. Congress on U.S.-Greek issues more effectively than the State Department can usually manage. For complex social and historical reasons, however, Greek-Americans and their counterparts elsewhere are never as influential in the motherland as they and we sometimes naively expect.

Maintaining America's overseas constituencies and relationships requires more investment than the U.S. government will make unless it is prodded. Bureaucracies are seldom exuberant, but the Americas Division of the Greek Foreign Ministry radiated depression. The Americas Desk was not a dumping ground for losers—the U.S. relationship was too important. But everyone there was always trying to wangle another assignment. The U.S. embassy had a bad habit of going around the desk directly to the minister or, worse, to some rival ministry. Friends of the United States were too often blindsided by offhand decisions made in Washington that caused them to look like chumps to their peers. This is the price of dealing with a self-absorbed and secretive superpower.[1]

Over twenty years I watched the European Union (EU) gradually overtake the United States in the competition to attract officials and politicians able and willing to make their organization work effectively for both themselves and their foreign partners. An official who masters Euro-jargon and "comitology" (the arcane art, unknown to better dictionaries, of mobilizing the EU committee structure to generate policies and regulations) is guaranteed postings in comfortable European capitals, frequent business trips to cities with fine restaurants, and the smugness of belonging to a morally superior club. The Americas Desk has less to offer in terms of career advancement. To persuade foreigners that Washington is still the world's most challenging and rewarding diplomatic assignment it helps to have a less nationalist and inflexible U.S. administration than the current one.

## *Paring the Enemies List*

The counterpart of helping America's friends is neutralizing hostile constituencies. A healthy enemies list is good for keeping the competitive juices flowing and convenient for bureaucratic self-promotion safely back in Washington. Enemies are a dangerous nuisance overseas. I tangled with my last ambassador in Athens over my insistence that America pay attention to its foes as well as its friends.

As a junior officer I used to make the long drive every few months to the Greek Communist Party (KKE) headquarters in an outlying working-class neighborhood of Athens. I would walk past the huge bust of Lenin and argue for an hour with Comrade Kolozof, the Politburo member in charge of international relations. I would point out all the areas where U.S. interests and KKE policy converged, such as Balkan stability and human rights, and ask the KKE's perspective on political events such as the ongoing collapse of world communism. Kolozof probably never believed a word I said, but we both enjoyed our arguments. When the 1989 Greek parliamentary elections deadlocked and the Communists joined the governing coalition, I had relationships I could call on and knew there was no need to panic. The KKE was far less obstructive a governing partner than its official ideology should have made it, partly because senior KKE leaders were not entirely the victim of their own propaganda regarding U.S. policy.

Clinton's post–Cold War cuts in the State Department had an impact. The embassy in Athens was leaner and busier when I returned for my second assignment.[2] Greece's election law had also changed, weakening the influence of smaller parties. The KKE had regressed intellectually and morally since the end of the Gorbachev era. But I remained stubbornly convinced that ordinary prudence and good diplomatic manners required the U.S. embassy to maintain a working relationship with every party in Parliament.[3]

Respect for democratic rules means respect for the outcome of democratic processes, and sometimes—as the Pentagon discovered in early 2003 when the Turkish parliament narrowly refused to allow the Fourth Infantry Division of the U.S. Army to invade Iraq via Turkey—every vote counts. The future is predictably unpredictable. Last year's lunatic fringe will be next year's government somewhere in the world. A couple of hours every few months of preventive diplomacy, like preventive dentistry, is a wise and certainly affordable investment for the richest superpower in human history.

Diplomacy can resemble a visit to the dentist in other respects as well. One speaker of the Greek parliament was a punctilious patriot who believed part of his national duty was to make sure that American official visitors understood why so many ordinary Greeks felt betrayed by the United States. The beneficiaries of his lecture tended to be spitting mad by the end of it. Greek journalists watched each U.S. ambassador to see whether he would overreact. One of mine did. The embassy released a blistering statement rebutting the speaker's remarks and complained to the foreign minister. The Greek government looked around for somewhere to hide, but in the end it backed the speaker. The Americas desk officer sighed mournfully to me. What had we expected?

The executive branch was not going to quash the speaker for us. The speaker of Parliament is a senior politician of the governing party, the head of one of the three branches of government. Ministers needed his cooperation. The next U.S. ambassador, after two months of gentle nagging by the Foreign Ministry and his own Political Section, dutifully put on his dark suit and made a pilgrimage to Parliament. He listened to the speaker politely for forty-five minutes, long enough to take the issue off the table for the watching Greek media. The same excessive sense of duty that inspired the speaker's lectures to visiting Americans also drove him to support Greek-U.S. cooperation, provided it was based on the appearance of mutual respect. His daughter lived in New York, and he visited her often. But he was the speaker, and he would do business with us by Parliament's rules, not ours. And ultimately, by those rules, America's business—bilateral agreements that needed parliamentary ratification—got done reasonably well.

A sensible superpower does not permit itself the luxury of publicly denigrating foreign politicians. Demonizing foes, a rewarding exercise in machismo for the home front, is always counterproductive abroad. Foreigners do not expel or even discipline their wayward leaders at U.S. request. Unless war is our predetermined outcome, then the U.S. government will eventually have to pursue its goals through negotiation with a foreign leader powerful enough to make a deal. A leader who has been publicly insulted is a leader with a domestic political duty to exact some satisfaction for the insult before he comes to the table (see the Bolton–North Korea episode in chapter 12). Given the choice between war and an apology, U.S. national interests will usually require some senior State Department official to come hat in hand to atone for the immaturity of some posturing opportunist.

## Footing the Bill for Good Relations

One of my old bosses had a plaque on his wall from his time in the Personnel Office. It quoted Louis XIV complaining, "Every time I appoint someone I create one ingrate and 99 malcontents." In the period before a decision is finalized, those who stand to benefit from that decision treat politicians very well. A Greek defense minister who is weighing whether to buy his billion dollars' worth of tanks from France, Germany, England, Russia, or the United States will dine very well at the various ambassadorial residences until that decision is made. Afterward he will be systematically reviled, and awkward questions will be leaked to the press about the size of his divorce settlement and how he paid for the luxurious furnishings of his villa.

Politicians try to delay decisions as long as possible in hopes that only one unimpeachable course of action will be left on the table at the end. Superpower bureaucrats, impatient for a favorable decision, convince themselves that such self-interest is somehow disgraceful. I watched ambassadors try to force unenthusiastic politicians to make a difficult decision by threatening public condemnation and by brandishing "drop-dead dates," various U.S. bureaucratic deadlines. Politicians respect their own deadlines but not ours. A politician can occasionally be buffaloed by the U.S. government into doing something his people will see as illegitimate, but only once. A miracle of the democratic process is how often checks and balances prevent politicians from implementing suicidal decisions even when they have been coaxed or bullied into agreeing to them.

Diplomacy succeeds when it harnesses rational self-interest as a source of legitimacy. This is the reason the United States builds domestic constituencies and personal relationships. With logic, empathy, patience, and good information, it is often possible to find a moment—too often, as with counterterrorism cooperation, the result of some tragedy—when a foreign politician's immediate political interests and America's national interest coincide. The painless way is through "action-forcing events," high-level visits or meetings both sides look forward to as a chance to shine for their respective home audiences.

The U.S. ambassador represents an unpopular superpower whose mere existence is a challenge to the full national independence and sovereignty of other states. Therefore, to enjoy the normal fruits of diplomacy, the burden is on him or her to be twice as diplomatic as anyone else. The most persuasive U.S. ambassador I ever met, Frank Wisner in India, always offered his interlocutors three crisp reasons why the U.S. position served India's national interests. He knew the domestic opponents his partners would face were no less ignorant and vicious than America's Ann Coulter or Rush Limbaugh. A basic task of U.S. diplomats is to give their local allies strong arguments to defend themselves against facile charges of treason.

### *Sovereign Equality*

Diplomacy relies on one rigid and indispensable rule of diplomacy, the rule of sovereign equality. All states are equal, all heads of government are equal, and all ambassadors are equal. National flags are arranged by alphabetical order, not by the number of nuclear warheads of the state they represent. In order of precedence, George W. Bush ranks only one-hundredth in the world, behind Gloria Macapagal-Arroyo of the Philippines, who took office a few hours earlier than he. This rule, alas, is one the United States is doomed to break every day.

When the U.S. president visits Greece, Athens grinds to a complete halt. In addition to the state dinner with the Greek president and the working meeting with the prime minister, the U.S. president will address the Greek parliament, give a speech to the business elite, and meet a select group of editors and star journalists. The prime minister and foreign minister drop everything to dog his footsteps, even during the Acropolis tour, and the archbishop and rival shipping tycoons will do decorous cartwheels for an invitation to the private dinner at the residence.

When the prime minister of Greece wants his return visit to Washington, the Greek embassy will call in all its chits to squeeze a forty-minute meeting with the president in between the visiting Baptist choir and the mountain bike. Representative Mike Bilirakis of Florida will host a coffee with a few burly Greek-American donors. Retired foreign service officers and a handful of lobbyists, congressional staffers, and Balkan diplomats will attend the speech at a Washington think tank. When the president and the prime minister pose for the television cameras in front of the White House, no U.S. journalist will show the slightest interest in U.S.-Greek relations. And Greece is a country Americans care about.

U.S. diplomats try to keep the disparity between foreigners' treatment of our leaders and our treatment of theirs as unobtrusive as possible. For the pope's funeral, the Vatican protocol office found a version of alphabetical order that would give the U.S. president a seat near the front. A prudently punctilious superpower welcomes such artifices but does not insist on special treatment.

It is physically impossible for the U.S. president to devote a half day of relationship building to each of the dozens of foreign counterparts who parade through Washington every year. Still, with each new administration the State Department must fight the battle to set aside a reasonable number of presidential hours each week to the care and feeding of foreign visitors. More important, the State Department must prepare the president and everyone beneath him well enough to ensure that the precious hour of presidential time allotted to the visit generates a television message the visitor can safely use back home.

A good U.S. ambassador will put the screws on every Washington acquaintance to make sure someone more important than the Romania desk officer attends the gala dinner for the visiting Romanian president. The Public Affairs Section will fight to find a senior U.S. official prepared to tell Romanian journalists on the record that their president's visit was important even though neither the *Washington Post* nor the *New York Times* saw fit to mention it.

In preparing for a visit or any other piece of business, successful U.S. diplomats use most of their tact and ingenuity not on foreigners but rather on their bureaucratic allies and rivals back in Washington. The State Department negotiates for the whole U.S. government, not just itself. Every other bureaucracy can take a maximalist view of its particular interests, with no regard for U.S. national interests as a whole. Whenever a U.S. diplomat advocates a compromise based on a realistic appraisal of what the other side can agree to, he or she will be accused of having gone native.

The State Department tends to crumple preemptively at this charge. But crumpling is a mistake. When the State Department does not advocate on behalf of the vital interests of foreign partners, those interests will not be taken adequately into account in the competitive process that generates U.S. policy. Trampling on the vital interests of foreigners often has unpleasant consequences down the road. A U.S. president may decide to accept those consequences, but it should not be because the State Department was too patriotic to warn him what they were.

The rules of effective diplomacy are similar to the rules of effective persuasion in any society. A superpower gets what it wants by paying the price for it. Fortunately, that price is seldom very high in absolute terms, once America recognizes that the currency politicians value is not dollars or even Kent cigarettes but rather their standing with their own population against their political rivals. Successful diplomacy depends, therefore, on a close, accurate reading of local politics. Through the personal relationships they build with foreigners who share some common aspiration, diplomats learn to read and predict the swirling patterns on an all-too-different, all-too-similar foreign playing field.

# 5

# ★ *Diplomatic Character and the Art of Curiosity* ★

*I am glad the American Vandal goes abroad. It does him good.
It makes a better man of him. It rubs out a multitude of his old
unworthy biases and prejudices. It aids his religion, for it en-
larges his charity and his benevolence, it broadens his views of
men and things; it deepens his generosity and his compassion for
the failings and shortcomings of his fellow creatures. Contact
with men of various nations and many creeds teaches him that
there are other people in the world besides his own little clique,
and other opinions as worthy of attention and respect as his own.
He finds that he and his are not the most momentous matters in
the universe. Cast into trouble and misfortune in strange lands
and being mercifully cared for by those he never saw before, he
begins to learn that best lesson of all—that one which culminates
in the conviction that God puts something good and something
lovable in every man his hands create—that the world is not a
cold, harsh, cruel, prison-house, stocked with all manner of selfishness and hate and wickedness.*

Mark Twain's Speeches, *ed. Albert Bigelow Paine*

To be named the U.S. ambassador in a European embassy, it
helps to be a political friend of the president. Closeness to the president is supposed to make up for lack of local expertise and to some
extent it does. A wealthy businessman can pick up the phone and
inform the president that his foreign policy has a problem, without
jeopardizing his career.[1]

The professional diplomats get the remaining 65 percent of
ambassadorships, the lively and interesting posts with schistosomia-
sis and civil unrest. By calling up obsolete memories of choking smog,

terrorism, and Balkan wars, the State Department has generally persuaded the White House to reserve U.S. Embassy Athens for a career diplomat, despite the well-equipped residence, excellent climate, and opportunity for island cruises. The department nominates respected professionals at the peak of their Foreign Service careers, people who have worked their way up from the bottom as junior consular officers, typically with thirty years of experience in a variety of countries and positions.

I served as political officer for four different U.S. ambassadors in Greece, and I knew the work of two others. A seventh arrived in January 2005. The odds seemed poor that I would ever join their number. I was a good analyst, a good drafter of telegrams, with better than average aptitude for finding common ground with skeptical foreigners outside the embassy; I thus possessed some of the rarer skills of good diplomacy. But there were other skills of management and self-presentation I never mastered. As a political officer, I had many opportunities to watch my superiors in action.

Ambassadors and their subordinates line up on a spectrum that runs from pure diplomats to pure bureaucrats. The diplomats' playing field is the foreign country in which they are posted. Diplomats do not compete with their foreign hosts. They derive their job satisfaction from achieving America's goals through understanding and exploiting the political and bureaucratic competition that takes place in the host country. The audience they aim to charm and impress is made up of foreigners, and cooperative local relationships are their currency.

A bureaucrat's playing field is the corridors of Washington. The goal is personal influence. Bureaucratic job satisfaction is based on performance in the competition. The standards of success are pay grade, size of budget, and number of subordinates. The bureaucrats' audience is their bureaucratic allies, superiors, and rivals in Washington.

It would seem sensible to lock America's bureaucrats safely inside the Beltway and exile its diplomats safely abroad. In practice, this is impossible. No foreign service officer can succeed without some mixture of diplomatic and bureaucratic instincts. Building relationships with foreigners requires some ability to persuade Washington to pay for those relationships. Busy foreign counterparts will write off diplomats who fail to understand their own bureaucracy, no matter how brilliant their understanding of the local scene. On the other hand, bureaucrats posted abroad who ignore foreigners will quickly discover that inability to play by the local rules makes them useless to their bosses.

One-third of the average Foreign Service career is spent in Washington being reminded which government the officer works for and what its preoccupations are. The more ambitious the officer, the more time spent in Washington close to the center of power. This has a mildly perverse effect, at least in recent years. The officers who rise fastest to the rank at which they can demand an embassy of their own tend to be those who have become most absorbed in Washington's competitive culture and least interested in talking to foreigners. Such ambassadors are seldom the most effective ones.

All U.S. ambassadors enjoy automatic deference and near-universal access as the representative of the superpower. They are treated like celebrities whether they choose to act like celebrities or not. Each of six remarkably different characters I watched in Athens won over the course of three or four years more than one fervent Greek admirer, who insisted to me that this U.S. ambassador was the best one they had ever met. All but one of the six acquired a rather larger number of fervent critics. Greek responses to each ambassador varied so wildly that it is tempting to dismiss the issue of diplomatic character as purely a matter of taste.

But common threads link both the praise and the criticism. Successful diplomats need a very high energy level and a sense of the importance of their mission. Being smooth, sociable, and articulate is a gift, but smoothness is not in itself persuasive. Giving good parties helps, but most parties at the residence were tepid and powerful Greeks still came to them. Being ideologically compatible with the local political party currently in power is a minor convenience.

What separates the effective diplomats from the less effective ones, I concluded, is a permanent and patient curiosity about the country they work in, a willingness to listen as well as talk, and—crucially—the ability to recognize the moral underpinnings of foreign interlocutors and articulate our shared interests as an appeal to shared values rather than a competition between their value system and our own. Few diplomats achieve that sympathetic understanding of foreigners without having some ability to detach themselves from their home society, at least for analytical purposes.

Among the Greeks I knew, the consensus view was that the most effective and respected U.S. ambassador to Greece of the past twenty-five years was a man with the improbably ambassadorial name of Monteagle Stearns. As a junior officer in Athens in the late 1950s, he and his equally gifted wife Toni had befriended and earned the intellectual respect of a brilliant Greek-American academic named Andreas Papandreou, the socialist son of a prominent center-left politician. When Papandreou was elected prime minister in 1981, he did not fulfill his campaign promises to throw out the U.S. military bases or pull Greece out of NATO and the European Union (EU). Instead he called Stearns, his old friend, now the U.S. ambassador, for a long, private talk. Papandreou asked America's help to prove to the Greek people that a new, equal era had dawned in the U.S.-Greek relationship. There were many rocky moments—to dimmer elements of the Reagan administration, Papandreou was a satanic crypto-communist—but America kept its military bases and all its vital interests intact thanks to a calm, patient ambassador who respected the messy rules of Greek politics.

Another diplomatic hero I worked with was John R. Davis, whose final posting was as U.S. ambassador to Romania in 1992–94, when I was the desk officer in Washington. Davis had won eternal glory among fellow diplomats and the Poles when, as chargé d'affaires and then ambassador in Warsaw, he used his close friendship with Solidarity leaders and the respect he had earned from the Polish government to help mediate the talks that brought the end of Communist rule and the peaceful accession of Solidarity to political power. On a visit to Bucharest, I watched him sharply rebuke a visiting U.S. congressman for threatening to hold Romania's trade status hostage to U.S. dealers in Romanian orphans for adoption. Romanians, like the Poles before them, knew from public demonstrations of Ambassador Davis's moral courage that he put their welfare and U.S.-Romanian friendship above his own bureaucratic comfort. Romanians had few opportunities in their public lives to safely follow their moral instincts. In John Davis they found a diplomat whose fine character it was safe to mirror back.

### The Need to Be Understood

The primitive human instinct for justice implies a yearning to be understood by the powerful. My brother and I were seven and eight respectively the evening we ran away from home. Our rebellion was not triggered by the minor punishment we had just received or because we were innocent, strictly speaking. We rose up in revolt because what our mother said as she punished us revealed a massive failure to comprehend the fundamental logic underlying our transgression. We wandered back three hours later, hoping our rebellion had inspired a respectful curiosity in the sole superpower of that era.

Effective superpower diplomacy accepts and exploits this demand to be understood. The working visit of Romanian president Ion Iliescu to Washington in 1993 was an excellent illustration. As Romania desk officer at the State Department, I was too junior to be included in the meeting with President Clinton at the White House.

My boss, the office director for Eastern Europe, rolled his eyes as he described how Iliescu, the initial pleasantries completed, had launched into a thirty-five-minute history lecture on his country's struggle for independence and self-respect, complete with bitterly restrained references to old Hungarian oppressors, the Russian threat, and the general backwardness of his difficult region. President Clinton could do nothing but listen politely while his guest rolled on, and only five minutes or so were left for a rushed discussion of the official agenda when Iliescu finally stopped.

From a bureaucratic standpoint, the meeting had been a disaster. My friends at the Romanian embassy bewailed Iliescu's failure to take the excellent advice we had worked out jointly on how to engage the president on issues we knew Clinton cared about. The National Security Council made it clear that Iliescu would never darken the president's door again. We should not have worried.

President Clinton was a natural diplomat and took Iliescu's lecture in stride. He wasn't going to pay close attention to Romania under any circumstances. But Iliescu had climbed the mountaintop and made the appeal of his people and had not been rebuffed. Iliescu returned to Bucharest with the serenity that comes with believing that the relentless U.S. insistence on democratic and economic reforms in Romania was not driven by implacable U.S. ignorance of Romania's special history and circumstances. That security helped give him the courage to lose an honest election in 1996, confounding his many critics.

American diplomats listen to many such tirades. Unlike a president, they can sometimes steal enough time for a real discussion afterward, one that begins: "yes, we understand your history, we respect your national struggles, we agree that you have suffered many injustices, but now it is time to look forward rather than backward, and this is how." Use of the local language makes that assurance of superpower understanding seem more credible.

My favorite book is *Kim* by Rudyard Kipling, a novel I rediscovered when I needed a crash course on India to become India desk officer in 1994. Kipling sets forth a seductive ideal of familiarity with local language and culture so deep and intimate that British agents could infiltrate themselves undetectably into India's immensely rich cultural and political pageant. Kipling's standard applies to fiction only. The number of homebred Americans or British who could pass for twenty-four hours as natives even of Toronto is small. No amount of training can alter that fact that American diplomats are— and should be—recognizably American.

Almost every foreign ministry in the world demands that its

junior diplomats be fully fluent in English and at least one other foreign language when they come on board. The State Department is equally strict about fluency in English. Otherwise, it simply demands that foreign service officers demonstrate, sometime during their first four years of service, that they have acquired moderate fluency in one easy language or survival knowledge of one hard language. The State Department has an excellent foreign language institute. Most U.S. diplomats emerge from intensive language training able to understand the gist of television news stories, read newspapers slowly and laboriously, cope with restaurants and cab drivers, and make polite chitchat with foreign officials to prove that the United States cares about their country. For most personnel in a given embassy, this is enough.

Embassies have local employees to scan the newspapers and translate the important stories. But as locals the translators view information through a different set of filters than an American diplomat would. No matter how brilliant (and some of my Foreign Service national staff were frighteningly so), they have blind spots about their own society. Foreigners say different things, and think different things, when they speak in English rather than their own language.

Every U.S. embassy needs at any given time one or two officers whose grasp of the language is good enough to read local newspapers and watch local television for pleasure, good enough to cultivate talented politicians who will express their real views and values in their native language rather than in a sanitized English version. A U.S. embassy without a couple of trusted American diplomats immersed in the local political scene is an embassy vulnerable to unpleasant surprises, such as being taken hostage at the Tehran embassy in the wake of the shah's fall.

I was one of the State Department's best Greek speakers, thanks to a background in ancient Greek. I knew Greek history. I read the political gossip section of the newspapers and could follow the slangy, half-obscene accounts of who was doing what to whom. I had complex, rewarding conversations with Greek politicians who spoke no English. Still, like my colleagues, I gravitated toward English speakers. My few public statements in Greek were either written out painfully in advance or else were agonizing for their audience. Most of the useful diplomatic relationships I had were built on English. But my ability to engage in small talk in multiple languages entitled the country I represented to respect as a superpower that valued what foreigners thought.

The world is full of Greeks and Armenians and Israelis and even homegrown Americans who put my linguistic skills to shame, people genuinely fluent in five or six different languages and able to do business deals across five continents. Skill at languages does not, however, automatically make people good diplomats. I was ignobly comforted to discover that the most linguistically gifted foreign service officer I ever met was only an average diplomat. His amazing fluency in Arabic, Russian, and five other difficult languages was not matched by a burning curiosity to lift the barrier that language interposes between the U.S. government and the inner workings of an alien political system. At the end of a conversation with the third most powerful person in the country, his insights into the man's political sensibilities paralleled with suspicious fidelity his assessment of the man's good Russian.

Diplomatic sensibility, not the degree of assimilation to local culture, gives a superpower privileged access to the local political system. Foreign-language learning burnishes the diplomatic temperament. An outsized ego is helpful in bureaucratic competition, but diplomats who thrust their ego into a foreign pecking order fall on their faces. Someone whose ego has been sandblasted by the humiliations of learning a language successfully from scratch as an adult is better at risking the reciprocal vulnerability required for relationship building. Diplomats cannot always be charming in a foreign language, but they can be charmed, and that is half the battle in winning foreign allies.

Knowledge of history is some protection against impassioned tirades. During the fleeting instant when a politician draws breath for the grand assault, a prepared diplomat can slip in some magic phrase that implies intimate familiarity with the negotiating history of the Treaty of Trianon. Surprised and gratified, the politician may allow the narrative to be brought up to the present without the tirade. But effective diplomacy requires that somewhere in the course of building a working professional relationship the substance of the sacred national history will be mutually acknowledged as one of the bases of mutual understanding.

## *Rank Consciousness*

U.S. ambassadors, because of their superb access, neglect their local counterparts in age and diplomatic rank—other foreign ambassadors and the heads of divisions in the Foreign Ministry. By dealing directly with the foreign minister on even ordinary technical issues, a U.S. ambassador can send a steady stream of first-person cables to Washington to remind bureaucratic bosses and peers how seriously Washington's requests are taken. This attitude trickles down to lower level U.S. diplomats as well.

A superpower is automatically guilty of arrogance until it proves otherwise. As I jogged from office to office in the Greek Ministry of Foreign Affairs in 1990 trying to report on Greece's foreign policy, I had a difficult time figuring out why diplomats of vast experience and senior rank refused to give straight answers to my questions about Greek business ties to Iraq or the progress of Greek relations with Slobodan Miloševic's Serbia. I wrote off most of them as obstructionist, ill-informed, and ridiculously rank-conscious. Though a mere second secretary, I was still the only U.S. diplomat they were likely to see, so they should have been grateful.

A diplomat who routinely goes over the heads of his local counterparts will find them as ill-informed and obstructionist as the worst Balkan bureaucratic stereotype. Only when I showed Greek diplomats the respect they were due as equals or superiors did I begin to elicit the level of cooperation the importance of the Greek-U.S. relationship entitled me to expect. This, alas, takes a good deal of time, more than prudent bureaucrats care to spend away from their office mates.

## *The Perils of Long Apprenticeship*

The least popular ambassador of the six I worked for in Greece was appointed by an unpopular U.S. president to faithfully carry out the unpopular policies of that president. His personal views were civilized. An effective way to play the poor policy cards he was dealt would have been to burnish his personal character as the decent representative of a demanding but well-intentioned superpower, admit that American policies caused difficulties for our Greek allies, and ask sincerely how we could work together to make the best of it. Instead, with one eye fixed firmly on Washington, he tried to bluff the Greeks by using arguments he did not himself believe. Tom Miller had the disadvantage of knowing Greece well enough from two previous tours to have lost some of the respectful curiosity that might have bought those arguments a gentler hearing.

Part of the long apprenticeship of foreign service political and economic officers is service as a silent note-taker at meetings of the ambassador or deputy chief of mission (DCM) with host-country officials and politicians. Understandably, many officers are tired of being good listeners by the time they become ambassador. Miller was certainly not the only ambassador I watched who was too busy talking to notice the clues that the minister had something he would tell us if we stopped to ask him. This is bad diplomacy, not only bad manners, but few foreigners call us on it.

Pounding out the obligatory reporting telegrams on meetings, I was troubled all through my career by the attention U.S. embassy officers devoted to reporting what the ambassador had told the minister. As far as I was concerned, Washington already knew U.S. policy. If the State Department did not trust the ambassador to convey that policy accurately to foreigners, the president should never have appointed the person. To me, reporting what the ambassador said seemed necessary only when the embassy had come up with new and better arguments than Washington's own or had responded effectively to the minister's counterarguments. The goal of an embassy report, I thought, was to analyze the local reaction and suggest ways to refine the U.S. approach in light of that reaction.

Ambassadors rise to become ambassador by overcoming that automatic suspicion that accrues to anyone who spends too much time talking intently to strangers. Loyally restating the talking points in messages back to Washington is proof of reliability. It is also self-protection in bare-knuckle interagency games, in which █████████ ██████ other agency heads might retaliate for attempts at ambassadorial oversight by sending back-channel messages to imply that the ambassador puts foreigners' interests ahead of America's own.

The implications for U.S. interests of perceived ambassadorial arrogance were minor. Greek officials generally did what needed to be done because the government was committed to transatlantic cooperation. The scathing press commentary and political cartoons, however, meant that America's Greek friends paid more of a domestic political cost than would have been necessary if diplomats had couched U.S. policies in terms to impress a skeptical Greek public rather than a Washington audience.

Diplomacy is the art of presenting Americans to foreigners and foreigners to Americans in non-zero-sum terms, of creating personal relationships that encourage risk taking in the collective interest by otherwise cautious and selfish politicians and bureaucrats on both sides. Those relationships cannot be counted upon until a diplomat has proved his willingness to invest personal prestige in arguing successfully with Washington on behalf of his hosts. A U.S. diplomat who trims his messages to reassure his Washington audience, who is too self-protective to advocate compromise even when the alternative is no deal at all, will ultimately be written off by the locals as no diplomat at all.

### *The Blessings of Diversity*

The State Department has long had the goal of creating a Foreign Service that "looked like America." This is not a bad idea. The U.S. Foreign Service is now an incredible mix of shapes and sizes, races, creeds, colors, national backgrounds, sexual orientations, skills, personalities, and ideological preferences. Indeed, diversity is America's best diplomatic attribute. Many different, mutually incompatible skills and characteristics serve vital purposes with different foreigners under different circumstances. The qualities that make someone a brilliant diplomat in Kabul may make him a completely ineffective bureaucrat in Washington. As long as the United States correctly matches the talent to the position, it has an advantage over the impeccable, semihereditary diplomatic clones some countries still try to generate.

Evolutionary reasons explain why diplomats tend to be modestly more liberal than the general population in the range of ideological positions they stake out. People who believe their country's welfare is inseparable from the planet's are more able to cooperate constructively with foreigners than those who are locked into a zero-sum chess match between competing nation-states. America's conservative nationalists, no matter how loyal and lovable they may be to their bosses back home, come across to many foreigners as closed-minded, condescending, and uncooperative, triggering a mirror-image response. Shared liberalism makes for freer exchange of information.

Like any diplomat, I was enough of a chameleon to maintain reasonably cordial relations with nationalist local politicians and officials in Greece. But we did not seek one another out. I always learned more in less time from Greek diplomats and politicians who valued international cooperation as an end in itself. They tended to be brighter and more interesting than their nationalist colleagues. More important, idealistic internationalists have a strong motive to collaborate with the United States because America has the logistical and political resources to help them make the world a better place. Still, I would have benefited as political counselor in Athens from a conservative Greek-speaking junior officer eager to work the other side of the aisle in the Greek parliament more effectively than I could. If the State Department attempts to impose the same ideological rigor as some domestic U.S. bureaucracies, it will cut itself off from many of America's best diplomatic allies around the world.

## *Management* Versus *Diplomacy*

Misinterpreting the meaning of diversity, State Department bureaucrats routinely attempt to define the characteristics of the perfect foreign service officer. Predictably, because this exercise is driven by the Administrative Branch, renamed the Management Branch in 2002, the conclusion is that the State Department needs to emphasis good management skills as the most important criterion for promotion to senior ranks and service as a U.S. ambassador. This shift coincides with a self-serving confusion between management and administration spread by administrative specialists and security officers.

It is a fine thing when an embassy is well run, when all the office equipment works, when the resources are clawed out of Washington for in-country travel and entertaining our contacts, when morale is high. But the purpose of an embassy is not to be well run, to make its personnel happy, or even to guarantee that all of them stay alive. The purpose of an embassy is to promote U.S. interests with foreign governments and publics.

A successful U.S. mission depends on senior diplomats who understand the full spectrum of competing U.S. interests and can weigh the demands of competing U.S. bureaucracies in terms of what is possible and affordable in the context of host country law and politics. Without this rare and precious set of analytical skills, tough and disciplined administration leads as often to protracted administrative nightmares—such as trying to fire an unproductive local employee in the teeth of local labor laws and unfriendly courts—as to successful promotion of U.S. interests.

The "old" Foreign Service overemphasized general amiability as the key to assignments and promotions. The current Foreign Service personnel system focuses on identifying potential managers—bureaucrats of unusual energy and ambition—and promoting them rapidly to policy and personnel management positions as DCM or deputy assistant secretary in Washington. The less-forceful colleagues of these managers are pensioned off at age fifty or so.

Competent diplomats without management pretensions will be retired at the height of their functional expertise. The high-fliers are dropped into make-or-break positions, such as DCM, in which they are judged for promotion by standards skewed to favor administrative skills over diplomacy. A diplomat who has served a whole career as a lightly managed political officer talking brilliantly and persuasively to foreigners about foreign policy may well go fetal when elevated to the rank of DCM and called upon to adjudicate interagency disputes over parking spaces. DCMs who remain faithful to their diplomatic instincts make themselves and their embassies miserable. Those who flourish tend to sacrifice their curiosity about foreigners.

The triumph of administrative aptitude over policy judgment is logical for a domestic bureaucracy, with influence that increases proportionally to the resources it can absorb. In the State Department, with only a tiny budget for programs and thus little ability to rent a domestic constituency, competitive advantage resides in the ability to get things done overseas for itself and the dozens of U.S. agencies it supports. Downgrading diplomatic skill and local expertise in favor of generic bureaucratic skills is a suicidal mantra. Applying it, the State Department becomes what its bureaucratic rivals in Washington would like it to be, the docile concierge for other agencies that set foreign policy in accordance with their own bureaucratic convenience.

## *Diplomacy as a Career*

Diplomacy is a great adventure, but it is not for everyone. The necessary specialized knowledge can be (indeed must be) learned on the job. Americans with the generosity of spirit that inspires skeptical foreigners to respond with similar generosity are plentiful. Analytical curiosity about the world is somewhat scarcer. The discipline and energy needed to budge a huge, self-absorbed, bureaucratic organization back in Washington are the rarest traits. Those diplomats who thrive in every posting and at every level of responsibility are few. Some of them are freaks who need only four hours of sleep a night. But plenty of room remains for lesser mortals, for gentle souls with a gift for hard-nosed political analysis or for charming American tourists out of jail.

Life overseas imposes personal and other costs, including a real risk of estrangement from the people diplomats grew up with. As Mark Twain warned, foreign travel liberalizes a person. Substantial parts of the U.S. government justify their existence by presenting the world as "a cold, harsh, cruel, prison-house, stocked with all manner of selfishness and hate and wickedness." One of the most necessary but perilous parts of a diplomat's job is to take U.S. officials by the hand and explain to them how the rules that govern foreign societies serve the same purposes as the rules that govern America. The world then becomes considerably less frightening, its unsolved problems less immediate a threat to U.S. interests. This is diplomatic realism, but in Washington people call it by the uglier name "clientitis."

Some foreign service officers protect themselves from the liberalizing impact of travel by making their American embassy compound as faithful a replica as they can manage of a gated community in suburban Virginia. The real diplomats, however, embrace the intellectual adventure of each new set of unwritten rules. The stigma of clientitis is a small price to pay for the honor of representing America to the world and the duty of interpreting the world to America.

# 6

# ★ *Bureaucratic Fantasy and the Duty*

# *of Dissent* ★

*What is official*
*Is incontestable. It undercuts*
*The problematical world and sells us life*
*At a discount.*
                    *Christopher Fry,* The Lady's Not for Burning

*He'll sit behind that big desk and say, "Do this," and "do that."*
*And do you know what will happen? Nothing.*
                    *Harry S. Truman in 1953, referring to Dwight D.*
                                                      *Eisenhower*

By studying the rules of political and economic competition of
a given group of foreigners carefully enough, curious, dispassionate
U.S. diplomats can make reasonably accurate short-term predictions
about the foreigners' behavior. The U.S. government is a set of strong,
relatively virtuous institutions. American bureaucrats are as well
meaning and hardworking as any in the world. Armed with accurate
information, they will, if so requested by their president, propose
and implement policies that have a high probability of promoting
the welfare of the American people. So why does the United States
blunder into foreign policy quagmires?[1]

The fact that "Cassandra" is an epithet Americans use to reproach pessimism, not to applaud accurate prophecy, should be a
tip-off. One morning in Athens late in 2001, the ambassador gave
the Embassy Country Team, the heads of the various sections and agencies at post, a pep talk on the impending Greek purchase of main
battle tanks. Hundreds of U.S. jobs hung in the balance. My realist
eyebrows rose. Did the United States in fact have any chance of persuading the Greek government to buy M1A1 Abrams? For a political

officer with no career stake in the outcome, the answer was obvious. I quietly polled the defense attaché and the head of our Office of Defense Cooperation. Their sources were better than mine, and they were specialists while I was not. They shook their heads.

If generals made the decisions on arms purchases, America's share of global arms exports would be more than the 50 percent the country enjoys currently. Our military hardware is expensive, but soldiers are rightly happy with it. All governments, however, see arms deals as politics by other means. Each big weapons purchase curries favor with some foreign ally. Each purchase also means a commission that enriches a specific group of friendly local businesspeople, who will kick back some share to fund the governing political party.

A government is bound by some notion of "fair share" in dividing up the surplus wealth of its citizens. By late 2001 superior U.S. technology and gentle political pressure had won U.S. companies and their local business partners several big Greek weapons orders. European Union (EU) arms manufacturers and their Greek middlemen were complaining. Germany had supported Greece in other EU issues. My Greek contacts hinted, and Athens newspapers indirectly confirmed, that Prime Minister Kostas Simitis felt he owed German chancellor Schroeder the tank deal. The U.S. and German tanks were close enough in quality and price that the Greek military had no problem with a decision to buy Leopards.

A wide-awake analyst could have detected the Greek government's political decision the moment the procurement specifications were released. The scoring system gave the Leopards a slight edge over the Abrams, even without French cheating (they planted a global positioning system jamming device at the test site to sabotage the Abrams navigation system). The arduous procurement process that followed was designed to reassure even the most skeptical Greek taxpayer, plus the British and U.S. governments, that the competition was fair and genuine. By keeping General Dynamics officially in the running until the last possible moment, the Greek government could squeeze the Germans to sweeten their offer. The Defense Ministry spent many months scraping together the money to pay for its purchase. Meanwhile, many business lunches were eaten at fine restaurants.

I did not see myself as a pessimist. The United States was not going to win this deal with any arguments an ally and friend cared to make. However, ringing up a big sale for General Dynamics was not America's only national security interest. My uniformed colleagues agreed that Greece was wasting the money it spent on tanks. No land army was going to invade in the next two decades. NATO had many more tanks than it could transport to any plausible battlefield. At NATO headquarters in Brussels, the United States was urging European NATO members like Greece to spend their limited defense budgets to meet more serious operational gaps, buying the transport and communications gear the alliance needed desperately. Why, I wondered, when the tank sale was a lost cause for U.S. business interests, was our embassy still feverishly endorsing the idea that Greece needed tanks? Why not use U.S. influence to steer Prime Minister Simitis toward a more appropriate shopping list, in this case NATO's Defense Capabilities Initiative? U.S. companies had a fighting chance of selling the hardware on that list.

In retrospect this was not a prudent question for me to ask, even in a private email to the ambassador. I thought I was being patriotic and realistic. He reacted as if I were subverting him personally.

The tank deal was large enough to draw welcome high-level Washington attention to U.S. Embassy Athens. Washington officials would judge the ambassador not by whether the embassy had read the situation correctly, or even by its success or failure in promoting the tank deal. They would judge him and his team by the same measure ordinary human beings use, by their perception of character. How aggressive, competitive, and self-assured did the U.S. ambassador seem in the pursuit of the goals that had been set for him? Relentlessly positive salespeople will be respected and promoted, no matter how much they actually sell. An ambassador who admits defeat, even to propose a better policy option, will be savaged. Retired ambassadors, former members of Congress, and an assortment of three-star generals—the General Dynamics Washington lobbying team—will spread the word that he is a loser. Bureaucratic realism, for this or any ambassador, means fostering the fantasy in Washington that a phone call from the president to the Greek prime minister might still tip the balance for the Abrams.

I shut up. The U.S. government had no vital interests that would suffer from ignoring Greek political realities. I, however, had a career that would suffer from my ambassador's wrath.

University professors used to teach their students that "realism" competes with "idealism" in international relations. The academic debate is more subtle now, but journalists and politicians still speak as if pessimistic, amoral realists and moral, optimistic idealists wage permanent war for the soul of America. For polemical purposes, realism is synonymous with selfishness and extortion. Most Americans recoil. Some do not. Either way, putting the debate in such terms misrepresents the planet we inhabit.

When America understands its real-world interests correctly, idealism and realism seldom conflict. The United States and Greece have a shared interest in Greece's spending its defense budget wisely. More generally, the U.S. government sincerely (and correctly) believes it has a selfish interest in building peace, prosperity, and liberal democracy worldwide. The clash most academics ignore, the clash that dominates the foreign policy process in practice, is the permanent tactical struggle between realism—the diplomatic art of the possible abroad—and self-aggrandizing bureaucratic and political fantasy at home. In 2001 an inexperienced American president allowed fantasy to prevail.

When Greece bought its Leopards, a very decent local General Dynamics representative limped sadly home but the sky did not fall. When a heavily armed superpower pursues a fantasy aggressively enough, the sky does fall. The sky fell for the families of the thousands of American men and women who lost their lives or limbs in Iraq. It is still falling for 25 million ordinary Iraqis.

### The Real World Is Knowable

President Bush's official excuse for America's debacle in Iraq is that "everyone thought . . . " Nonsense. Detailed, accurate knowledge of the world is available to anyone who looks for it. The course of human history is an open book of strategies that work and strategies that fail. Ninety percent of the world's population knew instinctively that invading Iraq was a bad decision. The other 10 percent could have reached that same correct conclusion, if they had asked the right questions of the experts whose specialty it was to understand Iraq and its people.

On key questions regarding Iraq, the experts most closely involved in studying the issue had answers that were reasonably correct. The UN inspectors on the ground were not surprised when the United States found no weapons of mass destruction (WMD) threat in Iraq. The CIA and State Department officials who had worked on Iraq during the 1990s knew that Ahmed Chalabi, the neoconservatives' candidate to replace Saddam Hussein, was a liar ordinary Iraqis would not follow. Army Chief of Staff Erik Shinseki made very clear that the U.S. military could not maintain order in Iraq without twice as many troops as Secretary Rumsfeld was willing to send. Consultants to the Department of Energy had said publicly that it would take years of work and billions of dollars of investment to increase Iraqi oil output to a level that could finance postwar reconstruction.

One of the joys of a diplomatic career is discovering that the human ecosystem still has multiple niches capable of supporting a reasonable number of people whose intellectual curiosity about their planet is intact. Sometimes they will be journalists, sometimes scientists, sometimes engaged businesspeople. Asked with respectful curiosity about their area of interest, they will give accurate information to the American diplomat who tracks them down.

The U.S. government pays a huge army of federal employees to find out about the world. Many of them do their job brilliantly. In every U.S. embassy I ever visited, I always found at least one U.S. diplomat committed to the intellectual and emotional challenge of understanding the politics that drove the behavior of the local society. With the help of the local staff of the embassy, he or she could assess correctly whether America's strategy for the given country was working or could work. Washington swarms with people intimately familiar with the inner workings of every country in the world and desperately eager to share that knowledge with anyone who will listen. From conversation with its own experts, the U.S. government has access, when it asks for it, to all the accurate information it needs.

### The Social Construction of Foreign Policy Realism

The State Department's Bureau of Intelligence and Research invited me to more than my share of foreign policy conferences. At these conferences, a stream of distinguished experts would get up and competently describe the foreign policy situation. I would nod approvingly. Yes, the academics understood the problem the State Department faced in making policy, its need to balance multiple, conflicting U.S. goals spread across many different agencies and constituencies. As they wound up their presentation, the speakers would all stress that India (for example) was a crucial regional player and that it was vital that the U.S. government adopt a clear policy toward it. I would wait expectantly for their policy prescription, but the speech was over. I would ask a pointed question to which the customary response was that the purpose of the conference was to frame the further study that would propose the policy I sought.

When the speakers were ex-officials, they would often suggest that a new bureaucratic organization be created, with some well-known ex-diplomat to lead it and a funding allocation of its own. I would ask in my convoluted way what the United States expected the organization to do. The answer was important to me: if someone had an idea that would work better than what the United States was doing already, I or the embassy in New Delhi should get to work on it. Besides, I could not understand how it was possible to structure an organization and assign it a funding level without first specifying at least in general terms a workable strategy to achieve its purpose. A couple of State Department colleagues would nod approvingly, but the panel moderator would change the subject. One speaker told me firmly that it does not behoove senior experts and bureaucrats to "get down in the weeds."

Experts become experts by virtue of studying messy real-world problems. Most of these problems have no tidy solutions, certainly not solutions that can be imposed from outside by a democratically governed superpower with a huge budget deficit and an addiction to its creature comforts. No prudent person would voluntarily stake his or her career advancement on successfully transforming the real world. Most of the time, no one is asked to. The real world seems to be, and generally is, safely far from America's shores. There are more urgent bureaucratic matters to deal with any given morning than extracting workable foreign policy guidance from someone whose expertise is problems rather than solutions.

Successful—because ambitious, disciplined, and competitive— bureaucrats gradually lose interest in the outside world, no matter how curious they were about it when they started. Rather than torment themselves with an intractable intellectual puzzle, they plunge into a narrow, winnable game of funding and influence in their own capital. Washington is incredibly competitive. High-level bureaucratic competition, like that of the advanced levels of video games, takes place at a blinding pace. A bureaucrat rises not by formulating initiatives likely to achieve their stated purpose overseas but by successfully silencing some buzzing alarm going off inside the U.S. political world. The most valuable expertise is the ability to generate immediate, plausible bureaucratic responses to the political challenges posed by each morning's headlines. Plausibility is measured, however, by a purely internal, self-referential process. In practice, bureaucratic victory means having advocated whatever course the president ultimately adopts.

An effective bureaucrat takes an unnecessary risk, therefore, in exposing peers and superiors to the views of experts, even the experts the U.S. government pays for. Effective bureaucrats accumulate instead a roster of presentable, credentialed persons with views likely to reinforce what they perceive to be the prevailing inclination of the chief policymakers. Lurking in some obscure or less obscure university is all the intellectual underpinning required for any fatuous scheme.

In the run-up to the Iraq War the neoconservatives scored a major triumph by introducing Vice President Cheney to Bernard Lewis, the eminent Princeton emeritus professor of Middle Eastern studies. Lewis's ethnic slur that Arabs could best be controlled through fear of force proved no more useful in practice than the similar slur ("either at your feet or at your throat") directed against the Germans during the early twentieth century. But because Lewis's advice mirrored his own prejudices, Cheney did not question whether an expert on the Ottoman Turks was really the most reliable guide to the behavior of Iraqis. An expert on fifth-century BC Athenian farmers and their wars, Victor Davis Hanson, was likewise trotted out to reassure Cheney that militarization of American foreign policy around the myth of U.S. ethnic superiority had impeccable classical antecedents. When actual Iraq experts intruded into the policy process, a quick call to the vice president's office assured that they would be smoothly removed.[2]

As a rule, senior bureaucrats in Washington either do not know who their experts are, do not invite them to the meetings where their expertise would be useful, or do not trust them to speak when key policymakers are present. Often they can point to a justification: experts are too divorced from high-level bureaucratic thought processes to speak in a language that validates their advice in the mind of their audience.

The U.S. government is enormous and complex. Keeping abreast of its inner workings is a full-time intellectual commitment. Senior officials form a series of interlocking groups of close colleagues. Among themselves they speak a private language of funding levels and bureaucratic acronyms. Rare geniuses aside, an expert who has devoted similar intellectual intensity to the inner workings of some foreign country will not communicate effectively with them.

Bureaucrats are social animals. By the time bureaucrats have climbed high enough on the career ladder for their opinions to be heard directly, the successful ones are fully immersed in the study of their superiors and rivals, not the behavior of foreigners. Sitting in the Country Team meeting at the embassy or in a meeting of the South Asian Bureau at the State Department, my colleagues and I slowly learned that Greek or Indian internal politics were not of general interest. Fresh gossip on the views of the secretary or undersecretary, of the White House, or of our Pentagon rivals was the currency that purchased respect.

### Superpower Narcissism

Most Greek bookstores carry Greek translations of all the latest books by Noam Chomsky, an American intellectual gifted at connecting all the dots of U.S. behavior into a tidy picture. In 2001 I assured Mr. Tegopoulos, the publisher of Athens' most popular leftist daily newspaper, that his favorite American philosopher was "clinically insane." Chomsky, I said, had deduced a vast, invisible mechanism of systematic U.S. oppression and exploitation, one that was not true to human nature and could not have operated over decades without becoming visible to its employees. I reassured Tegopoulos that the U.S. foreign policy apparatus could not conspire its way effectively out of a paper bag.

I feel more charitably disposed toward Chomsky now. The Iraq War proved that the United States does have a small group of extremely intelligent, disciplined, highly competitive individuals competent enough to mobilize the U.S. bureaucracy around a single mission such as regime change in Iraq.[3] Chomsky's favorite conspirators, the former Trotskyites turned neoconservatives, might even have read Chomsky in their youth. Certainly they made the same mistake he did. They confused mastery over the U.S. bureaucratic system with U.S. power to triumph over the real world. The State Department inadvertently contributes to that delusion.

Every spring the State Department and all its far-flung outposts convulse themselves in an exercise called the Mission Program Plan (MPP). The ambassador exercises his authority as the president's personal representative to compel the U.S. government agencies at post to contribute to a unified set of mission goals and objectives. Accordingly, the local representatives of (I've forgotten a few) the ████████████████, Office of Defense Cooperation, FBI, Foreign Commercial Service, Foreign Agricultural Service, Drug Enforcement Administration, Immigration and Naturalization Service, and Transportation Security Administration join the chiefs of the State Department sections (Political, Economic, Public Affairs, Management, Consular) sitting glumly in the ambassador's ugly living room while a designated MPP coordinator attempts to organize everything the United States  does in Greece in tidy categories defined by the State Department.

The MPP process is a necessary, even noble exercise—reexamining what America is doing in terms of what U.S. priorities are likely to be over the next four fiscal years. The participants venture predictions about where Greece and its neighbors seem to be heading. More important, they attempt to match resources to goals. Each agency makes its claims regarding the correct mix of people, office space, equipment, and budgets to promote U.S. national interests most efficiently in light of how Greece is expected to change in the coming years. And various offices suggest objective indicators to measure how well the mission attains the goals it sets.

Fortunately no local citizens are present during the MPP process. If there were, they would reserve a locked ward for us at the nearest mental hospital. The internal bureaucratic processes of a superpower are almost indistinguishable from megalomania. A living room full of experienced, dignified, sensible men and women will speak to one another as if the U.S. government, simply by having the right mix of bureaucratic resources in place, can end terrorism, instill respect for human rights, double U.S. exports, and become universally beloved in the course of the next three fiscal years. No one notices anything amiss in the implication that the collective action of foreigners is the product of tireless, infinitely acute U.S. bureaucratic readjustments.

MPP participants are perfectly sane. The MPP is a competitive process for allocating scarce bureaucratic resources worldwide, not actually a blueprint for changing the world. Humility, no matter how appropriate, means loss of resources. The grandiosity of U.S. Embassy Athens's claims for the effectiveness of its diplomacy are a direct result of the need to persuade Washington that Athens, rather than Tirana or Mogadishu, is the correct recipient of additional Foreign Service personnel slots and additional millions of dollars in program funds. The real world is only a scenic backdrop for this particular bureaucratic competition. When that world does not cooperate with our instinctive human desire to hold on to what we have, sensible bureaucrats touch it up slightly for Washington's benefit.

A month after the MPP, each foreign service officer receives an employee efficiency report (EER). Promotion in the Foreign Service is a competition against other officers of the same rank and functional specialization. These reports are almost the sole basis for career advancement, and supervisors agonize over them for days to get their subordinates promoted. It goes without saying that all U.S. diplomats are brilliant, charming, and good team players. The EER form is designed to squeeze out these empty adjectives in favor of specific accomplishments.

Competitive pressure sharpens the wits. The State Department will not notice that three different political officers at U.S. Embassy Athens simultaneously deserve sole credit for eliminating Greek domestic terrorism, brokering Greek-Turkish rapprochement, ending the sex trafficking of women and children in the Balkans, selling the Greek Air Force a billion dollars worth of F-16s, and managing one-half of a local employee with firmness plus exemplary devotion to equal opportunity principles.

"He believes his own EERs" is a Foreign Service cliché that applies to almost every successful bureaucrat. The overall effect of the EER and MPP is to reinforce each employee's comforting illusion that being a well-regarded American bureaucrat is the same thing as running the planet. This rosy picture of U.S. efficiency inspires "the meddling spirit that rarely sleeps in the breast of a diplomatist."[4] A taste for activism is commendable, provided the people at the top are experienced and tough enough to quash the natural self-promotion of their subordinates.

As the Soviet empire collapsed under resurgent nationalism, outside efforts to hasten that collapse amounted to fleabites on a dying mastodon. One of the most courageous services George H. W. Bush ever did his country was to demonstrate how helpless American influence was to change the fate of a fellow superpower. He traveled to Kiev in July 1991 and appealed to the Ukrainians not to give way to "suicidal nationalism." Conservatives in the United States slammed his "Chicken Kiev" speech as the betrayal of Ukraine's sacred aspiration to freedom. Their criticism was ridiculous. The Ukrainian people still voted overwhelmingly for the independence they would seize a few weeks later. Bush's cautious advice, however, had a positive impact on a Moscow audience that was listening very carefully. By publicly taking the United States out of the Soviet death struggle, Bush yielded the floor to Russia's own reformers. Had he pandered to Washington narcissists, the outside challenge from the rival superpower would have goaded the Soviet security mastodon to crush its local tormentors in its last dying spasms. The United States was helpless to protect Gorbachev from his generals, and Bush knew it.

Noam Chomsky is not the only American who imagines that the United States is a more effective superpower than it is. Had President George W. Bush any experience in foreign policy, he might have been able to discount the competitive boasts of his cabinet secretaries. But when he decreed the invasion of Iraq, he and Vice President Cheney apparently genuinely believed that the United States had intelligence officers with reliable information about Saddam Hussein, soldiers who know how to fight, and teams of civilian experts with the skills to occupy, rebuild, and democratize foreign countries.

Thanks to sixty years of massive defense spending, the U.S. military had the ability to make mincemeat of any foreign army it chose to destroy. U.S. intelligence agencies, however, were led by officers whose prized expertise was no longer the behavior of foreign governments but rather the political requirements of their superiors. America's corps of state-building experts did not exist and never had. Instead, the United States had a medium-sized herd of international development bureaucrats, who over decades of Third World floods, famines, and earthquakes since the Marshall Plan, had become efficient lifesavers in humanitarian relief work. The development expertise that was most highly rewarded, however, was the bureaucrats' ability to write checks in a way that would spend all the foreign aid money Congress allocated without annoying any influential member of Congress or violating U.S. accounting regulations. U.S. Agency for International Development officials did not dare admit that they had no idea how to put Iraq back together again. If they had, the president would have handed over exclusive responsibility for state building to a more optimistic agency, specifically the Pentagon.

It took me almost two decades in government service to realize a simple truth. Washington's bureaucratic competition for resources was just like the political competition I watched in Greece. Policymaking everywhere is fixated on two basic questions: how much money should be spent on a given issue, and who will have the right to decide which contractors get to spend it. A global superpower cannot defend its interests competently, however, until it factors into this policymaking process the likely effect of its actions on the intended beneficiaries.

## Challenging the Fantasy

President George W. Bush, enabled by brilliant bureaucrats like Rumsfeld and Wolfowitz, launched the Iraq War based on calculations judged false by the nonbureaucratic experts who looked in detail at Iraq and the threats it posed. U.S. diplomatic and military personnel then strained every sinew to achieve the admirable, doomed goal of a stable, democratic, united Iraq. They would have been justified in defending their failure publicly: the task they had been given was objectively impossible to achieve by any means tolerable to ordinary Americans. In public, at least, they said nothing of the kind. America's competitive bureaucratic system guarantees that each struggling U.S. soldier or diplomat will personally have far more to lose than to gain from admitting to the American people or even to him or herself that American power is limited.

Idealistic young Americans join the U.S. government with the idea that one day they will have a role in shaping the policies on which America's welfare depends. Foreign service officers hear their words spoken by presidents and see their ideas in instruction cables signed by the secretary of state and sent to embassies around the world. But these accomplishments will seem trivial if the worst should happen. When the vast mechanism, of which they are loyal, vital cogs, goes hurtling toward some folly their diplomatic expertise allows them to recognize, what is their duty?

America is a superpower partly because the American political system gives more power to its president than most democracies entrust to their leaders. American voters put their security and prosperity and that of their children and grandchildren in the hands of a single person. The consequences of a bad decision by the U.S. president can be catastrophic for American citizens and the world. Even small mistakes have dangerous consequences years later, as America learned when it created a battle-hardened Islamist resistance in Afghanistan and then forgot it had done so.

Foreign policy requires a massively complex balancing of competing interests, too many judgment calls in too little time based on too much contradictory information. A huge bureaucratic apparatus supports the president in making his decisions, but the big decisions are his alone to make. No one else is in a position to see all the pieces of the domestic and international puzzle on the table before him. Even a stupid gamble can sometimes succeed when it is pursued with absolute unity of purpose. And therefore a patriotic government employee puts aside bureaucratic self-interest, moral squeamishness, and intellectual vanity to defer honorably to the foreign policy determined by the president.

Despite the whining of outside critics, the U.S. president can take for granted the loyalty of the State Department, CIA, and Pentagon. Bureaucrats fight unscrupulously to set the stage for a favorable presidential decision. Once the president has decided, however, they implement the decision with a stiff upper lip, even when vital U.S. national interests are being harmed. American bureaucrats are less disciplined than the German generals and diplomats in World War II, who loyally helped the Third Reich commit suicide by invading the USSR. But they come reasonably close.

I served four successive presidents and the six secretaries of state they appointed. Any diplomat who tamely agreed with every policy decision of every one of those figures would be a slippery character indeed. On areas of disagreement peripheral to their expertise, diplomats keep silent. But in their specific area of responsibility, there is a permanent tension between loyalty to country and loyalty to career.

Bureaucrats control the decision-making process by shaping the information that reaches the president. Usually they do so by simplifying a complex world, not by falsifying it. In the process of reaching the rank of ambassador, foreign service officers develop an unconscious aversion to being the bearer of bad news. Every ambassador I ever worked for, and every secretary of state, announced at the beginning of his or her tenure that he or she wanted the plain, unvarnished truth. All of them thought they meant it. But the official paper trail emanating from every embassy was relentlessly upbeat. The depiction of the host country would be accurate enough. No matter how bleak the situation, however, the embassy's policy prescription would be to allocate more resources to keep doing more of what it was doing already. Sometimes ambassadors let bad news from subordinates die in their in-box. More often, the members of the ambassador's Country Team of senior staff understand that it is not their job to write awkward answers about the appropriateness of U.S. policy until someone wiser than they has asked them.

Protecting America requires the president to make full use of America's vast array of expert knowledge of the world. The unique expertise of diplomats about foreigners and their vital interests and probable reactions gives them a compelling moral duty to fight as hard as humanly possible to make sure that the decision-making process gets it right, regardless of the personal cost. But loyalty to bosses is a competing moral claim. The most damaging allegation leveled in Washington against Colin Powell was that his State Department troops were disloyal. What finally lost CIA director George Tenet his job was not getting Iraq wrong. It was being unable to control his employees when they began leaking their policy dissent to the media.

The State Department, to be sure of getting the accurate advice it needs, tries to reduce to a minimum the cost, both to the dissenter and to the State Department, of free expression of opinion by anyone with a claim to useful insight. Scarred by the debacle of Vietnam policy, which included the resignation of a number of talented foreign service officers who recognized the United States was fighting a lost war, the State Department created an excellent institution called the Dissent Channel. The Dissent Channel is a safety valve for frustrated diplomats and a protection for the secretary against his relentlessly upbeat ambassadors. Any State Department employee can send a message to the secretary of state on any policy issue. The policy planning staff of the State Department must respond in writing. The existence of the message, its content, and the identity of its drafter will be kept rigorously secret, including from the White House, unless the drafter specifies otherwise. Retaliation against the dissenter is a violation of official regulations, punishable with a career-blighting reprimand.

I used the Dissent Channel in early 1992, on an issue that is now a minor historical footnote, except to Greeks. I had experienced the full force of nationalism in 1990, when the U.S. embassy in Athens was brave or foolish enough to mention Greece's officially nonexistent Slav Macedonian minority in the State Department's annual human rights report. In September 1991 an independent Republic of Macedonia appeared on Greece's northern border as Yugoslavia slid into civil war.

The modern Macedonians are Slavs who arrived in the geographical area known as Macedonia (in northern Greece, western Bulgaria, and southern Yugoslavia) many centuries after the Greek-speaking warlord Alexander the Great put Macedonia on the map by conquering the Near East. The Slav Macedonians consolidated their own identity as a distinct nation and language too late, after Greeks and Bulgarians had already locked up most of the region's heroes, history, and real estate. In a belated spasm of nation building, the Macedonians rewrote history to turn Alexander the Great into one of their own.

Local politicians in northern Greece realized that there was political mileage to be gained from fanning the Greek public into a nationalist frenzy in response. Blackmailed by an ambitious young foreign minister who controlled enough seats in Parliament to topple the government, Prime Minister Konstantinos Mitsotakis felt he had no option but to demand that the Macedonians abandon all use of the name "Macedonia," even though it was the only name this people had for themselves, their language, and their country. By doing so, Greece made an enemy out of what should have been a helpless client state next door and turned itself into an international laughingstock. What could the United States do to remedy the situation?

The rumor from a colleague in Washington was that Acting Secretary of State Larry Eagleburger was under pressure from well-connected Greek-Americans to lean on the Macedonians to change their name to something the Greeks would accept, without the word "Macedonia" in it. I could not judge how strong that pressure really was, but I was convinced that by undermining Macedonia's fragile state identity, America would harm Greek interests in the Balkans as well as its own. Though few of my Greek contacts dared admit it publicly, many of them quietly agreed that their rational course was to help the Macedonians consolidate their state under Greek tutelage. But they were helpless. Greek voters knew the EU operated by consensus. The Greek government would be toppled if it failed to use its veto power to block EU diplomatic recognition and assistance to the Macedonians. With the EU stymied, only the United States had the power to broker a compromise that would keep

Macedonia stable. But a long and useful U.S.-Greek relationship was at risk if the United States intervened.

What justified use of the Dissent Channel in my own mind was my certainty that only U.S. Embassy Athens could credibly analyze the impact on U.S. interests in Greece of U.S. policy toward Macedonia. If the U.S. embassy took an official position, America's own short-term self-interest would force it to exaggerate the strength of Greek arguments. My Greek-American ambassador would ruin his life by doing otherwise, and U.S. diplomats would briefly be in danger. America's decision on what to call Macedonia was one only America's political leadership could make, but I did not want that decision to be made on the basis of incomplete information.

I trusted the system and wrote a Dissent Channel telegram laying out the arguments for U.S. recognition of the Republic of Macedonia by that name or by a compromise name like "Nova Makedonija" (New Macedonia). I couched my argument in brutal, realist terms: Greek prime minister Mitsotakis, an excellent U.S. partner on many issues, was politically a walking corpse, doomed to lose the next elections whatever he or the United States did. He was thus immune to any further U.S. harm. America would have to do the right thing on Macedonia eventually in any case. By waiting, America would pay an inflated price, reduced ability to work with the next Greek government.

As it happened, the administration was unwilling to antagonize Greek-Americans in an election year but also unwilling to hurt America's other Balkan interests by blessing the Greek position. Thus it played for time. If anyone resented my unsolicited advice I was oblivious. My action kept my ambassador out of the awkward position of having to block or comment on my message. The secrecy of my Dissent Channel telegram was well protected and the U.S.-Greek relationship did not suffer.[5] My message kept my professional conscience clear and gave me some modest stature later in the eyes of colleagues with similar views.

Twelve years later the State Department finally found a safe window of opportunity to recognize the Republic of Macedonia by its own name, two days after the 2004 U.S. presidential elections. What broke the U.S. internal deadlock was the desire to encourage a positive outcome for a crucial Macedonian referendum. Greeks and Greek-Americans, however, were furious at the cowardice and cynicism that the timing and lack of forewarning seemed to imply. They could do nothing to retaliate against President Bush. The U.S. ambassador was a lame duck, in his last weeks in Athens. The opposition party turned on the Greek prime minister and foreign minister, pummeling them brutally for failing to prevent the U.S. decision. After a few days they got tired and moved on.

In 1994, back in Washington, I was rewarded, albeit by the American Foreign Service Association, not the State Department, for participating in another act of dissent. Serbs, Croats, and Bosnian Muslims had been slaughtering one another to redraw the map of Bosnia to correspond with their ethnic aspirations. Publicly, U.S. policy toward Yugoslavia in 1992–93 was a pious bleat that the prior administrative borders of the original Yugoslav republics should be preserved. Senior State Department officials faithfully conveyed to us desk officers that the Clinton White House would not overrule the Pentagon's reluctance to intervene to stop the carnage.

Five State Department officials eventually resigned, citing their disgust at U.S. inaction in Bosnia. It never occurred to me to join the resigners. I had fleeting contact with George Kenney, who resigned as the Yugoslav desk officer in August 1992, a few days after I arrived as the Romania desk officer next door. Kenney's sacrifice sent little ripples through Washington and prompted a high-level pep talk for our office, but nothing seemed to change in policy terms.

Angry at the Yugoslav killings, our office focused on the one step that was bureaucratically uncontroversial—enforcing UN economic sanctions against Serbia. Sanctions turn out to be a frustrating, even demoralizing, tool of foreign policy. They did not save the Bosnian lives they were supposed to save. They cost my Romanian clients more than their struggling economy could afford in lost trade. They impoverished ordinary Serbians. Meanwhile, the Serb nationalist mafiosi we diplomats despised were the ones who profited. They got rich off smuggled oil and cigarettes, while the Greek and other neighboring governments turned a blind eye.[6]

In a well-run bureaucratic universe, the desk officers do not wait passively for guidance from above, from senior officials whose core expertise is their knowledge of the president's inclinations. Instead desk officers volunteer the best guidance they know, confident that their bosses have confidence in them to carry out loyally whatever policy is adopted, no matter what they personally had argued. Sometimes the U.S. government works this way.

In April 1993 activist colleagues recruited me to join their coordinated effort to persuade the U.S. government to change its Bosnia policy. A dozen regional and functional experts sat down together to draft recommendations to rebut the self-protective pessimism of the Pentagon. Based on our collective knowledge of the situation in Bosnia and the surrounding region, we knew the Bosnian

Serb militants could not set their own limit to the ethnic cleansing of the Muslims. The Serbs would make peace only when they lost hope of further territorial gains. Our specific recommendation was to allow the Bosnian Muslims to rearm, while U.S. airpower struck the Serb artillery batteries above Sarajevo. I contributed a paragraph to our memorandum to Secretary Warren Christopher, arguing that the government would reduce the odds that U.S. military intervention would be needed if it kept the threat of that intervention as immediate, credible, and open-ended as possible, not excluding the use of U.S. ground forces.

Warren Christopher was a distinguished lawyer with sensible views. When a confederate on his staff placed the memo in his hands, he invited us all to a meeting with him. He shared the memo with cabinet colleagues. Still, he hesitated to put his personality on the line with President Clinton. Someone, though not one of us twelve, leaked our protest to the *New York Times*.[7] The leak might have come from the Pentagon to discredit the State Department as disloyal to the president's policy. Clinton's caution, however, was partly dictated by European hesitations, partly the result of massive exaggeration by the Pentagon about how much U.S. military force would be required. In any case we did not feel discredited.

Our dissent, public along with our names, had only a modest impact. We had suggested a policy that would probably work, but we could not prove that vital U.S. interests justified tangling with the Pentagon. We were given an award for trying. Ultimately Clinton was freed to act by a shift in U.S. and European domestic politics caused by the mounting anger of decent people at the civilian corpses they saw on CNN. As we had recommended two years earlier, Clinton rearmed the Bosnian Muslims and struck Serb artillery positions from the air. The Serbs were soon forced to negotiate. A peace deal emerged at Dayton, Ohio, in November 1995. The existence of the "Bosnia Twelve" had been, in the end, mostly a tiny additional ray of hope among Bosnian Muslims struggling for survival in their darkest days.[8]

### Strengthening Dissent Within the System

The Dissent Channel, and a State Department culture of tolerating if not taking unsolicited advice from working-level diplomats, is one of the State Department's strengths. Dissenting opinions offered confidentially within the system are or should be cost-free. There is no downside to U.S. national interests in looking at every angle of an issue before leaping into the dark. When naiveté, megalomania, or bureaucratic isolation fuels the dissent, a reply sent back through the Dissent Channel offers a discreet way to correct it gently. More often the dissent represents good foreign policy but bad domestic politics, and thus it must be discarded, but with no shame to the dissenter.

Dissent is seen as an urgent problem not by the State Department but by the White House, and the reason it raises hackles is a simple one. If no dissenting voices have spoken, then no one need pay a political price when policy goes badly wrong. President Bush and Prime Minister Blair both insisted that they were not to blame for claiming that Saddam Hussein had WMD when in fact he did not: no one had been rude enough to tell them differently.[9] Faced with the inherent conflict between their country's interests and their own political comfort, only rare, principled politicians leave dissent unpunished once it comes to their attention.

The higher one rises in the Foreign Service, even in a less ideological administration than the current one, the greater the career costs of dissent become. Sensitive management positions go to those disciplined and discreet enough to keep nonconforming opinions to themselves. For anyone dreaming of running an embassy, a recent Dissent Channel message is a serious career gamble. The White House controls those appointments, not the State Department, and its spies will warn it if an ambassadorial candidate is known for speaking bluntly.

In the Bush administration, possession of substantive expertise (membership in "the reality-based community" famously derided by an unnamed Bush aide) is in itself grounds for suspicion. Key positions in the U.S. occupation of Iraq went to College Republicans with no experience or credentials, while career civil servants with experience in democracy building and postconflict reconstruction were rejected because they had no way to document their loyalty to the president through service to his election campaign. A documented history of dissent is an even greater barrier to any senior position with multiple candidates vying for it.

Senior diplomats cannot dissent safely unless they resign, a sacrifice most do not care to make.[10] Thus, State Department management must look to bureaucratically immune civil service employees and to mid-level foreign service officers as the source of the analysis that might protect the United States from its fantasies. Below the political radar, both diplomatic training and the official standards for promotion in rank should emphasize analytical rigor in policy formulation as an end in itself. The State Department inspectors should assess each embassy on the critical curiosity and independent thinking showed by its political and economic officers. If empowered mid-level diplomats shoulder the burden of reality-checking on behalf of the American people, senior officers can practice with fewer qualms the loyalty and deference to conventional wisdom that smooth their path to bureaucratic influence. Once they reach the bureaucratic pinnacle, their integrity can reassert itself to reshape policy for the better.

## *Making Dissent Work*

In some sense the Dissent Channel is itself an exercise in bureaucratic fantasy, a harmless gesture of professional pride that pretends the State Department is the dominant player in U.S. foreign policy. How can State make dissent effective, when control of policy is centralized so thoroughly in the White House? Getting policy right is a matter of life or death for thousands or millions of Americans and foreigners. Late in 2002, as I contemplated the coming war and a diplomat's responsibility toward it, nothing in my own experience as a dissenter offered any hope of positive impact.

Effective dissent works by mobilizing the domestic political system as a force multiplier. In Greece, when the prime minister or Greek Pentagon took any liberties with the national interest, some Foreign Ministry watchdog would leak a distorted version of it to opposition journalists and members of Parliament. It would be a front-page story, picked up on television and by a united, vitriolic opposition. In the resulting uproar, the offending policy would go into the deep freeze or evolve into something less politically risky. Unfortunately, the hypercompetitive Greek parliamentary system did not make fine distinctions in its choice of ammunition: good policies were just as likely to be killed as bad policies. Greece is not a superpower, but it would have a hard time becoming one on this basis.

The same tactic is less effective in the United States. First, U.S. political parties are too weak to enforce discipline on their members of Congress. Secure in their gerrymandered districts and morally bound to earn a fair share of government largesse for their constituents, opposition members of Congress do not attack the president in unison or effectively. Secondly, commercial U.S. media outlets shrink from policy criticism that might be construed as partisan. But we sometimes owe it to our country to make the attempt.

## *Tactical Afterthoughts on a Resignation*

The State Department is neither ruthless nor efficient in punishing its dissidents. Still, foreign service officers censor themselves ruthlessly, as I did in Athens with my subordinates and most of my peers. Hundreds of U.S. diplomats knew better about the Iraq War, but each struggled essentially alone with that knowledge. When my two colleagues and I resigned, however, e-mails poured in from Foreign Service colleagues, almost all supportive. One colleague asked my advice on whether he should resign as well. I told him he should stay and fight on because the State Department needed able officers like him more than it needed another human sacrifice.

I had mistakenly thought when I resigned that I was part of a long Anglo-Saxon tradition of resigning over policy. British cabinet secretaries resign because they are independent politicians who sometimes need to separate their political future from that of their government. Ordinary civil servants rarely do. But resignation is a powerful gesture, one that automatically buys fifteen minutes of rapt attention from the world. Making the most of those fifteen minutes requires considerable forethought and discipline, the ability to be as relentlessly "on message" as the administration one is combating. I was too high-minded, docile, and disorganized a dissident, too little interested in U.S. domestic politics and not telegenic enough to constitute a prime-time attraction in the run-up to the war. The White House could ignore me safely. That was a pity.

Launching a war without leaving an incriminating paper trail is impossible. Skillful bureaucratic resistance would not have changed any minds in the White House. It might, however, have lured the administration into paranoia and dysfunctionality early enough to make a difference. As with the Iran-Contra scandal in 1983–88, stupid U.S. policies tend to cross a line into criminal behavior at some point, mostly because of the rigor and complexity of congressional oversight. Fear of leaks makes politicians lose their heads and stop trusting their bureaucratic allies. At a certain point they slip over to the dark side and unleash the White House Plumbers on some new Daniel Ellsberg.[11]

The willingness to lose one's job gives one freedom as a bureaucratic operator. Had I decided on resignation earlier, I could have used this freedom to track down a few more dissidents within the State Department before I went public. I had no access to incriminating documents or lurid gossip on White House policy regarding Iraq, but others might. U.S. journalists would have been far less subservient to the White House if they had sniffed a story of bureaucratic intrigue, something I could never supply from distant Athens. And fear of leaks would have triggered the White House immune system, with dire results.

Scooter Libby and Karl Rove's attempts to discredit the media-savvy Ambassador Joe Wilson for his revelation of the Niger yellowcake scam in July 2003 were ultimately disastrous for them and the White House image of competence.[12] If they had been goaded to such folly before the war began, the resulting outcry might have raised the domestic political cost of their march to war to the point where Bush would have been forced to demand an honest answer from real experts about the true costs of invading Iraq.

Conscientious American diplomats found themselves after 2001 relegated to the sidelines on policy decisions their professional expertise should have allowed them to recognize as harmful to U.S. interests. Humans tend to judge themselves by their standing in their own society. In a bureaucracy, loyalty to the chief is a key standard by which subordinates are judged. American diplomats cannot pledge allegiance to a higher standard—loyalty to the interests of the American people—without faith in their own analytical acuity that verges on megalomania. All but three U.S. diplomats (Mary Ann Wright, John Brown, and I) stayed at their posts during the Iraq War or retired quietly. The U.S. diplomats who stayed did vital work to reduce the damage. Because they followed the rules of a disciplined profession, they were not free to explain to the American people that the international system diplomats have labored so long and lovingly to build needs permanent protection from the self-serving fantasies that flourish in large bureaucracies.

The American people tend to be unfairly dismissive of their civil servants. If Americans traveled abroad to witness the performance of foreign bureaucrats, they would value the honesty, diligence, and efficiency of their own more highly. Dissent by patriotic government employees raises the political price ultimately paid for bad policies, but it almost always fails to preempt those policies. Therefore, Americans must protect themselves. The only way to do so is to elect leaders with brains, humanity, humility, skepticism, and commitment to open government, presidents brave and strong enough to hold the feet of competitive, inherently delusional senior bureaucrats firmly on the ground.

# 7

# ★ *The Cost of U.S. Unpopularity* ★

*We may be pretty certain that persons whom all the world treats ill deserve entirely the treatment they get. The world is a looking-glass, and gives back to every man the reflection of his own face.*
**William Thackeray**, Vanity Fair

A drawback of diplomacy as an instrument of American foreign policy is that it locks us into the obligation to maintain "a decent respect for the opinions of mankind." Some of mankind's opinions are wrong and despicable. Most are not. The vast wave of anger at the U.S. government that swept across Greece and Europe as the Iraq War loomed played a significant role in my resignation. Soldiers are paid to be thick-skinned, but diplomats cannot be insensitive to foreign public opinion if they are to do their job effectively.

People are polite. No tradition of hospitality anywhere in the world encourages too frank an answer to the American who asks "What do people in these parts think of America and Americans?" Until 2002 the answers were conventional and predictable. From rabid leftists I might hear a pointed display of enthusiasm for the writings of Noam Chomsky or Jack London.[1] The majority of ordinary Europeans, however, would have come up with one of the hundreds of positive things that can be said with reasonable honesty about the United States.

By February 2003, however, politeness toward Americans had frayed seriously. Greek leftist contacts stared at me with open reproach. Rightist politicians, except for a few fanatics who congratulated me for America's decision to join Orthodoxy in civilization's coming war against Islam, were politer but still convinced that the United States had broken the rules of international behavior.

Anti-American sentiment is not something new or particularly frightening. "Yankee go home" is an ancient cliché. For the past fifty years at least, in most cities on the planet, anyone who knows one hundred words of the local language and the location of the student district has been able to find anti-U.S. graffiti. As the junior political officer at the U.S. embassy in Athens in 1988, I wandered every few months through Exarcheia, the anarchist neighborhood, reading the anti-American slogans on the walls and figuring out the political context behind them. The wall-daubers in Athens and elsewhere were marginal groups with no ability to make themselves relevant to the U.S. government.

Old diplomatic habits die hard. In January 2005, caked with mud from the Hittite ruins of Shapinuwa, I stopped in the rural market town of Alaca, deep in central Turkey. Two separate, neatly photocopied fliers in shop windows on the main street were calling for local residents to boycott American products to protest U.S. policy in Iraq. One of them asked: "First Afghanistan, then Iraq. Is it our turn next?" Two shop windows do not a revolution make, and the shopkeepers were impeccably polite. But tourist shops in Ulus, the old quarter of Ankara, had also posted little signs after the U.S. liberation/demolition of Fallujah saying, "Americans not welcome." A Turkish human rights figure accused the United States of "genocide," a term so linked to the delicate issue of Armenia that it is normally unsayable in Turkey. In late December 2004 villagers in southern Turkey pelted U.S. military personnel with stones and eggs when they came to retrieve an errant practice missile and pay off the locals for the damage to their roofs.

Turks are extraordinarily patient and courteous people. Turkey is a staunch NATO ally. Turkish authorities do not reward misplaced manifestations of popular sentiment. The U.S. military is courteous as well, not to mention reasonably generous, experienced at civil-military relations, and very determined to keep the U.S. military presence at Incirlik Air Base from being an irritant to the locals. And yet, anger at the United States was intense enough to overcome the self-interest that normally locks the United States and Turkey closely together.

American travelers can assign whatever weight they like to random minor incidents and the presence or absence of "USA = (swastika)" graffiti on the walls. But the U.S. government needs to be more scientific. The State Department and various polling companies and foundations have been tracking global attitudes to the United States since the 1950s. The first four years of George W. Bush witnessed the largest decline in America's image ever recorded. For the first time in America's history, a majority of the world's population saw America negatively or very negatively.

The low point came in March 2003, when anger at the invasion of Iraq generated such widespread dislike for the U.S. government that ordinary Americans found themselves being insulted at dinner parties all over Europe. Though things have improved since then, America in 2006 is resented, feared, and/or disliked by half of the ordinary people of European countries it considers to be friends and allies. In most states of the Islamic world, almost 90 percent of the population has a strongly negative or negative view of the United States. Latin Americans profess opinions almost as negative. Views of the United States in Africa and Asia vary sharply from country to country and from year to year. Though Americans as people are less unpopular than their country and government, they too are less well regarded than formerly.[2]

So what? The world is not a beauty contest with college scholarships for Miss Congeniality. The U.S. government can seldom please more than half its own citizens, and Americans are bound together by strong ties of sentiment and self-interest. Foreigners with competing religions, languages, cultures, and interests are unlikely to put the world's most assertive and high-maintenance superpower at the top of their hit parade. Furthermore, among 6.5 billion human beings, billions (including some U.S. high school graduates) could not find the United States on a map of the world, billions could not name the U.S. president, billions have never in their lives had any meaningful contact with any American except as a flickering image on a television screen.

Do these people matter to us? The Cold War is over. We no longer are competing with the Soviets or any other dangerous rival for the affections of the rest of the planet. A majority of the American voting public considered George W. Bush and his policies successful enough to reelect him. America should be no less free than every other country in the world to behave selfishly in pursuit of its national interests. But what, exactly, are those interests?

### *The Goals of U.S. Foreign Policy*

One basic, even adequate, reason the United States should strive to be a popular superpower is that happiness is a legitimate foreign policy goal. Humans bask in kudos, the good opinion of others. In March 2005 I asked twelve American undergraduates in Athens to write an anonymous paragraph on how being in Greece had affected their feelings about being an American. Half of them confessed to feeling "ashamed." A leader who causes idealistic young people to feel ashamed of their country should feel ashamed himself. Americans have every right to take pride in their country, pride reinforced by the world's admiration for American achievement. Only a sociopath would take foreign vilification of America as somehow positive, somehow a confirmation of the rightness of our policies. Inability to convince the world of American virtues and accomplishments reduces the sum of American happiness.

A few Americans despise the general happiness. In their view, the world is a large pie and the U.S. government is a set of utensils to aid the strongest, shrewdest, and greediest in devouring that pie. That was Enron's corporate view. I watched the U.S. government help Enron dig itself deep into disastrous energy projects in India. Enron and its shareholders came to a sticky end and so will anyone who disregards the power of the public's moral sense.

Let us agree instead with the conviction of the overwhelming majority of U.S. government employees I talked to over my career, that their mission is the welfare of the American people. Properly skeptical of the government's ability to recognize welfare when it sees it, let us agree that the government's role in promoting Americans' happiness should be confined to the task of enhancing the physical and economic security of the American people over the next five, fifty, and five hundred years.

### Protecting Americans Overseas

One argument in favor of being a loved and respected superpower is that America has 300 million hostages to fortune alive at the moment. Nineteen strangers angry at the U.S. government killed twenty-eight hundred Americans in 2001 and cost the U.S. economy billions of dollars at a moment when the United States was significantly more popular than it is now. Basic social calculus tells us that people who hate and fear America are more likely to maim or kill Americans, especially overseas where the U.S. government is less able to protect them.

In twenty years I was directly involved with one American civilian victim of terrorism, as India desk officer in 1995. Don Hutchings, an American trekker from Washington State, was taken hostage in Kashmir along with five others. A covert U.S. special ops team flew to India, after much delicate diplomacy with the Indian authorities and at horrendous expense, to help the Indians look for him, in vain.[3] Kashmir was a war zone, but even in war zones, murdered Americans seldom form a noticeable part of the diplomat's workload.

Americans should feel more embarrassed at their fear of foreign travel. At least since the Vietnam War, parents have nagged their children to sew a Canadian maple leaf flag on their backpack before setting out on their grand tour. Texans are too proud to hide behind a false flag except for purposes of tax avoidance. A Texas travel executive instead told my Houston aunt to cancel her tour of Turkey because terrorism made it too dangerous. Fortunately, she had a diplomat to ask as well. My aunt had a wonderful time as an American in Turkey and so will anybody's aunt. Americans are no less the beneficiaries than any other tribe of the powerful instincts of hospitality that apply to respectable strangers in any society.

The State Department's global terrorism statistics prove that U.S. unpopularity has not made the world a more dangerous place for ordinary Americans than their own hometowns.[4] Worldwide one or two U.S. tourists are lost every year to an act of terrorism. In 2003, at the absolute height of anti-U.S. feeling, no American tourist was killed by a terrorist.[5]

The security threat to U.S. citizens increases significantly once they cease to be honored visitors. As residents they are expected to learn at least the basic rules of their host society's internal competition. Expatriate U.S. businessmen, diplomats, and military personnel are vulnerable when attitudes toward the United States go sour. One U.S. official, a long-time U.S. Agency for International Development employee in Amman, was shot dead outside his house when Jordanian anger at our Iraq policy reached its height in early 2003. That year thirty-five Americans were killed, all of them expatriates rather than tourists. They had chosen to work in dangerous places, particularly Israel, the Occupied Territories, Saudi Arabia, Afghanistan, and Iraq. Perhaps other American deaths were hushed up, or not recognized as political, but I doubt it. Some number of dead Americans is an inevitable result of America's huge global presence, but the numbers, mercifully small, correlate poorly with the rise and fall of our global reputation.

During the Iraq War, Americans around the world were involved in more bar fights than usual and suffered more acts of minor vandalism. The usual American response was a sensible one, to behave politely and to avoid talking politics. American service members at Souda Bay on the Greek island of Crete stayed out of certain bars. American businesspeople in Greece stayed away from crowded social gatherings for a few weeks, not because it was dangerous but because the political arguments—normally a pleasant pastime—were too one-sided to be enjoyable. If this were all the price Americans had to pay for U.S. unpopularity, they could certainly afford it. But it is not.

## Protecting the U.S. Economy

Various business groups have sounded the alert about the upsurge in boycotts of U.S. products around the world. In May 2003 I wandered the streets of Thessaloniki during the antiglobalization riots that accompanied the European Union summit nearby. Graffiti defaced most U.S. symbols. McDonalds and American Express had survived the firebombs pretty well, thanks to the sheet-iron barriers bolted up to protect the plate glass. The billboards for President cigarettes, studded though they were with American eagles, had not attracted the fury of the protestors. They were a Greek brand.

The threat to U.S. brands is real but very uneven. The U.S. balance of payments is a disaster, but no one has claimed that the small, local, disjointed boycotts of U.S. products since 2002 played a significant role in the sharp drop of U.S. exports in 2001. U.S. companies have adapted to foreign consumer sentiment by changing their advertising to emphasize their stature as local or universal rather than strictly American brands. In practice, America's traditional advertising imagery has become very difficult to find on the streets of Athens and other major European cities. This has a subtle foreign policy cost: private companies used to market certain American values—the Marlboro man version of rugged individualism—far more effectively than the government could. Post-Kyoto the once envied American lifestyle has taken on a darker connotation.[6]

More serious is the risk that America will cease to be the favored destination for the world's surplus capital. Without investment inflows from foreigners, the U.S. financial system would collapse in a few months. Anti-U.S. sentiment has limited effect on cold-hearted businesspeople when the U.S. investment climate is good. Should there be a U.S. economic downturn, especially one linked to the continuing shift of wealth toward energy exporters, the perception of shaky U.S. commitment to the rule of law would exacerbate the risk of capital flight.

### Other Practical Consequences

Anger at the United States has coincided with restrictive Homeland Security visa policies and the rising quality of the foreign competition to deal a setback to America's greatest competitive economic advantage: its ability to attract top intellectual talent from the rest of the world. The absolute number of foreign students studying at U.S. universities dropped 2.4 percent in 2003–4, the first such decline since 1971.[7] The decrease in applications from paying foreign students is beginning to be felt by all but top-tier U.S. universities. The resulting boost to foreign universities competing head to head with America's own for the most promising students will harm U.S. interests in a few years. Already, Indian software companies are proving that America's vaunted technological prowess is no longer a valid reason to prefer a U.S. firm over its Indian equivalent.

The justice system is a sector in which U.S. unpopularity makes Americans more vulnerable. As an out-of-state motorist in a Carolina speed trap can extrapolate, legal systems judge outsiders by different standards than their own people. Most foreign jurisdictions, fortunately, decline to prosecute minor charges against Americans because strict justice hurts the tourist trade. But something negative happens when local authorities conclude that, in their own small way, they can impose justice on a superpower regarded as oblivious to justice.

Anecdotal evidence suggests that Greek police and judges became significantly tougher on American law violators in 2003. Two U.S. service members found guilty of theft and assault were sentenced to ten years in jail for crimes for which a Greek would serve two or three. Rigorous justice for criminals, including its own, is something America thinks it believes in. However, in foreign commercial disputes, the erosion of foreign legal impartiality has serious consequences for the ability of U.S. businesspeople to compete successfully in world markets.

Diplomats pretend that all sovereign states are equal. This is a useful pretence most of the time, but sometimes a superpower has a good reason to exempt itself. Resentment of the United States makes it problematic for countries to bend the requirements of strict reciprocity. When in 2003 America started electronically fingerprinting foreigners on arrival, Brazilian authorities reciprocated with malicious zeal, at the instigation of an ambitious Brazilian judge. U.S. businesspeople and tourists, newly smeared with fingerprint ink, missed their flight connections. Since Brazil neither faced an identifiable terrorist threat nor was willing to implement the expensive record-keeping system to make such fingerprints usable, this was pure politics. Judges, however, are political animals.

### What Unpopularity Really Costs the United States

Even when whole continents seethe with fury at the U.S. government, ordinary Americans can and should continue to venture happily abroad, risking little more than inky fingers and an occasional random scowl in the hotel elevator. What harms an unpopular America's ability to protect its security interests is the reality that foreign states have domestic politics just like it does.

Frequently the U.S. government needs to make foreign governments agree to things that benefit U.S. interests: military basing rights, trade deals, law enforcement cooperation, shutting down a weapons program, or contributing money or troops to a coalition to intervene in some messy international situation. The U.S. government has a good set of tools—foreign aid, political support, military assistance, trade concessions, economic sanctions, armed blackmail—for making foreign governments recognize that compliance will serve their own national interests as well as America's. The U.S. diplomats who do the negotiating are normally fair-minded folk. Prudent acquiescence to the demands of a superpower will generally make a small country safer and richer.

When an unpopular superpower is unpopular enough, however, even the most fair and reasonable deal will be distorted through the filter of domestic politics as bullying. The appearance of kowtowing to the United States can turn into political suicide. Prime Minister Erdogan of Turkey preferred to risk America's wrath in 2003 rather than require his huge parliamentary majority to expose itself to the anger of Turkish voters by ratifying use of Turkish territory to invade Iraq. This decision to respect the strong antiwar sentiments of the Turkish Muslims on whom Erdogan depended for his electoral victory cost American lives, angered U.S. officials greatly, and soured a mutually beneficial U.S.-Turkish relationship. If U.S. unpopularity had not been so great, the powerful Turkish military might have stepped in to insist that the politicians find a compromise solution. The Turkish military kept quiet.

The U.S. government scratched its head wondering what incentive it could offer Erdogan to take the risk of bypassing his fractious parliament. In the old days, a state visit to Washington and a photographed handshake with the leader of the free world was a cheap and effective political tool. The United States could help a struggling politician against his intraparty rivals and perhaps win him a few additional votes by having the U.S. president praise him publicly. No longer.

Prime Minister Tony Blair of Great Britain was the best ally America could hope for in the world. His conservative rivals were unelectable, and so Blair had complete political freedom to put Britain's formidable diplomatic and military resources at U.S. disposal. He did, routinely, and America benefited greatly from his friendship. By 2004, however, Blair's misjudgments about the Iraq War had worn holes in his Teflon coating. "America's poodle" is a very uncomfortable nickname. In the fall, with U.S. elections coming, Blair found himself caught between the desire of the U.S. administration and Congress to remind Americans of Britain's loyal support in Iraq and his own knowledge as a gifted politician that accepting a medal from Congress would add more fuel to the political bonfire blazing around him. Blair was brave. He waited until after the U.S. elections to make his visit, and he traded the visit for U.S. concessions on trade policy and the Middle East.

The UK is America's closest ally, but the United States now has to pay British politicians to visit it. The United States loses a major part of its power if it cannot affordably reward foreign politicians for their cooperation. But this is the position that the United States has occupied since 2002. American praise is something leading foreign politicians currently prefer to hear only in private.

Dictatorships are not dramatically less sensitive to domestic politics than democracies. Pakistan derives many national benefits from supporting the U.S. goal of eliminating al Qaeda from the Afghan border: increased U.S. foreign aid, modern military hardware, and a blind eye to its nuclear program. But as President Pervez Musharraf has found, kowtowing to the will of a foreign state is politically costly, even for a dictator notionally accountable to no one. Musharraf must cope with the fact that not only his population but also many officers of the Pakistani intelligence service, police, and military have grave personal doubts about the acceptability of working with American counterparts perceived as plotting against their religion and their national sovereignty.

Musharraf's subordinates can and do sabotage joint counterterrorism efforts simply by going limp at crucial moments. In a country where the head of the Pakistani nuclear program can sell atomic bomb secrets to Iran and Libya for personal gain and not be punished, smaller fry can leak damaging information to the press, to opposition politicians, or even to terrorist groups with little risk. America's unpopularity with the people of Pakistan puts grave limits on Pakistan's ability to prosecute an effective war against al Qaeda.

An unpopular superpower can neutralize domestic political resistance to cooperation, but only by giving foreigners valuable things they want. The United States could gain Putin's support in Afghanistan by sacrificing its principles in Chechnya, or Beijing's by soft-pedaling its commitment to Taiwan's independent existence. This can get expensive, both in terms of U.S. national interests and U.S. domestic politics.

If politicians were corrupt in the manner many Greeks accuse them of being, the work-around would be simple. The CIA would bribe Greek politicians to do what the United States asked, buy them a pleasant retreat in Arizona when their enraged population threw them out, and then bribe their replacement. But human nature seldom cooperates. Fortunately for U.S. democratic principles, few politicians are willing to break themselves of their addiction to the narcotic of popular adulation. Even when they do, an enraged population will close the door to similar behavior while the replacement is still mopping up the blood in the presidential palace. A quarter century after the shah's ouster, Iranian politicians are still blaming the United States for the shah's inability to convince his people that he was serving their interests rather than America's.

A less obvious casualty of U.S. unpopularity is its diplomatic role as social arbiter. A remarkable number of people, seduced by the prospect of glittering receptions at the residence, will put useful information or influence at the disposal of the U.S. ambassador. During good times, embassy contacts can count on mingling with cabinet ministers, corporate chief executives, and cultural luminaries, people ordinarily inaccessible to them. As the U.S. government lost its charm during 2002, the Athens A-list became harder to recruit. Once social climbers discover they are socializing with one another, indifferent wine and leathery canapés cease to be adequate compensation for the favors they do the embassy.

Just as unpopularity deprives the United States of appetizing carrots, so it deprives it of many of the sticks normally wielded to punish politicians and bureaucrats who cross it. Public criticism is a weak tool at the best of times. Americans certainly did not turn against their politicians when the Soviet Union's press spokesman blasted the United States and its reactionary, imperialist policies. The USSR had no standing in American eyes to criticize U.S. behavior. Now, unfortunately, whatever limited standing the United States once had as global critic has evaporated in the eyes of the governments most in need of U.S. criticism. The State Department spokesperson can "quiver all over like Lionel Barrymore" (in James Thurber's felicitous phrase), but U.S. indignation, no matter how artfully expressed, does a foreign politician no harm when the domestic constituencies whose care and feeding is his first concern feel antipathy toward the United States.

Worse for U.S. interests is the ploy foreign politicians use when they are facing an internal uprising in their party: calling a press conference to claim that the United States is plotting their assassination or otherwise supporting their political opponents.[8] When this charge is even remotely plausible, the politician strengthens himself politically at further cost to America's reputation.

Except in countries where the United States enjoys popular respect, real U.S. sanctions are no more effective than rhetorical ones in promoting U.S. interests. Being denied a U.S. visa is a badge of honor to an ambitious Indian politician, not a political liability.

In Cuba Castro found American sanctions the perfect excuse for all the failures of his regime and is still comfortably in power decades after the United States swore to remove him.

America lost in four short years of the Bush administration much of its limited ability to reward and punish by peaceful means. This is an empirical observation but scarcely a counsel of despair. In Greece, a country where the United States has been an unloved ally for decades, the United States could protect all its vital interests by being patient enough. Mutual self-interest can always be found. More personal self-interest should push U.S. diplomats to make very clear back in Washington the full foreign policy costs America pays for its current negative image, so that their leaders will tolerate the domestic political and bureaucratic expense of refurbishing that image.

# 8

# ★ *Public Diplomacy and the Limits of Persuasiveness* ★

*All the figures have their heads on, and I cannot forbear reflecting again on the impudence of authors who all say they have not, but I dare swear the greatest part never saw them, but took the report from the Greeks, who resist with incredible fortitude the conviction of their own eyes whenever they have invented lies to the dishonour of their enemies.*
*Letter of Lady Mary Wortley Montague, April 10, 1718[1]*

Every couple years an angry mob storms the gates of a U.S. embassy somewhere to the surprise and indignation of the ambassador. Although the protests are sometimes unpremeditated—retaliation for America's accidental destruction of the Chinese embassy in Belgrade in 1999, for example—local authorities can usually prevent them if it is good domestic politics to do so. After every mob attack, the walls around U.S. embassies get higher and U.S. diplomats spend more of their time behind those walls attending Emergency Action Committee meetings and leaving protective paper trails.

When I broke free of the embassy compound for the real work of representing the United States to foreigners, it was usually to discuss something specific and operational. Many of the embassy's contacts read the same sanitized English-language abridgements of the local press that diplomats did or were grimly busy officials condemned to see the world through bureaucratic blinders like our own. The opportunities for thoughtful discussion of local attitudes were few and precious. A nuanced analytical view of what the United States was doing right and doing wrong to influence public opinion was something I heard in Athens a handful of times a year, from a talented Greek journalist or an unusually reflective politician. It takes

135

precious time to capture these insights in writing, and getting them to Washington requires the good fortune of having an ambassador brave enough to put his name on the report.

But what do foreign service officers report? Diplomats work in countries marked by "red state/blue state" cleavages as deep as America's own. The views of the "average Greek" tell them very little. Statistics do not blow themselves up at the entrance to a U.S. embassy. Statistics do not walk into that same embassy with the information needed to thwart that bombing. The decision to buy or not buy an American product is based on some subtle local agreement about what that product says about its individual purchaser. We live in a world of individual choices, and the task of U.S. public diplomacy is to identify and, if possible, counteract the influences within a given society that prompt choices harmful to U.S. interests.

As a sensible precaution diplomats talk to as many "real people" as they can. But diplomatic access to real people is not always easy, even when the language barrier is overcome. The confidence many Americans and Greeks have in divulging their political opinions to complete strangers is not universally shared. Diplomats find themselves pumping hairdressers and taxi drivers for the conventional wisdom they absorb, adapt, and rebroadcast into their society.

Taxi drivers in Greece, Egypt, or even the UK risk little disagreement with their clients today when they offer a conventional account of America that runs roughly as follows: "The American people have brought many good things into the world. I have nothing against them but their vote for President Bush. Power has bred arrogance. The American government does not care enough about justice or my country's unique culture as it tries to impose unbalanced, selfish, and dangerous policies. I respect local politicians who stand firm against U.S. pressure."

Whether the world's conventional wisdom accurately characterizes the U.S. government and president is debatable. That it harms U.S. interests is not. A principal goal of U.S. public diplomacy is to bring the world's conventional wisdom back toward a comfortable equilibrium in which America's exercise of power in its own interest is accepted as a reasonable price to pay for the peace, stability, prosperity, and democracy that American power helps ensure.

### Listening to Greeks

I spent seven years of a twenty-year professional life trying to eavesdrop on Greeks in a dignified manner. In March 2002, the embassy was anxious to change Greek perceptions that the United States was a legitimate terror target. We managed to persuade the

State Department to stop relying on cheap theorizing by its diplomats. A professional market research/polling company was hired to help us listen critically to ordinary Greeks in a small-group setting similar to the ones in which real human beings constantly test and recalibrate their opinions. It was a useful exercise.[2]

Proponents of unilateralist U.S. policies profess the belief, out of political or bureaucratic expedience more than stupidity, that foreigners who object to U.S. behavior are victims of a psychiatric disorder called anti-Americanism. In this view, negative foreign reactions to a given policy should not figure into the cost-benefit calculation for that policy, not necessarily because foreign opinions are irrelevant but because those opinions are irrational and unconnected with U.S. actions. A whole generation of conservative pundits claim that the source of U.S. unpopularity is not U.S. policies. Foreigners "hate our freedom" or envy America's ability to impose its will. More charitably, foreigners oppose us in a vain attempt to balance U.S. power. Because such a tiny percentage of American politicians and officials have any direct experience with foreigners in their native language and habitat, it is possible to sustain this narcissistic fiction that it is who we are, not what we do, that motivates the world's hostility.[3]

Anyone opposed to current U.S. policy finds the mirror-image argument—"It's the policy, stupid!"—a far more generous and logical view of human nature. Because it is bureaucratically useful to them as well, the policy argument becomes very seductive. The recent examples of the Arab-Israeli conflict, the Kyoto Protocol, the International Criminal Court (ICC), and the Iraq War, in which U.S. policy choices had a devastating effect on the U.S. image abroad, have made this argument seem more complete than it is.

To understand why limited changes in U.S. policy under President Bush had such violently negative effects around the world, a Greek focus group is an excellent place to start. Greece's geographical location, history, and culture are such that Greek attitudes bridge a broad spectrum of ideologies and narrative strategies, ranging from soberly rationalizing "Western European" to the most darkly conspiratorial "Middle Eastern" rumormongering. Greek conventional wisdom has been shaped by sixty years of close political and military association with the United States.

The twelve random Greeks around the focus group table, with only gentle prodding from the moderator, expressed a reasonable amount of admiration for the United States as a country, a people, and a set of democratic institutions. Years of snide commentary from Greek intellectuals had left me unprepared for the extent to which ordinary Greeks recognized and applauded the American work ethic, religious faith, and family values—traits often embodied in their Greek-American relatives.

Participants were conventionally critical of a standard list of U.S. policies. I had heard these criticisms before and could recite them in my sleep. Greek politicians feel a patriotic duty to politely remind visiting American officials early in the course of a formal meeting why Greeks are annoyed at the United States: U.S. intervention in Greek domestic politics in the 1950s and 1960s, support for the 1967–74 Greek junta, failure to prevent Turkey's 1974 invasion of Cyprus, pro-Israel policies, and the bombing of Serbia in 1999.

The focus group members knew America's foreign policy transgressions only vaguely and in many cases incorrectly. Harm to Greek national interests barely figured in the discussion. Wounded pride seemed to drive the focus group's reaction to America's "evenhanded" policy toward Greece and Turkey: the United States apparently recognized no fundamental difference between the democratic, peace-loving, civilized Greeks and the cruel, aggressive, authoritarian Turks. This was proof of injustice. The foreign policy decisions that had angered so much of the world were notable only for confirming the stereotype of an unjust superpower.

This should not be surprising. The November 2004 U.S. elections confirmed what every politician knows instinctively: perceived character counts far more than economic self-interest or any other rational assessment in human decision making. To maintain a plausible narrative of character and leadership once they have adopted it, people prefer to falsify the world. Since a moral president—and Bush voters were sure of their ability to judge character—could not have launched an immoral war, Saddam must have been implicated in the 9/11 attacks. Many Americans still believe, despite official denials, that U.S. troops found chemical and biological weapons when they invaded Iraq.

Foreigners are no smarter or more rational than Americans are, nor are their sources of information more objective, complete, or intelligible than Americans' own. Both foreigners and Americans are drowning in information, true, false, irrelevant, contradictory. Blinders make the world intelligible. In practice, information that does not harmonize with some underlying narrative about human character does not get processed, while information that suits such a narrative will take on exaggerated importance.

National interest arguments do not explain why the United States plummeted so fast and so far in the world's opinion after George W. Bush shifted U.S. foreign policies rightward in 2001. Once the intrinsically negative narratives of American power are factored in, America's current image becomes more understandable. Recognizing the power of such narratives, the United States can improve both its policies and its salesmanship to change its image for the better.

## Superpowers and Lesser Powers

The United States could never win an international popularity contest against a small, generally virtuous country like Finland or the Netherlands. Even sheer size matters. The United States generates 25 percent or so of humankind's surplus carbon dioxide. When a record European heat wave kills ten thousand people or a record number of typhoons hit the Philippines, humans look for a lesson, or at least a scapegoat. It does not matter that the Kyoto Protocol was only an imperfect first step in a process that might not prevent catastrophic climate change even if fully implemented; what matters is that President Bush opted not to sign the agreement. At some psychological level, President Bush's evident callousness toward climate change made the United States guilty of the weather, a problem no small-country politician will ever have to face.

Power drives a universal moral narrative. The ancient historian Herodotus used it to make sense of the Persian invasions of Greece in the fifth century BC: power corrupts its holders. They overreach, transgressing divine justice and bringing down the wrath of Nemesis, who will destroy them as she destroyed the Persian fleet and army in 479 BC. Avenging Nemesis is a fixture in the folk tales and action-adventure movies that constitute an American moral education as well as a Greek one. But unlike most Greeks, most Americans grow up to see power in relatively positive terms, as the ability to control their environment. Not even after a catastrophe does their instinct for justice necessarily push them to find the overlooked evidence of prior hubris.

For six-sevenths of the world's population, the ordinary experience of power is far more negative than it is for Americans. A petty official, unconstrained within his limited domain, can and will make the life of an average Pakistani or Chinese or Nigerian living hell. Saddam Hussein is certainly not the only dictator in recent history from whose household no beautiful woman or profitable business was safe. Greeks too are hostile to power. After grieving the victims of 9/11, many Greeks quietly told one another, "*kala na pathoun*" ("It served them right"), and began to remind themselves of past indications that American arrogance had been riding for a fall.

The United States is seldom an overreaching empire. But given any assistance at all from U.S. rhetoric, the narrative of American arrogance becomes instantly dominant in scores of countries around the world. Once it does, Greek archbishops and taxi drivers cheerfully edit the world to make American behavior fit the paradigm, cherry-picking a handful of U.S. policy blunders, Rumsfeld sound bites, and presidential tics. As the Iraq War loomed, every hint of superpower hubris was seized upon and magnified. Countervailing American acts of idealism, generosity, and self-limitation no longer penetrated foreign blinders.

One of the worst political deformations of Muslim elites, as of Greek elites until the 1990s, is the belief that unlimited American power absolves everyone else of moral responsibility. Few Muslims accept America's legitimate argument that peace and justice in the Middle East depend first and foremost on the people who live there. America could have prevented Israel from colonizing the West Bank, but it did not. The CIA is an allegedly all-knowing intelligence service, so ignorance is no excuse. Therefore, America is an evil superpower, and evil must be resisted.

## Us Versus Them

Another universal folk narrative defines relations between us and the Other: "We Greeks are simple, sincere, romantic people wedded to our land and traditions. Carried away by noble but old-fashioned emotions—courage, loyalty, hospitality, generosity—we fail to calculate our long-term interests. The Other lacks our virtues but also our vices. Coldly rational, selfish, and well-organized, the Other takes advantage of our disunity to methodically pursue a unified goal at our expense."

The narrative of systematic victimization is too useful a tool in identity politics to discard no matter how mature a state becomes. Greeks once defended their status as full Europeans by exaggerating their differences with the Turks. Now Greece's European character can be asserted, on the very rare occasions when anyone challenges it, through exaggerating their differences with a relentlessly "globalizing" American Other. Most Greeks still assert that the Other has maintained since the 1950s a constant, consistent long-term policy to keep Greece bitterly divided and dependent on the United States.

This narrative is not completely unfounded. The legacy of old American missteps in Central America and Iran will be felt in their domestic politics a century from now. Thirty years after the fall of the Greek military dictatorship, Greek political activists of all shades of opinion commemorate the antijunta resistance by marching on the U.S. embassy, not the Greek Pentagon. The only issue that unites these hundred disparate groups is their choice of destination.[4]

Every whisper America makes abroad is taken up and amplified in local politics. Even when the United States is a passive and oblivious spectator, assertions of U.S. engagement serve useful tactical purposes. Greek politicians cheerfully accuse their rivals of being in America's pocket. Al Qaeda mobilizes nationalist/religious support against the House of Saud by claiming that the corrupt Saudi monarchy will fall once the United States stops propping it up. When the United States emulates Switzerland and refuses to take sides, its evenhandedness does not win it the rights accorded smaller neutral states.

Anyone who has worked with or for the U.S. government would scoff at the idea that Americans are fiendishly well organized or that the U.S. government wants a weak and fragmented Greece. After twenty-four years of membership in the European Union (EU), Greece's Self-versus-Other victimization paradigm can be sidestepped. But in every country of Africa and the Middle East, the assumptions made about the Other are more dire than they are in Greece. Each postcolonial state teaches its schoolchildren that foreigners engaged in systematic divide-and-rule, that current political divisions are a product of outside manipulation. Amazing conspiracy theories flourish, and as the only halfway plausible heir to European colonialism, the United States is near the center of most of them. Proving innocence is impossible. All the U.S. government can reasonably do is keep its various covert agencies under tight control and keep its ambassadors from playing too heavy-handed a public role in local politics.

### American Exceptionalism

American politicians' self-congratulatory assertions of American uniqueness are a mistake because they play into the narrative of the hostile Other. President Clinton had a rare gift for expressing American values in a way that recognized that foreigners had them too. President Bush prefers, for domestic political reasons, to imply that America is a uniquely virtuous and legitimate purveyor of freedom and democracy. The original context of his statements was the intended war to the death against Muslim zealots allegedly intent on America's extermination. When the president changed his tune to emphasize democracy building rather than weapons of mass destruction, his hoped-for democratization of the Arab world was already firmly embedded into a narrative of methodical, long-term efforts by the selfish Other to destroy a traditional, virtuous, and beleaguered society. The best service the United States can provide Arab democrats who wish to avoid being gunned down in the streets of Baghdad is to keep firmly silent while they themselves point out that the roots of democratic decision making can be found centuries ago in their own society.

U.S. claims of moral superiority are easy enough to rebut, and the world is full of people who feel it their absolute moral obligation to rebut all such claims. Historical lapses such as slavery aside, foreigners usually focus on localized U.S. oddities, such as infatuation with the death penalty, attachment to handguns, and public displays of sectarian fervor, to prove that America is out of the moral mainstream. But sometimes the rebuttal is more pointed.

U.S. television stations choose film footage to reinforce the pious myth that U.S. wars are tidier than other wars because much of their audience will change channels rather than disbelieve it. Those who have experienced war on their own continent know, however, that enlightened military doctrine and high technology still fall far short of making war tidy enough to be a policy tool of other than a last resort. Unable to rub American noses in the collateral damage, European and Arab television made a special effort to expose their own populations to the horrors of the Iraq War, to confirm them in their own moral superiority.

The U.S. abuses at Abu Ghraib and Guantanamo, abuses less serious than those every Middle Eastern government routinely engages in, were catastrophic for U.S. interests. Had U.S. claims of commitment to the rule of law been less immodest, the abuses would have been less newsworthy and the harm to U.S. image less. Israel, for example, has found itself better able to cope with the foreign policy impact of its intermittent atrocities against Palestinians now that all but a handful of fantasists have abandoned the myth that the Holocaust had made Israelis incapable of committing them.

## *The Unhistorical Superpower*

Plumbers in Athens condescend to their American clients about America's comparative lack of history. This is nonsense. Every country in the world, including the United States, produces more history than it can consume, as the humorist Saki quipped about the Cretans. Greeks are easily as adept at ignoring twenty-six hundred years of their recorded history as Americans are at ignoring their own mere four hundred. There is no country in the world where one need reach back further than fifty years to illustrate all the basic lessons of human folly. But alleged lack of history is a powerful emotional argument for discrediting U.S. international leadership.

Ignorance of history is supposed to give Americans optimism to match our alleged skills at practical improvisation. Americans attempt the impossible and sometimes achieve it, but this boast plays badly abroad. Worse is the deliberate distortion of history. In the public diplomacy of a superpower, the stern classicist A. E. Housman's precept applies: "Accuracy is a duty, not a virtue."[5] An American might forgive President Bush for saying as late as July 2003, "Did Saddam Hussein have a weapons program? And the answer is, absolutely. And we gave him a chance to allow inspectors in, and he wouldn't let them in."[6] Historical simplification for the home audience is a morale-building exercise. Thoughtful Europeans, however, drew dire conclusions. Either the U.S. president was a liar, or else he was massively unqualified to conduct foreign policy in the Middle East.

## *Prying Eyes*

This level of external scrutiny is one of America's principle foreign policy handicaps. The world paid little attention in 1990 when Saddam Hussein made clear to his own population that he was prepared to ratify Kuwait's status as Iraq's nineteenth province by force of arms. Iraq had the luxury of keeping messages for internal consumption distinct from the more reassuring messages Iraqi diplomats spread to the international community. Likewise, only a few diplomats will bristle when a Greek minister panders to his domestic audience in Greek. Small-country politicians are seldom forced to make a painful choice between promoting their personal ambition at home and defending their country's foreign policy interests abroad.

When the U.S. president is speaking, his audience is always the whole planet. George W. Bush was elected by a constituency that prized plain language. After 9/11, most Americans wanted to wallow in the nationalist rhetoric other countries enjoy every day. Efforts by the State Department and National Security Council to craft a different, gentler presidential message for foreign audiences produced some excellent presidential speeches, but the international media routinely subverted them with video clips of what the president told the American people at home.

American officials do not even have the right to boast about how diplomatic they are being. During her confirmation hearings in January 2005, Secretary of State designate Rice correctly highlighted the catastrophic December 26 tsunami as a diplomatic opportunity for the United States. Fast, generous U.S. assistance indeed contributed enormously to improving America's image in Asia. Watching on CNN half a world away I winced, because in her zeal to seem pragmatic to the Senate Foreign Relations Committee she had forgotten that Indonesians were watching. Senator Barbara Boxer correctly called her on her apparent callousness. The foreign beneficiaries of U.S. diplomacy are watching like hawks for proof that U.S. generosity is a sham.

## Reforming the Messenger

In October 2002 I flew to Brussels from Athens for a one-day conference of political counselors from U.S. embassies in EU countries. The focus of the closed meetings was how America could most effectively influence the arcane inner workings of EU foreign policy decision making. At a certain point we started talking about the difficulties of convincing our EU partners about the coming war with Iraq. The U.S. political minister-counselor from Rome rebuked the prevailing mild defeatism, volunteering his own superbly articulate summary of the U.S. case for war. Already in sacrificial mode, I raised my hand to reply: "Yes, Tom, we know the arguments. We make them. We use all the credibility we have built up with contacts over the years to convince them, and often when we leave the room they are convinced. But the next day President Bush or Secretary Rumsfeld appears on TV and blows to hell all the work we have done." Silence fell . . .

The U.S. president is by an order of magnitude America's public diplomat in chief. He is the face and voice of the American state to the world. President Bush firmly believes that he leads an enlightened superpower with the world's interests at heart. He does not convey that impression to the world.

A BBC/PIPA/GlobeScan poll in twenty-two countries in November/December 2004 reported that only 26 percent of those surveyed saw the reelection of President Bush as positive for peace and security in the world, with 58 percent seeing it negative and 8 percent volunteering "no effect either way." The most alarming finding of the poll was that a large plurality of those asked said that Bush's reelection made them feel "a little worse" (26 percent) or "much worse" (16 percent) about the American people (versus 8 percent "much better," 18 percent "a little better," and 23 percent "no effect either way"). Normally, foreigners insist that they distinguish between the American government and the American people. When anger at the United States blurs into anger at the American people, this undermines the work of U.S. diplomacy. With luck these poll results reflected transitory disappointment about the U.S. election results rather than any more basic shift in attitudes against Americans.

Much of the world views U.S. policies through the prism of highly negative assessments of the character of George W. Bush. The president branded himself with a number of public diplomacy missteps. His indifference to executing criminals chilled the blood of European humanists: renouncing judicial murder has become the price of admission to the club of civilized nations. Bush's justification for rejecting the Kyoto Protocol on Climate Change ("it would hurt the U.S. economy") established him as selfish head of a selfish superpower. Phrases like "dead or alive" and "well, they're not a problem any more" presented the frightening image of a man who seemed genuinely to believe that the world's most ancient and thorny problems could be solved by killing enough people. Bush's mangling of history and refusal or inability to explain political slogans such as "liberty" in policy terms convinced much of the European center-left intellectual mainstream that he was the puppet of others more cerebral than he.

Bush is, of course, no one's puppet but his own. European diplomats who have met him attest that he is not a fool. His speeches drafted for foreign audiences are fine, when he sticks to the script. What he is, however, is a man achingly unable to project himself to foreigners, at least in unscripted public sessions, using the humane, Enlightenment values they expect and demand from the leader of a state powerful enough to wreck the security and prosperity of the whole planet with any miscalculation.

President Bush is not likely to seek or receive a personality makeover. Minimizing his visibility on the world stage is not an option. The American president cannot hide in the White House and let the secretary of state run the world. Even if he tried to hide, the media would drag him out again. But from a public diplomacy perspective, Bush could make a few useful adjustments.

President Bush can limit the harm he does to U.S. global interests by separating foreign and domestic policy in his public events, so that when he is speaking to Americans in the populist language they appreciate, foreigners will have less reason to listen in. President Bush should pass more of his foreign policy messages in speeches delivered to foreign audiences, speeches influenced by the political and public diplomacy specialists in the local U.S. embassy to signal that the United States recognizes and is correcting some of the gaffes of the past.[7] The smirk and swagger are tics that he can suppress when necessary.

Bush should not hold press conferences. First, those conferences blend domestic and foreign policy. Second, his inability to articulate a logical response to a difficult question frightens the world more than he wants the world to be frightened. He should leave to his diplomats the job of answering the unanswerable questions about the contradictions inherent in the foreign policy of any great power.

The president should also spend less time in photo opportunities with the troops. Bush's apparent militarism harms U.S. international interests. Those troop visits are aimed purely at a U.S. domestic audience. Bush is not up for reelection. He should cede to Republican senators and governors the political benefits of appearing alongside television personalities at American military bases. U.S. soldiers who depend on presidential pep talks to boost their morale should look for another career.

The Bush White House doctrine of rigorous communications discipline is a mistake where public diplomacy is concerned.[8] The internal U.S. government policy debate should be lively and public enough to reassure foreign observers that most Americans are not knaves and many are not fools. With official voices silenced in the run-up to Iraq, a relative handful of neoconservatives just outside the administration, the Richard Perles of the world, took advantage of the information vacuum to seize the headlines in the U.S. policy debate. This radical fringe framed the war on terrorism, Iraq, nonproliferation, and many other issues in terms of glorifying the exercise of naked U.S. power. These threats had no visible positive results on their intended targets, but fueled damaging foreign public narratives regarding the United States. Senior U.S. officials have a duty to counteract that message with one of intense, morally committed debate on the policy options the U.S. is realistically considering.

### Rearranging the Deck Chairs

In 1999 the once-independent U.S. Information Agency (USIA) and its foreign service, the U.S. Information Service (USIS), were absorbed into the State Department, under a new undersecretary of state for public diplomacy (PD). President Clinton signed the death warrant of USIA, a liberal outpost, as the price of prying loose America's unpaid UN dues from Jesse Helms, the virulently conservative chairman of the Senate Foreign Relations Committee. U.S. politics are full of such odd transactions.

Most of my former USIS colleagues fought absorption, fearing that their unique corporate culture and promotion system would be subordinated to a relatively tougher and more bureaucratic State Department mindset. They predicted that U.S. ambassadors, given direct supervisory control over public affairs officers, would take away their separate motor pool, reassign their designated houses, plunder their representational funds, and make them drowse through embassy staff meetings when they should be outside charming local literati. All those predictions came to pass. Some ambitious and dynamic USIS officers, however, welcomed the change because it put public affairs officers more firmly in the chain of command that leads one day to ambassadorships and influence on policy.

USIA loyalists can be forgiven for noting that the collapse of the U.S. international image began short months after USIA ceased to exist. *Post hoc ergo propter hoc* is impeccable bureaucratic logic and has a whisper of truth. The broader structural and policy reasons for American unpopularity, however, offer poor foothold for even the most agile bureaucratic climber.

I liked the old USIS. Their best diplomats were smart, lively, interesting people, freer than their State counterparts to use their frankness to gain credibility. However, the foreigners America has lost and needs to regain do not judge the credibility of the message by whether it comes from a pure and beautiful little agency, or from the State Department, the White House, or the Pentagon. No amount of rearranging the bureaucratic furniture will make our existing public diplomacy presence measurably more visible or more persuasive to Greeks conditioned to disbelieve whatever they hear from any representative of any government. Nor can the problem of how the United States presents itself be separated from the problem of what it is presenting.

Policymaking is a competitive process. Different agencies have different missions to assert and protect specific U.S. national interests. Those interests conflict, and therefore so do the different agencies. The president watches the battle and judges from how hard each agency fights how serious the stakes really are for the competing U.S. interests involved. America's global image is one of those national interests.

The senior official in charge of PD must be part of the policymaking process, someone with the mandate to improve America's global popularity as an end in itself. That person, out of bureaucratic self-interest, becomes an advocate for policies that least alienate the planet. If that person has the moral courage to fight hard enough, and the bureaucratic savvy to build tactical alliances with other agencies whose own agenda happens to coincide on a given issue, he or she can improve the odds that the U.S. policy that emerges will be one that can be marketed successfully to foreigners.

It is difficult to imagine finding anyone in Washington genuinely qualified for the job: both intimately familiar with the way foreigners understand the United States and tough-minded enough to have an impact on U.S. policy. That person would have such invidious tasks as explaining to the cabinet that America's moral superiority over terrorists and tyrants, something it takes for granted, is not taken for granted by the people the United States needs as our allies and that this will have consequences for U.S. counterterrorism policy. A successful head of PD would soon become the most hated figure in Washington, pilloried by all as a cheese-eating surrender monkey and closet Islamic extremist. U.S. poll numbers would change, if at all, too slowly to redeem that person's lost reputation. But patriotism requires that someone make the attempt. Accordingly, the president chose his trusted adviser Karen Hughes, and she loyally accepted.

### Making the Best of a Bad Message

Given the balance of power in American politics, Karen Hughes will not succeed in dragging U.S. policies into even superficial alignment with the prevailing sensibilities of its European partners during this administration.[9] Though partly masked by the president's crusade for Muslim democracy, Washington's "realism" in most issues is not so different from that of China: toughly nationalist, suspicious, relatively indifferent to human rights and the environment, and determined not to be seen by domestic rivals as giving anything away for free.

President Bush spent key formative years among Texas businesspeople who pretended to see hypocrisy as a sign of weakness. In most societies it is a sign of good manners not to say exactly what one thinks when that thought is too unpalatable to the audience. In addressing the foreign publics of key allies, the president and his subordinates must either share the ordinary humane hopes and aspirations of decent people around the globe, or else make a plausible pretence of it. U.S. lives and U.S. alliances depend on it.

The least discreditable form of diplomatic hypocrisy is to take advantage of the size and diversity of the U.S. government. Most officials in the U.S. government care sincerely and passionately about human rights. Plenty of officials are absolutely devoted to the environment. A handful will still fight grimly for international law and a strengthened, credible UN. Silencing such people in the name of a unified and disciplined U.S. foreign policy is cruel and counterproductive. Let them build international cooperation with their commitment to U.S. and universal values. They can then be quietly overruled when American domestic politics require it.

America's constitutional separation of powers is likewise a powerful negotiating tool. State Department negotiators who believed firmly in the treaties they were working on made effective use of the threat of congressional veto to extort the changes to the Comprehensive Test Ban Treaty, the ICC, and the Kyoto Protocol they hoped might make these treaties ratifiable by the Senate. President Clinton supported them, mournfully aware that congressional ratification would take a miracle. Clinton's use of American polyphony was far less costly than the Bush technique of supinely identifying U.S. government policy with the crude prejudices of congressional chauvinists.

More generally, when America cannot for domestic political reasons go along with the aspirations of its allies, its representatives must make a virtue out of the world's complexity. For a domestic audience, politicians prosper by simplifying the world, but for foreign publics that strategy is disastrous. If foreigners cannot recognize their own situation in America's description of it, they will assume the worst of America's intentions. An effective foreign affairs message tells foreigners that, yes, we understand the urgency of your problems and share your noble aspirations and are confident that in the long term we will realize them together. By showing enough grasp of the details, the United States can convey to foreigners, not that America is virtuous but at least that it is mindful of the many competing interests at play, including its allies', as it labors to keep the world balanced precariously on its axis.

## The Message of America Itself

America will never train a special corps of traveling salespeople skilled enough to "sell iceboxes to Eskimos," not in an age when Inuit groups are taking the United States to court claiming U.S. global warming is destroying their livelihood.[10] No brilliant marketing can solve America's current image program. The structure and funding level of PD are important mostly to the extent that they signal to the Pentagon, CIA, and State Department the president's genuine policy commitment to repairing the damage he has caused. Good PD programs do indeed serve U.S. national interests and at a very reasonable cost, but to measure their effectiveness America must make a virtue out of the patriotic truism that America will still be around in twenty years.

The only public diplomacy message compelling enough to counteract the interlocking hostile narratives about American power is prolonged contact with a broad spectrum of America and Americans. This is not a miracle cure. The world's prejudices about the

United States can be confirmed rather than dispelled by a poorly crafted visit. Still, people who have spent time in the United States tend at a minimum to be more careful in their choice of conspiracies and more thoughtful about the interplay of U.S. foreign and domestic policies. After an extended visit, most foreigners return with both a pragmatic and a sentimental stake in the success of the United States in portraying itself positively in their home country.

PD International Visitor (IV) programs have a respectable track record. Embassy sections identify potential leaders in politics, economics, various academic fields, journalism, and culture, and PD ships them off to the United States for an all-expenses-paid tour. In the old days, when allies were poorer and travel more expensive, it was easy to persuade a junior politician or journalist to take a month off to see America. A remarkable number of embassy selectees, at least in Greece, later rose to positions of influence. They remembered their IV program fondly for decades afterward, and sometimes wondered out loud why the United States had not been more aggressive in seeking a direct return on its investment.

The world is richer and busier than it was when I nominated my first IV candidates in 1986. A free trip to the United States is no longer an automatic godsend. Those already clearly marked for future glory are hard to break loose for even two weeks away from work. They accept the trip and cancel at the last minute. But less than three weeks is not enough time to imprint on an adult the breadth and complexity of the United States.

The simplest answer to the visitor problem, not ideal, is a shotgun approach. From each of the Middle Eastern countries that matter to us, the United States should be sending hundreds of people per year rather than tens, recent university graduates with a sprinkling of religious and business counterparts, identified by the recommendation of friendly officials, businesspeople, and academics (including those in American studies programs, in the rare universities that have them), for five-week tours including home stay with an American family (by universal admission a key transformational experience). Far more of the American people would happily volunteer for the role of hosting foreign visitors if their president asked them.

In terms of long-term transformation of poor, authoritarian states, high school student exchanges are the best investment in creating the core of a new generation of democratic technocrats. A sixteen-year-old wrested from his or her peer group will return from a year in the United States speaking perfect English and keenly aware that the way Uzbekistan is now is far from the only way a country can be. Fulbright and other higher-level academic exchanges are excellent, but not as radical in their impact. University students are too set in their ways to rewrite the rules by which they understand the world.

The U.S. government has substantially increased its funding for student exchanges since 2002. This is progress. The government should be funding thousands of student exchanges in key countries. One serious handicap, alas, is the peculiar nature of the U.S. high school system, which teaches young Americans many wonderful skills but not math or science or world history. Unless absolutely brilliant, a foreign student who spends junior year at a U.S. high school is condemned to repeat the year at home, hire an expensive tutor, or else fail university entrance exams. So exchange programs should factor in funding for remedial education on return to the home country.[11]

USIA tried moving away from cultural diplomacy under the mistaken impression that American culture marketed itself. There is a crucial difference between the entertainment industry—a gargantuan complex of multinational corporations, some U.S.-based, producing films, music, and other content in the English language—and American culture—an incredible pageant of musical and other regional artistic idioms, most of them hopelessly noncommercial. The version of the American image pandered to by the entertainment industry is part of America's image problem, not its solution. The entertainment industry does a good job making sure that in video shops all over the planet Oliver Stone conspiracies and dubbed versions of old Sylvester Stallone films compete successfully with wet sari musicals from Bombay and Hong Kong martial arts revenge fantasies. The shelf space left over for Cajun music documentaries is limited, and few Uzbeks would pay to rent them. They will watch them with pleasure, however, if American diplomats invite them to their homes.

American culture is a cheap, easy, agreeable, and useful reminder to skeptical foreigners that America is an old and varied country with a rich and sophisticated cultural life rooted in many different and reasonably interesting traditions. American culture is also a perfect excuse to pry smart, charismatic American public affairs officers loose from the embassy and send them around the host country to remind foreigners that Americans have neither horns nor tails. In the process the embassy smokes out the businessman whose secret passion for Elvis Presley makes him the perfect U.S. honorary consul and sponsor of U.S. trade promotion missions.

### Speaking Directly to the People

It is not a routine matter for the U.S. government to get out a simple message even to the American people. At critical moments it succeeds by devoting massive resources to the task. No matter what resources it devotes to the problem, the United States will be disappointed in the results when it attempts to go over the heads of foreign governments to appeal directly to mass public opinion in foreign countries.

Media access is difficult but not impossible. The U.S. government can gain some access to foreign television audiences even without buying its own satellite television stations like al Hurra. The problem is not even lack of the right people. The numbers are painfully small, but the State Department can field a handful of diplomats who are sufficiently fluent in the local language, culturally sensitive, appropriately idealistic, of presentable appearance, and trainable in mass communications techniques. But the cultural and intellectual barriers to successful communication are high.

In Athens at the beginning of 2003 the embassy put its fine young press officer on a major talk show to defend Iraq War policy. He spoke in Greek, looked good, bravely counterattacked against hostile questions, and defended U.S. motives behind the invasion. Greek friends commented sympathetically on his courage. No one thought his or any similar performance would persuade any measurable number of ordinary Greeks that the Iraq War was a good idea that Greeks should support.

Even when the U.S. government speaks the gospel truth, ordinary people in the larger part of the planet will not believe it. The smoother the performance, the more the U.S. message will be resisted. First, American diplomats are outsiders implicitly challenging a society's hard-won consensus understanding of the world. Second, they are from a government, and foreigners do not see why America would be an exception to the rule that governments routinely lie. Third, they are doomed by their status as bureaucrats to sacrifice their foreign audience to their domestic one. Washington watches its spokespersons like hawks, including (Americans learned recently) through clandestine eavesdropping, to make sure they stick to a narrow set of talking points designed to avoid trouble inside the Beltway.[12] Abstractions like "freedom" and "democracy" are safe, and so diplomats rely on them too heavily whenever they speak for the record. These abstractions are, alas, debased currency to the billions of foreigners who noticed long ago that such slogans are used impartially by democrats and autocrats alike. Greeks or Jordanians or Russians who bother to watch a representative of official America being smoothly diplomatic on their TV screens will congratulate one another on not being taken in.

This is not an argument for silence and passivity. Diplomats speaking on television will never persuade Greeks of benign U.S. motives for invading Iraq, or induce Indonesians to believe George W. Bush a better human being than Osama bin Laden. Still, television is the only window the world has to see American officials showing genuine, knowledgeable concern for the fate of the world and the welfare of their foreign hosts. The attempt to be persuasive, particularly in a difficult foreign language, is proof of respect for the decent opinions of mankind. It is the perception of such respect that makes American power palatable.

As I discovered to my chagrin from my own limited appearances on Greek TV, almost no one responded to the substance of what I said. I was like Samuel Johnson's dog "walking on his hind legs. It is not done well; but you are surprised to find it done at all." Quietly sincere American officials who speak the host language and display knowledge of the culture usefully undermine preconceptions. Bureaucratic prudence, however, is counterproductive to this exercise. Sticking to the generic talking points Washington provides will be perceived as an attempt to manipulate rather than persuade. American diplomats make good television only when they take risks. U.S.-controlled television channels like Al Hurra can hope to change hearts and minds abroad only through years of faithfully portraying America in all its complexity.

## The Curious Superpower

America has a million fine stories to tell about itself, dozens of excellent narratives to compete with the hostile ones that shape its current image. One of the key jobs of U.S. public diplomacy around the world is to find American narratives that strike local chords and to make certain that local journalists, artists, and storytellers are exposed to them. But talking is not the most important part.

The hardest anti-U.S. narrative to combat is the narrative about the arrogance of power. Unfortunately, there is more than a grain of truth to it. Even when U.S. policy is firmly multilateral, strict reciprocity is impossible. Well-meaning and egalitarian American officials will routinely be misread as arrogant by foreign colleagues because, as overburdened employees of a heavily bureaucratic superpower, they cannot afford the time required to go through the rituals of proving they are not.

Where possible, America must enlist time as its ally, slowing the pace and allowing two-way conversations to take place. Americans think they worship efficiency, but their diplomatic shortcuts are not particularly efficient. The best disproof of arrogance is genuine curiosity. More than by talking to foreigners, a superpower proves its good intentions by listening to them. But the overwhelmingly negative response to the first Middle Eastern tour of Undersecretary Karen Hughes in October 2005 is a reminder that intelligent, effective listening takes an enormous amount of homework to carry off successfully.

The realistic goal of public diplomacy is not to make America loved. The United States will be loved by a plurality of the planet again only if and when enough countries recognize a need for its assistance and it responds wisely as well as bravely and generously. Pending such redemptive crises (earthquake diplomacy is, as Secretary Rice noted, an excellent opportunity), the attainable goal of public diplomacy is to foster a U.S. image that is tolerable enough to ordinary, conventional human beings that foreign governments, whether fundamentalist tyrannies or liberal democracies, can easily afford the political cost of cooperating with the American superpower on terms close to those it seeks.

The stories the Greeks and others tell about Americans are too compelling, too rooted in the human experience of power, to be rebutted by any bureaucrat's sales pitch. Occasionally Americans will elect a president with the ability to convey to foreigners U.S. reverence for life and law. A less nationalist, more responsible Congress might some day scrape together a budget for foreign assistance proportionate to America's wealth. Festering sores like the denial of a viable Palestinian homeland can be healed. Still, unless it enlists character narratives that make American power seem humane and American society less self-absorbed, the U.S. government could blanket the globe with brilliant, balanced, generous policies and find that the vision of America's leadership of the community of nations was continuing to recede over the horizon almost as rapidly as it did during President Bush's first term.

# 9

# ★ *Diplomats and Journalists* ★

*If you can bear to hear the truth you've spoken*
*Twisted by knaves to make a trap for fools . . .*

*Rudyard Kipling*, If

I spent my second year in the Foreign Service at a tiny desk sandwiched between the much larger ones of two formidable foreign service specialists, the secretaries to the ambassador and deputy chief of mission. I was the staff aide to Sam Lewis, then in his eighth and final year as U.S. ambassador to Israel. I didn't know much about diplomacy. I knew, however, that Ambassador Lewis was a strong, confident, unerring, and occasionally angry God.

One afternoon the ambassador's secretary shook her head when I brandished my stack of paper. I should keep out. The ambassador wanted to be left alone. A very long time passed. Finally, some pressing paper needed to be retrieved, and I went in. God was hunched over his desk, writing a letter in longhand, one that had already consumed more than one attempt. This was very unsettling to my theology.

Ambassador Lewis had given a lecture at Tel Aviv University about the stalemated Arab-Israeli peace process. Led astray by his approaching retirement and his analytical acuity, he had couched an accurate conclusion about the failure of President Reagan's major Middle East peace initiative in terms too elegant not to quote verbatim: "The timing was . . . abysmal, the tactics of presentation worse, and the outcome, so far, nil."

An Israeli journalist in the room alerted Tom Friedman, then the *New York Times* correspondent in Jerusalem. He sent in a front-page story, headlining Lewis's catchy phrase, a few days before the 1984 U.S. presidential election.[1] The White House was not amused. Now a man of fifty-five, near the pinnacle of a distinguished career, Lewis was writing a personal apology to President Reagan and radiating the godlike self-assurance of a ten-year-old writing to apologize for the broken window. Reagan was gracious about it.

Over the centuries the diplomatic tribe has evolved a self-protective upper-class contempt for the mass media. Diplomats, even the most literate and humane ones, learn to use in public a hideously boring and obscure language designed to cause the eyes of prying journalists to glaze over as rapidly as possible. In the short term, fending off the media is prudent. But is it the correct approach for a superpower?

## On (Not) Handling the U.S. Media

In the permanent identity struggle over whether to be a diplomat or a bureaucrat, attitudes toward the Fourth Estate are a litmus test of loyalties. U.S. diplomats are conditioned by service overseas to value journalists as a vital information source as well as a way to communicate with host-country elites. Washington bureaucrats learn to exploit journalists as tools in their internal rivalries; other times they despise them as a dangerous nuisance.

A major shift from the Clinton era to the Bush era was in the relative importance given domestic and foreign publics and their right to know. Clinton was a confident political animal who embraced the media's role as his conduit to and from the world. Bureaucrats resented being forced to bend to media pressure (the CNN-driven international intervention in Bosnia, for example), but that was a price they paid for the public's access to information about the policies affecting its welfare.

Under an inarticulate president and a strong press secretary—such as Ari Fleischer during the first thirty months of the George W. Bush administration—the battle for overall control of the U.S. policy process was largely a battle for control over how stories appeared in the U.S. national media. Strict media discipline was especially vital to the administration when the gap between bureaucratic fantasy and the real world was starting to widen.

Journalists are not fools or knaves and will happily report that reality is about to bite an administration on the butt—provided they can find an official to confess it. Journalistic livelihoods depend on access to reliable sources of sexy information. Starved of leaks by a disciplined administration, journalists consciously or unconsciously shape their reporting with the expectation that faithful reproduction of bureaucratic dogma will win them back their access. And thus the incuriosity and credulity of the Bush administration regarding Iraq passed unchallenged until the war was safely begun.

Inside the State Department, the liberal instinct toward openness is permanently at war with bureaucratic self-preservation. Where the U.S. media are concerned, bureaucratic instinct prevails. The career consequences of getting crosswise with the White House domestic media strategy are too great for an ordinary desk officer to do more when a U.S. journalist calls than simply confirm publicly available facts. Secretary Powell could maintain his private ties to journalists, leaking without attribution the occasional counterpunch to some jab from the Defense Department. Most of his subordinates, however, loyally funneled U.S. media inquiries to an official in Public Affairs skilled in the art of lulling journalists to sleep.

A given mantra is decided upon, generally by the regional bureau in conjunction with the relevant functional bureau, and disgorged at the daily State Department noon press briefing.[2] Ideally a spokesperson's repetition of this mantra—something short, easy to remember, and ruthlessly uninformative—will cause the U.S. journalists the government fears to go away and write about something else. This system may not coincide with Americans' vision of informed democracy, but it is the one we have.

## Why the Foreign Media?

For diplomats from small countries, the cost-benefit ratio of spending time with foreign journalists is not much better than it is for Washington bureaucrats. The insider political information local journalists provide is not vital for the ordinary diplomatic business of trade promotion and arranging official visits. The Greek public's hazy public image of Bolivia plays little role in the success or failure of the Bolivian embassy's work. If the Bolivian ambassador needs a press clipping badly enough, a handful of Greek newspaper editors are willing to do the needful at a price he can afford.

The United States does not have Bolivia's option of neglecting foreign journalists. Persuading U.S. journalists in Washington that Greece is not really a story this week is easy enough. Foreign policy stories tend to hit the front pages in the United States only when there is a major political or bureaucratic battle feeding them. But it is absolutely impossible to persuade Greek journalists that the U.S.-Greek relationship is not an interesting story. No amount of bureaucratic obfuscation will deter a journalist whose livelihood depends on seeing through it. The U.S. government cannot operate outside the media spotlight. There will be a story about the United States, whether diplomats talk to journalists or not.

Every day the United States asks some foreign government to do some alarming and newsworthy thing like sending troops to Afghanistan or Iraq. In an ideal world, the United States makes its foreign policy requests privately and nothing appears in the media until the local government has decided to agree to the request and has come up with a public relations strategy for explaining it to the public. Few governments, however, have an Ari Fleischer strong enough to stonewall the media and make it hold. Any policy issue of major importance to the United States will become the subject of press stories written in Athens by Greek journalists based on leaks by Greek politicians and bureaucrats.

America normally has legitimate reasons for making its requests, and its allies normally have legitimate reasons for agreeing to them. However, the information Greek officials obtain from U.S. diplomats about U.S. policies is swamped by information they obtain from their own media. In Greece or anywhere, one of the most effective weapons of a Defense Ministry bureaucrat determined to prevent his budget from being poured into a sand dune in Eastern Iraq is an article in a semirespectable Athens daily newspaper implying that his Foreign Ministry rivals have buckled to American pressure, been diddled by the Americans, or are in the pay of the Americans. The content and tone of the article will reflect competing Greek internal bureaucratic and political interests, not those of the United States. The opposition political parties will take up the question in Parliament, more media coverage will follow, and the government will eye the exits.

It takes a brave prime minister to send his country's sons and daughters to Iraq. When America cannot get its own story across to justify a shared policy, its local negotiating partners lose their nerve. Diplomatic partnerships flourish when American officials can persuade influential local journalists to report that the result of long, tough negotiations with patriotic professionals is a deal that serves local interests and falls short of U.S. hopes. This is a diplomat's self-abnegating message, not a bureaucrat's self-promoting message.

Neither kind of message, however, will get out unless the U.S. embassy has solid ties to local journalists. Unlike many Greek politicians, the U.S. government does not subsidize flattering stories in the Greek media. To get America's story out it must be a good story, plausible, and told by a source with whom the journalist has some reciprocal relationship of favors given and received.

If another inducement is needed for U.S. diplomats to build ties to the media: the local journalists diplomats talk to are often their best source of priceless information, the stuff too sensitive to print, about what is really happening in the internal policy struggle over who gets sent to Iraq, what they will be qualified to do, and what their presence will cost the United States down the road. Local journalists will also warn American diplomats, when no one else dares, that U.S. public diplomacy is failing dangerously. Failure to engage with local journalists is dereliction of a U.S. diplomat's duty.

### *Keeping Our Expectations Realistic*

How does the United States use foreign journalists to strengthen America and its friends and to weaken its foes? Successful human communication is difficult enough even with one's immediate relatives, without barriers of language and culture. Making oneself accurately understood to a foreign journalist is more difficult than most Americans imagine. The rules of attribution are slippery. Editors can change the spin of even the most reasonable story. And foreign journalists react as ferociously as their U.S. counterparts to obvious efforts to manipulate them.

I cringed when I read the (rare) articles that emerged from my conversations with Greek journalists. The headlines would contradict the text. Of my sincere, eloquent, and logical presentation of the U.S. position only the barest traces would survive. Offhand comments about personalities would achieve embarrassing prominence. When the U.S. ambassador, in whose hands my career resided, raised his eyebrows at bizarre opinions attributed to "an experienced Western observer," my ingenuous response was to panic, to complain that Greek journalists were irresponsible scum to be treated in future like mushrooms. But I took a deep breath and moved on.

I take some comfort from the fact that even the State Department's most expert media-handlers could not make the foreign media dance a jig on command. I served in Athens one year under an ambassador who had been the State Department spokesman in Washington. Nick Burns had enormous experience in dealing with journalists. He liked the role and spent a huge amount of time on it. He knew their names and remembered their articles. He flattered them by asking their opinions and learned in the process an enormous amount about Greece and its internecine political struggles. He offered a balanced and sensible view of U.S. policy for local journalists to use or not use. Mostly they didn't.

Burns was an experienced professional doing a professional job of public diplomacy. He was backed by an excellent press officer and a local staff with decades of experience. He was far from a patsy and would punish irresponsible journalists and reward their more responsible colleagues. It is difficult to picture any American diplomat doing the job better. But the best he ever achieved was a draw. Headlines routinely distorted American positions. Journalists cited official U.S. views only to make a point of distancing themselves from them. Television news coverage would backdrop factual reporting from Washington with pictures of wounded Serb or Iraqi babies. We at the embassy got our message across when we needed to, by using personal relationships to sweet-talk or guilt-trip journalists and editors. From time to time we accidentally handed them a bigger headline than a self-protective bureaucrat would have preferred.

Inability to make local media a docile instrument of U.S. diplomacy is a worldwide reality, not an artifact of particular Greek perversity. America sends its best professional diplomats to U.S. embassies in the Middle East. They are skilled and work hard at their task of persuading local journalists. But, putting it very mildly, Middle Eastern media coverage of American foreign policy fails to do justice to America's good intentions.

When the United States needs the local media to get a certain message out to the broad Greek public, the only sensible way is to have the Greek government do the asking, letting it sweeten the request in whatever way seems best to it. The audience the United States can reach through its own journalist contacts is a narrower policy elite.

U.S. diplomats cannot directly change mass attitudes. They can change the attitudes even of friendly journalists only slowly and subtly. After fifteen years the memory of the pitying smile a young and attractive Greek reporter gave me as I challenged the tortured assumptions behind her latest article on U.S. connivance in the breakup of Yugoslavia still stings. I had fatally disgraced myself in her eyes by making clear that I believed the information I was conveying.

In American, "faith" is practically synonymous with "virtue" and "social respectability." Born into a state church that has been hand in glove with the civil power for centuries, Greeks have a less rosy view of faith. The virtue that matters most to their standing with their peers is not to be played for a *malákas* (a chump—literally, one whose wits have been dulled by excessive masturbation). No rational argument will change the social conditioning that makes refusal to believe official truth as valid a sign of journalistic integrity as the readiness to challenge official falsehood.

A self-respecting journalist will never be a passive conduit for official U.S. positions, even if an American diplomat acquaintance warrants the information to be true. Neither editors nor colleagues nor readers would forgive it. Journalism is a cutthroat business. In Athens a dozen or so highly politicized daily papers use hysterical banner headlines to fight for market share in city kiosks. Any message the United States wants to get through the noise must have some compelling local hook. Journalists who report the official government line, their own or America's, without giving it an interesting spin, will not be read, and eventually they will not be paid. When bribes, threats, supremely gifted persuasion, or—most reliably—friendship get a helpful article published, the journalist whose name appears above it will savage the United States on something else as proof to peers of journalistic objectivity.[3]

Often, the most important result of a successful conversation with a local journalist is that journalist's grudging recognition that a reasonably thoughtful American official seems to believe his own arguments. Such conversations between hundreds of U.S. diplomats and thousands of journalists over the decades have killed tens of thousands of damaging stories, mostly without our knowing about them.

In November 2001 Embassy Athens found itself caught up in the great anthrax scare. A suspicious mailbag from Washington was tested for bacteria. Bacteria, of course, are everywhere. Premature efficiency in warning the embassy staff of the ambiguous preliminary results was not matched by similar efficiency in informing the Greek government. Predictably, within a couple of hours every news program in the country was announcing that American anthrax had struck the cradle of Western civilization. It was the lead headline of every paper except the influential political daily, *To Vima*, whose senior correspondent thought to call me on my mobile phone and accepted my less sensational view of events. It wasn't anthrax, and there had been little reason for thinking it would be. One set of elite readers was spared the image of an embassy full of diseased prevaricators.

The benefits of building bridges to journalists go beyond article placement. Extended off-the-record talks with journalists gave me a treasure trove of useful information on Greek domestic politics, including foreign policy, arms sales, and the rising and falling reputation of the U.S. embassy. Much of that information made its way back to Washington as analysis of the Greek political situation. Some of it was helpful, on the rare occasions when the U.S. government was compelled by some crisis to take an interest in Greek domestic politics.

### Risky Business

Discretion is a painful necessity in a world in which any off-hand remark by a U.S. ambassador can be misused by some local faction in its internal political battles to its own profit and America's detriment. Dealing effectively with the media is a high-risk skill, like downhill skiing. It takes a whole career to learn to do it gracefully, and even experts impale themselves on trees from time to time.

When I arrived in Casablanca as a lightly supervised young economic officer in 1985, I did not think very deeply about why the Moroccan newspapers were full of turgid tripe about official visits and dubious economic statistics. I knew this was a country in which cautious bureaucrats controlled the sources of information. I did not realize how much power they had to punish media that strayed from the official line.

Fumbling for information beyond the worthless official statistics in *Le Matin du Sahara*, I met a Moroccan junior journalist who shared my impatience with the obsessive secretiveness of the bureaucrats. I learned a good deal about Moroccan economic life from her. Anxious to uphold my end of our exchange, I one day tipped her off on the conditions the International Monetary Fund was imposing on the next loan program for Morocco. I had the fuzzy notion that such information, not secret in the United States, had no business being secret in Morocco either. The story was an important one, and her editor put it on the front page.

Word quickly came down that someone in Rabat, the capital, was gravely upset. Presumably a population that is unaware that austerity measures are in place is a population that will not complain about them. My friend was a marked woman. Family friends relayed word that Driss Ben-Hima, the all-powerful interior minister, thought she would be happier back in France, where she had studied, rather than fraternizing with foreign diplomats in Casablanca. After weeks of hesitation and watching her sources dry up, she took the hint.

I had violated an elementary diplomatic rule by not understanding beforehand what the political stakes were. The problem was an internal Moroccan one. There was no embassy witch-hunt. I did not come forward to confess and be punished. The harm to a friend (and the loss of a well-informed local contact) was more than punishment enough.

The journalistic gaffe that hit me personally stemmed from a lengthy, frank conversation with a well-placed journalist regarding the waning fortunes of Greek Prime Minister Simitis. The United States had no dog in this fight. I took away some valuable analytical insights about the internal dynamics of the Panhellenic Socialist Movement (PASOK), Simitis's political party. I offered some minor correctives of my own. I neglected to consider, however, that my interlocutor's thirst for influence in Greek domestic politics might outweigh his friendly concern for my bureaucratic comfort. I was off the record, but not off the record enough.

The lengthy article that came out was designed to protect me, in the sense that the journalist had an anonymous source in Washington willing to take the credit for the journalist's and my shared analysis of the situation in Athens. But the U.S. government's alleged views were the hook for an editorial intervention on one side of the simmering succession struggle in PASOK. The State Department was portrayed as having concluded, along with many in PASOK, that Prime Minister Simitis was toast and that it should begin to assess the implications for U.S. policy of PASOK's dumping him.

Simitis was indeed toast, though it would take another year and a half to prove it. His replacement was Foreign Minister George Papandreou, the man the United States expected. But word came back to the ambassador from the prime minister's chief henchman that the prime minister did not appreciate Washington's sharing bleak opinions of his political future with the media.

The harm to U.S. interests was too small to measure. Simitis had little use for the U.S. ambassador even before the article. The U.S. government had no standing in Greek domestic politics either to help or harm Simitis, for whom there was guarded respect and certainly no U.S. malice. Simitis could and did regroup the party. When he finally stepped down, it was not because the United States had undermined him but because the public opinion polls convinced him and his party that PASOK had absolutely no hope of winning another election under his leadership but had a tiny hope under his successor. My gaffe, however, was seized on within the embassy as an argument for tighter media control.

### Getting the Bureaucratics Right

The policy damage done by diplomatic indiscretion is hard to quantify. Ambassador Lewis's indiscretion in 1984 had no impact on Reagan's crushing electoral victory or on the fate of U.S. efforts to bring peace to the Middle East. The indiscretions of lesser diplomats below the ambassador are generally almost invisible. The United States is so self-absorbed that banner headlines in the Greek press, even headlines revealing a major rift in U.S. policy, will have not the slightest ripple in the U.S. media.[4]

The harm to loquacious diplomats is not inflicted by journalists—who have little interest in destroying their sources—or even by host governments. Generally it is inflicted by a diplomat's superiors, out of an excessive concern with perceived personal loyalty and discipline. This distortion of values leads to a number of diplomatic failings, such as allergy to risk taking. The State Department errs by not setting a forward-leaning philosophical and practical framework for embassy management of relations with local media. This failure leaves each ambassador free to dictate his own approach or to leave a vacuum that subordinates will fill.

As a young political officer in Athens I took advantage of the too-great freedom I was given by a liberal ambassador and languid press section. I concluded that local journalists were one category of Political Section contacts, to be managed accordingly. I did not ask permission but simply read the Greek press to identify journalists who sounded useful and then called them up. A gratifying number were willing to talk to me, despite my youth and ignorance, and I learned a great deal from them. How far I shaped their opinions I do not know, though at the time the journalists protected me from whatever blunders I made. I was junior enough for my unformed opinions not to be newsworthy, and in any case I let them do 90 percent of the talking.

I later worked at the opposite extreme, with a Public Affairs Section that insisted that the embassy speak with a single voice, that of the ambassador and his press officer, and that journalists were the exclusive property of their section. The result was bemused local journalists and ineffective working relationships.

Public affairs officers have a legitimate concern with maintaining a seamless embassy facade to outsiders. The ambassador is—indisputably—the official face of the embassy. Flattering an ambassador's fragile self-importance by suggesting that he alone can successfully convey America's message to the host country is a wise bureaucratic move, although not strictly true. An overexposed ambassador becomes, as happened in Greece, a communications liability rather than an asset.

Political and economic officers view local journalists as partners in a subtle barter arrangement. They exchange information about U.S. policies for unpublished insights about the local situation. The official "talking points" sent from Washington are threadbare and unconvincing, the compromise product of an interagency bureaucratic process that strips them of any language that might prejudge some bureaucratic battle in Washington. Such points will not convince a skeptical foreigner, no matter how crisply they are delivered. Nor will they elicit any interesting information in exchange.

Press officers defend the value of their own expertise by harping on the genuine pitfalls that lurk for amateurs who talk to the press. The integration of Public Diplomacy, the old U.S. Information Agency, into the State Department in 1999 did not end the bureaucratic battle over the relative merits of diplomatic improvisation versus sticking closely to the agreed public line produced in

Washington. An officer with no previous knowledge of the subject can read a set of talking points. Ambitious political officers claim such points are useless. Ambitious public diplomacy officers exaggerate the dangers of going beyond such points.

In the end a leap of faith is necessary to accept that in a superpower diplomatic service, all foreign service officers, of every foreign affairs agency, should contribute to the U.S. government's permanent quest to influence foreign hearts and minds. From their first steps outside the visa window, junior diplomats should regard local journalists as an embassy asset to be cultivated, and performance evaluations should reflect that skill. Junior diplomats are bird dogs looking for talent. Senior diplomats keep senior journalists as well informed as possible, ideally exploiting friendships built during previous service in the same post. And no career ambassador should go before a pack of hungry Greek journalists without having had previous experience when the stakes were lower.

There will always be glitches, as naive young officers attempt to replicate with naive young journalists the calculated indiscretions of their ambassador. But their and America's best protection is long-standing embassy relationships with local editors and publishers, relationships monitored and enforced by a Press Section that accepts its role to teach junior officers, to coordinate overlapping contacts, to serve as institutional memory, and to enforce the ground rules on journalists who take advantage of embassy openness. The worst trap is a system that penalizes risk-taking activism but not passive incompetence.

A bland, opaque ambassador—a type many in Washington prefer—will never build the credibility the United States needs. Occasionally indiscretion is a vital part of diplomacy. Real, dangerous secrets leak. Journalists published less than they knew on the counterterrorism campaign against the Greek terror group 17 November because the U.S. ambassador and the Greek minister of public order were willing to share enough additional information to convince their friends that publishing then would harm an ongoing investigation. Only a chief of mission with the full picture of embassy operations can accurately assess the cost and benefit from buying silence in this way.

## A Free Press

The democracy the United States wants to spread throughout the world is meaningless without an informed citizenry. States conceal information from their own populations, seldom for altruistic reasons. The U.S. government, by virtue of its sources of information, can help remedy that lack. The United States is rich and powerful enough to withstand the official irritation that results when the local media are better informed than an autocrat likes, but at the same time, the superpower risks losing its sources. This is a difficult trade-off, and diplomats become too cautious as they age.

What diplomats cannot be, however, is cautious in their defense of a struggling free press wherever they find it. The clearest mark of freedom in the public's mind, alas, is the freedom to criticize not only the local government but also the superpower that works with that local government. I watched ambassadors "punish" local newspapers and journalists for their hostile coverage by disinviting them to embassy press conferences. This tactic is effective in Washington with the White House press corps. Overseas, it is as effective a tactic, short-term or long-term, as slashing our wrists to bleed on our tormentor's shoes.

# 10

# ★ *Democratizing an Oligarchic*

# *Planet* ★

*4) WE MUST FORMULATE AND PUT FORWARD FOR
OTHER NATIONS A MUCH MORE POSITIVE AND
CONSTRUCTIVE PICTURE OF SORT OF WORLD WE
WOULD LIKE TO SEE THAN WE HAVE PUT FORWARD
IN PAST. IT IS NOT ENOUGH TO URGE PEOPLE TO
DEVELOP POLITICAL PROCESSES SIMILAR TO OUR
OWN. MANY FOREIGN PEOPLES, IN EUROPE AT
LEAST, ARE TIRED AND FRIGHTENED BY EXPERI-
ENCES OF PAST, AND ARE LESS INTERESTED IN AB-
STRACT FREEDOM THAN IN SECURITY.*
*George Kennan,* The Long Telegram, *February 22, 1946*

Government by the consent of the governed is a principle that can be extended to cover a multitude of sins. After an elected government has floundered badly enough, a large majority of the population will sit placidly at home through a military coup and the resulting dictatorship. This happened in Greece, the birthplace of democracy, in 1967. In Argentina until 1983, ordinary good citizens turned in their democratic activist neighbors to the police as dangerous radicals who could be dropped into the ocean from airplanes at five thousand feet. The U.S. government did business with despots on both occasions. American standards of what constitutes acceptable governance for U.S. allies have become stricter since the end of the Cold War. What the United States lacks is a clear sense of how to promote those standards effectively.

"Democracy" is an easy applause line for American presidents. President Bush took for granted in March 2003 that his subordinates knew how to install democracy in Iraq or anywhere else America was bold enough to try. As a diplomat, I had the honor of working alongside brave Americans and Europeans who had proved their genuine commitment to democracy by attempting to build it in countries not nearly as divided and difficult as Iraq. I did not share my president's confidence.[1]

### *Chilly Lessons From an Armenian Election*

Armenia was my schoolroom for democracy building. When the 1998 Armenian presidential elections were announced, the U.S. embassy in Yerevan mobilized to support the democratic process. Diplomats, drivers, and English-speaking Armenian staff fanned out across the country as part of the international election observer mission or manned the all-night control center back at the embassy. We put on blue and white armbands with the logo of the Organization for Security and Cooperation in Europe (OSCE) and joined colleagues from two dozen European countries in trying to keep the elections free and fair.

As I huddled with Alla, my wise and wonderful political assistant, in an unheated Yerevan kindergarten with broken windows, Renik, our driver, kept tabs on what the men in the long black leather coats were muttering into their mobile phones outside. At 3:00 AM, after twenty hours of work, the election commission members took another break for cognac. They were too exhausted to make the numbers come out. I lent them my calculator, made diplomatic suggestions about arithmetic, and shared the dregs from my coffee thermos. I hoped the ultimate results would justify the hopes and sacrifices of the Armenians I had come to admire.

The polling stations run by the schoolteachers were the best. These formidable women were experts at making cold, confused children stand in line. Dazed veterans of the Great Patriotic War and even the swaggering young veterans of the 1992–94 war for Nagorno Karabakh obeyed them instinctively. The teachers could decipher the OSCE-printed booklet of polling instructions, handle a glue-pot to attach the paper seals to the ballot box, and keep a stove going with dried dung or whatever else would burn. They showed no hesitation barking at the local oligarchs when they loitered too close. Our little team would appear at one of their precincts, spend twenty minutes chatting politely with everyone, and leave feeling reasonably confident that there the paper ballots would be counted accurately and the voting materials delivered, neatly bundled and sealed, to the Regional Election Commission by three in the morning.

But it wasn't like that at half of the polling places we visited. At 8:00 PM, when the polls closed in the second round of presidential voting, I let myself be locked in with the election commission of a polling station in the Yerevan district of Achapniak. Contorted into a desk made for an Armenian six-year-old, I raised my eyebrows politely and scribbled notes while the balding bureaucrat from the state factory pulled, with increasing lack of enthusiasm as my interest grew, neat bundles of identically marked ballots out of the ballot box and read the name of the victorious incumbent over and over and over. The bureaucrat and his colleagues would not have stuffed this particular ballot box if they had known I was going to be there. But spending the night with them gave me lots of time to reflect. If Armenia could only be democratized by having a foreign diplomat guard each of eighteen hundred ballot boxes around the clock, then America had better revise its democracy-building aspirations downward.

Armenia conducted lots of elections when it was a Soviet Socialist Republic. Voting was mandatory. Voting against the official slate of candidates was perfectly legal, just antisocial. It suggested local problems that might require scrutiny from the capital. Every factory, every state farm, every family had its own little deviations from Soviet reality, and who really wanted to call a closer inspection down on the neighborhood? The socialist order was triumphantly reaffirmed by secret ballot. No one had any illusions that elections were the same as democracy.

The first post-Soviet election in Armenia, in 1992, was honest, Armenians say. Everyone knew who was going to win and was content. A respected intellectual named Levon Ter-Petrosian had headed the nationalist movement that lobbied for independence and to wrest the Armenian enclave of Nagorno Karabakh away from Azerbaijan. A national hero, Ter-Petrosian was easily elected president of the newly independent Republic of Armenia. His democratic legitimacy to govern was unquestioned, largely because it preexisted the election.

During Ter-Petrosian's first presidency, the Armenians defeated Azerbaijan militarily and seized Nagorno Karabakh and the territory around it, expelling hundreds of thousands of Azerbaijani civilians. Winning a war was a fine source of legitimacy—for the warlords who fought it. Ter-Petrosian was stuck in Yerevan struggling with the consequences of their victory. Azerbaijan and Turkey closed their borders. Communication to the outside world was disrupted by a Georgian civil war. One bad mountain road to Iran kept Armenia supplied. The Armenian economy collapsed. People burned the wooden slats on the park benches for fuel. To feed their children, women prostituted themselves to military officers who had enriched themselves by smuggling gasoline or looting Azeri villages. Ter-Petrosian was helpless against the corruption that began to run rampant.

This was not the democratic Armenia most Armenians had dreamed of when they claimed their independence from Moscow. In 1996 five feuding opposition parties unexpectedly united behind a single candidate to oppose Ter-Petrosian's reelection. Officially, Ter-Petrosian won with just over half the vote against Vazgen Manukian, the unity candidate, and Sergei Badalian, the communist. The OSCE observers realized from mysterious events late on election night that twenty-two thousand extra ballots had been crammed into Yerevan ballot boxes at the last minute, enough to put Ter-Petrosian over the 50 percent threshold needed to avoid a run-off against Manukian. What was not clear was how many other ballots had been stuffed in fraudulently during the day. The opposition took to the streets, sincerely convinced that it had won. The United States counseled the opposition to accept defeat meekly. Ter-Petrosian took office for a second term.

When I arrived in Yerevan ten months later as chief of the Political-Economic Section and began building my ties to opposition leaders, I dismissed as the usual whining of the defeated Manukian's certainty that he had won the 1996 election. Eighteen months later, poring late at night over a massive Excel spreadsheet that compared the precinct-by-precinct voter turnout of the 1996 and 1998 elections and charting the voting results against turnout in each case, I discovered that I had been unjust. The only logical conclusion from the data was that Ter-Petrosian had lost the 1996 election.

America's counsel of meekness in the face of electoral fraud turned out to have been bad advice. Ter-Petrosian had lost the respect of the Armenian people and put himself too deeply in debt to his "power ministers," the Karabakh war leaders who had rigged the election for him and now wondered why they had done so. The tainted elections gave Ter-Petrosian too little legitimacy to govern effectively. Ter-Petrosian was not a bad man. He wanted economic reform and a peace deal with Azerbaijan, but he could not deliver. After a year and a half of minimal progress, a mysterious flare-up occurred. When the dust settled early in 1998, Ter-Petrosian was out, his party was a shambles, and his prime minister, Robert Kocharian, the former president of Nagorno Karabakh, was about to elect himself president. Armenia had just wasted eighteen months, and U.S. interests had gained nothing from trying to legitimize an illegitimate president.

Kocharian was not particularly popular among ordinary Armenians. He was from Karabakh across the old Azerbaijan border. His Russian was better than his Armenian. He was respected for his role in bringing about Karabakh's independence, and he was seen as tough enough to control his ministers. His main electoral opponent, Karen Demirchian, had been the general secretary of the Armenian Communist Party during prosperous Soviet times. Demirchian's Reaganesque good looks and fondness for empty platitudes did not inspire enthusiasm among foreign technocrats, but many older Armenians worshipped him. Few Armenians believed Demirchian's promise to get the old Soviet factories working again—no manager on earth could make these dinosaurs competitive on the world economy. But ordinary Armenians thought that at least he would curtail the power of the economic oligarchs.

What constitutes a fair election? Fortunately, the U.S. government does not have to make that call on its own. In Europe, the OSCE's Office for Democracy and Human Rights does a valiant job of assessing whether a given election "meets international standards." OSCE monitoring teams descend a few months before a problematic election. They analyze the election law, the election mechanisms, the freedom to campaign, the access to the media, and then the actual conduct of the voting and counting. The OSCE mandate applies only in Europe, the United States, Canada, and the former USSR, countries that committed themselves to outside scrutiny by signing the Helsinki Accords. In the rest of the world, the UN and nongovernmental organizations monitor elections to the extent permitted by the local authorities.

The seventy-odd OSCE observer teams found that the March 1998 Armenian election campaign was rigged in favor of Kocharian, but not obscenely so. Many voters pocketed ten dollars or free electricity for their vote. Polling in a majority of precincts was honest. Still, my precinct-by-precinct turnout analysis suggested that Kocharian's 59 percent to 41 percent official margin of victory had been massively inflated and that honest voting would have given him a bare majority.

The day after the elections, Demirchian's supporters were not as morally certain of victory as Manukian's had been in 1996. They would challenge the results in court but not take massively to the streets in the absence of foreign encouragement. The international community had no vital interests in Armenia that pushed it to take sides. The path of least resistance was to accept Kocharian's victory. As the months progressed, it became clear that he had enough legitimacy to govern the country. At one point he came close to a peace deal with Azerbaijan. The mafias did not lose their power. Still, ordinary Armenians began to climb slowly out of the worst of their poverty.

The conventional wisdom of Armenian taxi drivers was that Demirchian would have won the election if Armenians had expressed their true personal preferences. Most Armenians did not feel they had that luxury. Some American voters felt in 2004 that during an ongoing war and terrorism crisis they did not have the luxury of changing presidents. Freedom to choose is relative, in elections as in everything else.

### The Oligarchic Threat to Democratic Elections

There are tyrants in the world, but few if any feel particularly all-powerful. Kocharian certainly did not. Looking at the Armenian elections through a statistical microscope, I began to realize that Americans misunderstand the world's huge democracy deficit. When I talked to Kocharian's adviser, it was clear that Kocharian would have preferred a close, credible victory, not the official landslide. The sharp variation in voting patterns from region to region and village to village showed that the fraud was not the outcome of one man's or one party's despotic control. The lopsided outcome was the collective result of private, self-seeking decisions by many individual local bosses, each using whatever power he had to put the new president in his debt.

When the Soviet and other colonial empires collapsed, they left behind weak national institutions, especially outside the capital cities. Local sheikhs or tribal leaders or factory directors seized the control imperial powers had relinquished, along with the local sources of wealth. Whenever the rule of law slips, local leaders exercise more arbitrary control over the lives of local citizens than does even the most despotic central government.

In many established democracies, local chieftains see the votes of their district as theirs to bestow. Indians take for granted that poor, illiterate villages will cast 98 percent of their votes for one party in one election, then the same percentage for a different party in the next, depending on the will of their local strongman. My Houston grandmothers assured me that the same phenomenon occurred in border counties of Texas well into the twentieth century. Few American politicians, but many American preachers, still boast a similar degree of political control over their constituents.

In Armenia the commonest process for exercising that control was called "carousel voting." Each voter was given a premarked ballot before reaching the polling station. After signing in and getting a blank ballot, the voter would pocket the blank ballot, cast the premarked one, and then return the unused ballot to the men in long black leather coats waiting outside, to be marked and handed to the next voter. All across the planet, local equivalents of Armenia's black coats have similar ways to make sure each purchased or coerced vote stays that way.

When conducted as a straw poll of local warlords, elections give no guarantee to ordinary voters that their interests will be protected. Oligarchs do not see elections as a struggle between competing programs or ideologies. Except when they are positioning themselves for civil war, oligarchs want to make sure their district casts as many votes as the laws of physics allow on behalf of the candidate their informed calculation tells them will be their negotiating partner in the future. The warlords' reflex to herd around the preanointed victor explains why an outsider like Mikheil Saakashvili could win more than 90 percent of the vote in the 2005 Georgian elections with no recourse to fraud of his own.

In elections in post-Saddam Iraq there could be no such fore-ordained victor. The Baath Party, the only national institution that bridged the warring tribes and sects, had been destroyed. Warlords and sheikhs had no choice but to revert to more primitive personal and tribal forms of coalition building to safeguard their interests. This is democracy as Afghans and Pakistanis and many others know it. This is not democracy that achieves the goals of good governance Americans ask of it. A national government whose legitimacy derives from the vote-extorting talents of local oligarchs will not effectively perform its most important task, protecting the rights of ordinary citizens against extortion by those same oligarchs.

Since the 1960s election fraud in the United States has almost never been blatant enough to be provable. This is not because American political bosses are inherently more honest than their Armenian equivalents or because a token team of OSCE observers visited Florida in 2004 to defend our democratic freedoms.[2] Large, well-funded U.S. political parties mobilize armies of poll watchers to defend their national and statewide electoral interests against local power brokers. These parties can appeal to a once-respected Supreme Court any abuse that obviously perverts the will of the electorate.

In struggling new states, however, each political party starts out as the personal entourage of a single politician. Such parties are too small, disorganized, and regionally based to defend their interests effectively in the country as a whole. In their home region, moreover, they may be just as disgracefully antidemocratic as the ruling faction against which they are competing. The court system to which a defrauded candidate may appeal is simply the power structure dressed in dark robes.

Most OSCE member states, the United States included, have an ideological assumption that centralized authority is the problem. We reflexively try to weaken it. We tend to forget how recently—the civil rights movement in the 1960s—a strong federal government and Supreme Court wrote new rules that broke the stranglehold of some of America's own local despots. Only national institutions—well-funded political parties, an independent judiciary, and police and military loyal to the constitution rather than local paymasters—can temper the power of local oligarchy. If the U.S. government wants to build meaningful democracy around the world, it needs to teach its officials and contractors to turn national institutions into the ally of the population. The record of U.S. democracy-building efforts in Armenia suggests how easy it is to fail.

## *The Armenian Visitor and Other Perils of Democracy Building*

The world dispenses much of its wisdom in the form of dubious stereotypes. For Greeks an "Armenian visit" is when someone shows up at your house, is welcomed politely, and somehow never manages to leave. I arrived in Yerevan, on a scorching August night in 1997, six years after the Armenian Socialist Federal Republic had ceased to be a component state of the Union of Soviet Socialist Republics and five and a half years after Secretary of State James Baker had swooped in to open a new U.S. embassy there.

The major U.S. goal in the South Caucasus was to assure that the United States and its friends would benefit from the development of oil and gas reserves in Azerbaijan and the Caspian Sea. This goal was tied to our next goal, of weaning Georgia, Azerbaijan, and Armenia from their political and economic dependence on Russia. This implied the need to solve the Azerbaijani-Armenian struggle over the disputed enclave of Nagorno Karabakh. Democracy was a fourth goal, one that—in Armenia if not always in Azerbaijan—seemed to complement these other goals.

Thanks to an active Armenian-American community, the U.S. mission in Armenia had $100 million a year to spend in aid, more per capita than it spent anywhere else in the world except Israel. Much of that was humanitarian assistance, but the United States also allocated millions of dollars toward strengthening democracy. As the head of the Political-Economic Section at U.S. Embassy Yerevan, I had the agreeable task of providing political oversight to the organizations the U.S. Agency for International Development (USAID) had hired for that purpose: the International Foundation for Electoral Systems, which kept an election expert in Yerevan to help the Central Election Commission craft a fair election law and transparent voting system; the National Democratic Institute and International Republican Institute, which worked with Armenian political parties and grassroots organizations to teach them the skills of party organizing and voter mobilization; the Eurasia Foundation; Internews; and others. A dozen or so smart, idealistic, hardworking experts from the United States and all over the world were supporting Armenia's democratic transition. They did not have to overthrow a dictator when they arrived. Political parties and activist groups were numerous and vocal. The U.S. embassy had access and influence. There was adequate funding.

When I returned to Yerevan for another week of election monitoring in February 2003, Armenia still had opposition parties and human rights activists. The electricity worked. The cafes had new neon lights and better-dressed women. But in terms of visible progress on any key political indicator, whether media freedom, untainted elections, economic transparency, or human rights for political activists, after a billion dollars of U.S. assistance and eleven years of advice, energy, and dedication from U.S. officials and volunteers since 1992, Armenia in 2003 was almost exactly where I had first found it in 1997.

Armenia wasn't a fiasco. In Yerevan, citizens were still clearly freer than they had been in Soviet times. They were less secure economically, but they had more opportunities to use their talents. Elsewhere in the country, however, the firm grip of local economic oligarchs on Armenia's limited resources took much of the practical meaning out of "liberty" for average citizens. Reforms that might loosen that grip died a slow, mysterious bureaucratic death.

America and its allies did not find a magic formula to turn Armenia into a liberal democracy. The United States has fine aid organizations that can design programs, draw up budgets, hold conferences, evaluate grant applications, coordinate with other agencies, have regular meetings with Armenian counterparts, withstand regular audits from Washington, and produce quarterly reports to prove that they have met a series of bureaucratic benchmarks set by themselves, USAID, or Congress. This is not the same as democracy building.

When they were not writing mandatory progress and compliance reports, sturdy young democracy experts in Armenia did everything they could think of that the local authorities would permit.

These experts made a lasting and positive impression on the Armenians they met. They employed hundreds of idealistic Armenians who might otherwise have emigrated to Moscow or Los Angeles. At election time their work with political parties and nonpartisan grassroots organizations made the elections significantly more competitive. When the assistance funding was large enough to justify changing a bad policy to qualify for it, Armenian officials changed their policy, as least for the lifetime of the project.

Most of the U.S. democracy experts finished their one- or two-year contracts and moved on like I did, leaving behind them a pile of progress reports no one had time to read and dozens of obsolescent computers with USAID stickers on them. Some of the Armenian activist groups whose creation was catalyzed by U.S. democracy funds found new foreign donors after being cut loose. Those that did not died, with little to remember them by but tarnished nameplates outside crumbling buildings.

Looking for the reasons for these disappointing results, it is tempting to blame the lack of coordination of the assistance donors. The World Bank, International Monetary Fund, European Union (EU), UN, and United States seldom spoke with a single voice to the Armenian government on economic policy and political reform. They competed for the limited number of sensible aid projects that would appeal to donors and for the limited pool of trustworthy English-speaking Armenian partners. Armenian officials used this competition to weaken the leverage of each individual group.

Another excuse for the poor results was that the Russians were silent competitors. Russian companies and officials had no particular ambition to transform Armenian society and were happy to pursue their economic interests with friendly oligarchs. When the United States pushed the prime minister too hard on reforming the electricity sector, a Russian company would purchase a blocking share of the power company. Americans' superior selflessness did not confer the advantage my colleagues and I expected. Many locals were convinced, wrongly I think, that America was trying to pull the strings of local politics just like the Russians did, only less competently.

The real problem was that the United States and its EU partners were not giving Armenian decision makers any reason to act against their short-term economic interests. In a closed society, a cartel generates more wealth for its members than does free, market-driven competition. The United States and its partners could not explain how the EU-inspired rules they promoted would benefit the people whose wealth made them indispensable to Armenian politicians. Therefore they could not persuade the politicians to put their personal or institutional prestige behind those rules.

At the current pace of progress, idealistic young Americans will continue to find employment as democracy-building experts in Armenia for as many decades as U.S. taxpayers maintain their enthusiasm for the idea. Until they find more effective strategies for redressing the power balance between weak central institutions and strong local personalities, being stereotyped as an Armenian visitor is one of the many moral hazards that await them.

### So Why Try to Democratize?

U.S. foreign service officers learn to see democracy and human rights as U.S. national interests to be weighed against other interests. Few Americans feel morally at ease when a dictator ruins a country and brutalizes its population. Still, U.S. passivity in the face of the Rwanda genocide is a reminder of how rarely the American people demand intervention without some motive of self-interest to supplement their humanitarianism. Can we make a true and compelling case that authoritarian regimes harm U.S. interests enough to justify the cost of changing them?

The costs and benefits of doing business with dictatorships are not equally distributed. The State Department enjoys a slight advantage in Washington bureaucratic competition when the U.S. government deals with fellow democracies. Diplomats are good at navigating the compromises and ambiguities of democratic decision making. When a dictator is in power, the advantage swings to the CIA and the White House. Dictators keep secrets that parliaments cannot and thus are less accountable politically for the cooperation they provide. The U.S. military is happy either way. It does not jeopardize cordial relations with foreign military officers by forbidding them to stage coups, but it does not encourage them either, because Congress puts limits on military cooperation with all but a few especially useful despots.

Most Americans agree instinctively with President Bush that greater democracy will reduce the threat to the United States and its allies. With regard to exporting terrorism, the practical difference between Islamic democracies such as Iran and Islamic monarchies such as Saudi Arabia is not self-evident. Israel, a vibrant democracy, is no more able than authoritarian Russia or tribal Sudan to grant an armed separatist movement the viable independence that would bring its insurgency to an end.

One of America's favorite platitudes is that democracies do not fight wars with each other. Until the 1960s democracies were sparse enough that they seldom bumped into one another. Greece and Turkey almost went to war over the rocks of Imia in 1996, for impeccable democratic reasons. Most wars are civil wars, and democracies are perfectly capable, like the United States in 1861 or the Philippines in 2005, of waging war on themselves. The most we can safely say is that leaders enjoying the legitimacy that comes from honest democratic election and good governance have no need for the legitimacy that derives from successful military adventures.

Dictatorships are dysfunctional. Most military officers are too rigid to be good politicians, tone-deaf to the trade-offs required to govern. After they seize power, they bankrupt their countries, launch little wars, and then end up in exile or dismembered by one of their rivals, like M. Sgt. Samuel K. Doe of Liberia. Often dictators condemn their country, like António de Oliveira Salazar condemned Portugal, to decades of stagnation and backwardness.

But what about Pakistan? Pervez Musharraf's elected civilian predecessors tolerated as much corruption, brutality, tyranny by local landowners, and general incompetence as Musharraf does. If history is any guide, Musharraf's democratic successors will be at least as likely to lead Pakistan into some unpleasant new adventure with India. How do we judge between them?

At some point, even without U.S. intervention, dictators die or are run out of town. Their policies are overturned and their debts disavowed as "odious." This impermanence of dictatorships constitutes perhaps the best motive for America to insist on democracy. Democracies have long memories. Greek voters and politicians are still punishing the U.S. government's collaboration with the Colonels over thirty years ago. Democracies also fail, alas, but the regimes that replace them have no analogous political requirement to hold a grudge against the United States, no matter how galling America's support for the previous government might have seemed.

Over the very long run, therefore, U.S. interests are served by a consistent strategy of vigorously supporting democratically elected governments, whatever their views, and finding a cost-effective way to remove dictators, no matter how serviceable. It would take considerable courage for a U.S. president to invoke that principle. There is a middle ground.

## Fostering Regime Change

When a dictator has mastered the difficult art of keeping a reasonable percentage of his more influential citizens happy without antagonizing his foreign patrons, he can hang on until he dies, like General Francisco Franco of Spain. This is regrettable but understandable. Passionate adherents of "liberty or death" tend to get weeded out of the gene pool. Even a mild and successful revolution, like the ouster of the halfheartedly tyrannical Askar Akayev in Kyrgyzstan in March 2005, left Bishkek, the capital city, an ugly mess. Many citizens prefer to wait for nature to take its course.

Every regime has an expiration date. Over time, even freely elected governments become jaded and corrupt and lose their legitimacy to govern. Watching from my perch as political counselor in Athens late in 2002, I could see by the glassy eyes of Greek cabinet ministers that their superhuman effort to win the 2000 elections had been a mistake. The Panhellenic Socialist Movement (PASOK), which had governed Greece since 1981 with one three-year interruption, left office in 2004 with secret relief.

Affordable regime change is normally the result of a local population's concluding that the previous government has lost its legitimacy by governing too badly for too long. As a diplomat I had to be very diplomatic in how I noticed this because the United States had no standing with Greeks to be the arbiter of when their government had outlived its legitimacy. By the time it is true enough to be useful, the message is obvious without us.

When the United States intervenes, it runs the risk of giving a precious lease on life to a leader who should be packing his bags. Superpower criticism triggers a nationalist reflex to rally around the embattled leader. More damagingly, a dictator who has burned his bridges decisively with his own population may find a foreign government willing to prop him up if the United States allows him to frame his misrule in a context of great-power rivalry. Fidel Castro was brilliant at using U.S. pressure to manipulate Moscow into giving him more aid during the Cold War. All the Central Asian dictators pay a visit to President Putin whenever the United States makes noise about human rights and free elections. They move closer to America again when Russia gets too greedy or when the situation in Afghanistan deteriorates to the point where the United States will pay the price they seek for use of their airfields.

Dictatorships collapse spontaneously, but only when they have done something so stupid that it leads to national humiliation. The 1967–74 junta in Greece collapsed when the dictator Dimitris Ioannidis sponsored a coup against the legitimate government of Cyprus and then watched helplessly as the Turks invaded and partitioned that island nation in response. Argentina's more brutal

1976–83 military dictatorship ended with the fall of Gen. Leopoldo Fortunato Galtieri after he invaded the Falkland Islands and was humiliated by Margaret Thatcher and the British navy.

Not even catastrophic incompetence and draconian international sanctions are enough to force out a dictator who is brutal and independent enough. Germany remained loyal to Hitler until the Russians entered Berlin. The grotesquely vicious Idi Amin of Uganda was driven out only when the Tanzanians counterattacked after Amin's failed invasion of Tanzania. Vietnam forcibly rusticated Pol Pot of Cambodia once his murderous repression spread to ethnic Vietnamese as well as his own people.

Outside military intervention works, but it is terribly costly and has another crucial disadvantage. Over decades of independence, a state's political system evolves to reflect the intensity of the internal competition it must regulate. When a population drives out its own dictatorship, enormous legitimacy accrues to the leaders of the successful movement. A national liberator, like George Washington, Mahatma Gandhi, or Kim Il Sung, can successfully unite the quarreling tribes. His heirs will enjoy some of that same legitimacy. Democratization from outside deprives the local population of its liberation struggle.

In Romania, Nicolae Ceausescu had purged one capable deputy, Ion Iliescu, under circumstances that left Iliescu the least tainted leadership figure in the country when the dictatorship fell. Exiled politicians rushed back from Paris and London but discovered that the Romanian people had forgotten them in favor of a man who had been present and visible when their world changed. Iliescu had the legitimacy to keep his wounded country united and to deflect the ultranationalism that would have blocked Romania's integration into Europe. Ahmed Chalabi, by contrast, had left Iraq as a young man. When he returned to Iraq in 2003 behind U.S. Army tanks, he discovered that his remarkable contribution as puppet-master of the invasion did not inspire instinctive obedience from his fellow Iraqis. Managing a murderous ethnic mosaic like Iraq is no easy task. Self-appointed exile leaders must either use the same repressive measures as the dictator they persuade the United States to oust or else watch a generation's worth of social and economic capital disappear in the flames of civil war.

Covert action is cheaper than invasion and requires less congressional scrutiny but does not solve the legitimacy problem. Moreover, covertness is often illusory. In Armenia, Iraq, and most of the countries the United States would like to democratize, the head of the security services will report to his leader within a day or two whom a U.S. diplomat has met and more or less what was said. Covert scheming, to be successful, puts the United States in an unsavory partnership with the local security chief. His goals for the new regime may differ from ours.

Ceausescu fell once the Romanian military realized that it was under no pressure from its Russian partners to shoot its own people. When a dictator is foolish enough to let his people understand his dependence on foreign support, his legitimacy plummets. This makes him vulnerable to pressure from his outside benefactor. America's most effective and affordable contribution to democracy is to help persuade a friendly dictator to go into exile for the good of his country, as Ferdinand Marcos did in the Philippines in 1986 when faced with a non-violent popular rebellion.

Dictators think of themselves as patriots, no matter how greedy and depraved they also are. They tend to associate themselves with the nation they exploit and to assume the worst about any potential successors. To persuade a hereditary autocrat, Syria's Bashar Assad for example, to step down, the United States must make a plausible argument that the Syrian people will benefit. This question of popular benefit is not a rhetorical one. Destabilizing a country is cheap and easy. Democratizing even a small one is slow and expensive. If U.S. motives are opportunistically political, America will lose interest with the first setback or change of administration.

Afghanistan after the departure of the Russian Army in 1989 is a good example of what happens when one U.S. administration helps a divided country take the plunge from despotism into anarchy and the next feels no obligation to help it climb out again. A Syrian democracy project embarked on purely as a short-term tactical program to ease the president's conscience over imaginary Iraqi weapons of mass destruction, to break the OPEC oil cartel, to wrong-foot the Democratic Party, or to eliminate any lingering military pressure on Israel from its neighbors would be disastrous to its alleged beneficiaries. Innocent democrats who trusted the United States would die painfully in the civil war that followed U.S. loss of interest. Therefore, America's motives for ousting the Assad dynasty had better be clear, firm, and bipartisan, not (for example) a ploy to bathe Syria in fire and blood so that Israel can hang onto the Golan Heights forever.[3]

### Setting the Rules of Democratic Governance

Where democracy is not simply a slogan or an election staged for the benefit of outside donors, it is a set of rules giving a strong voice to the population in domestic political competition. When I put on my democracy-building hat in Armenia, I saw myself as an impartial referee standing outside the game, enforcing the rules with my whistle and with no interest except fair play. Of course this is nonsense. In every country of the world America has specific interests that affect its attitude toward the various local participants. The United States has multiple interests, in fact, and multiple Americans competing against one another to promote those interests.

It is difficult enough for foreigners to accept the U.S. role as referee. When America attempts to write the rules as well, problems develop. Very few Arabs believe the United States is interested in democracy for its own sake. Even if they did, their history tells them that outsiders' rules must be altered to take account of Islam and tribal balances. The host country judges U.S. choices not by their intent, which may indeed be to create timelessly valid conditions for fair play, but by their effect, which is often, as in Iraq, to give a decisive advantage to one tribe over another in its centuries-old struggle to control a given grazing ground or oil field.

In the 2005 Iraqi elections, the U.S. administration had a vital domestic political interest in holding an outwardly normal election, but little expertise in designing an electoral system that would promote fair, peaceful political competition among Kurds, Sunnis, and Shiites. The election law was skewed in favor of the major Kurdish and Shiite party leaders. Iraqi voters were proud to risk their lives for their right to vote, without realizing how little voice their courage gave them in how local oligarchs would divide up the spoils of office afterward.

Bad rules everyone is used to are often preferable to unfamiliar new rules and certainly better than no rules at all. Other things being equal, a more legitimate rulebook than even the most enlightened Washington-drafted constitution is the existing constitution of the host country, a document the United States should not allow to be thrown away lightly. Most constitutions are reasonably democratic on paper. The attempt to rewrite one may replicate on paper a civil war that already exists on the ground. The process also tends to align competing local factions with competing members of the international community, such as the U.S. and Iran in Iraq.

The UN was officially in charge of the election process in Iraq. This was an enormous boon to the United States, which otherwise would have borne the whole weight of responsibility. On its own, however, the UN is too weak and has too limited a mandate to successfully enforce the rules of democracy. Building up the democratic credentials of the UN should be a key goal of U.S. diplomacy, admittedly a difficult one. A parallel track to improve the environment for democracy is to encourage new binding regional compacts on the model of the OSCE. The existence of an accepted outside arbiter helps make the rule of law more enforceable in domestic power struggles. Without the rule of law, democracy offers no benefits to its citizens.

When a regime accepts the economic and security incentives for improving its international image through elections and other democratic trappings, it takes on a risk. Once fairness is introduced as an option, human beings begin to care passionately about the perception of unfairness. Breaking the rules too obviously in an election becomes proof for ordinary citizens that the leader who breaks the rules cannot have been a legitimate leader.

The 2004 Ukrainian presidential elections are an excellent example of the utility for U.S. interests of respect for the rules of the game. Local leaders in the western half of Ukraine were not overly scrupulous in the methods they used to promote the more Western leaning of the two candidates, Viktor Yushchenko; leaders in the eastern half of the country were fatally obvious in stuffing ballot boxes for the government candidate, Viktor Yanukovych. Democratic procedures, when so misused, provided no bridge between two populations divided down the middle by language, religion, and hopes for the future. The United States and EU supported Yushchenko, and Russia supported Yanukovych.

Seen in terms of power politics, the dispute had no outlet but schism or civil war. Fortunately, rule-based thinking prevailed. Rather than push the conflict, Russia agreed to accept the judgment of the OSCE, the legitimate arbiter of European elections, that a repeat election was necessary. This concession signaled to local barons that Yanukovych was finished. They trimmed their sails to give Yushchenko a clear victory in the rerun election.

The OSCE relies on consensus by its members. Its democracy programs are often blocked by Russia, acting reflexively to protect its strategic position and economic interests with its undemocratic client states. If the United States is serious about democracy, it will trade something to Putin in exchange for giving the OSCE a freer hand in punishing violations of democratic rules in the former Soviet republics. It will also strive to see the OSCE model replicated around the world.

## When Does Democracy Building Succeed?

During the administration of Bush the father, democracy seemed to be breaking out all over. Russia had let much of its empire slip free. South Africa made a brave democratic leap forward out of apartheid. African dictators left town, and many good elections took place. America had pushed for all these things, openly or secretly. As a State Department official, I shared the general optimism that America had demonstrated the strength of its influence for democracy. But U.S. gloating was premature. A number of African states soon reverted to civil war. The worst disappointment was Zimbabwe, once a jewel in the crown of conflict resolution and power sharing, now a one-party state dragging its population toward starvation.

But there were important triumphs. Over the past fifteen years, a whole group of countries has democratized thoroughly and apparently irreversibly. Poland, Hungary, East Germany, Slovakia, Slovenia, the Czech Republic, and the Baltic states joined the EU as full members. Romania and Bulgaria both earned membership in NATO as democracies that had successfully put their militaries under full civilian control. They expect to join the EU by 2008.

Central Europeans are grateful for U.S. support for their freedom from Moscow but do not see their new democracy as an American gift. As communism collapsed, the peoples of Central Europe were peering through the widening cracks in the Iron Curtain at the EU, fifteen prosperous, blossoming countries, militarily safe under the NATO security umbrella. As a role model the EU was overwhelmingly attractive: wealthy, secure, democratic, and free. Hungarians and Poles had a clear, obvious goal to aspire to. They would rally behind any national politician who offered them that prospect. In turn, NATO and the EU offered membership to any political leader in Europe who agreed to play by a rather strict, but fair and knowable, set of rules.

From the outset, the leaders of the former Warsaw Pact countries set out to learn those rules and to do at least the minimum necessary to comply with them. Those rules included open economic competition that reduced the stranglehold of the oligarchs who emerged from the fall of communism. Romania and Hungary swallowed their national obsession with Transylvania. Bulgaria forgot its sentimental Slavic attachment to Russia. The three Baltic states agreed to give rights to their ethnic Russian minorities. Croatia, to protect its EU candidacy, even handed over some of its war heroes/criminals to the International Tribunal for the Former Yugoslavia. All of them agreed to grant their citizens the right to appeal to the European Court of Human Rights, a high-minded international counterweight to chauvinistic national courts.

Ever since Turkey joined NATO in 1952, U.S. diplomats have pressed the Turks to be more democratic, to grant full human rights to the Kurdish minority, to reduce the role of the military in politics, and to stop torturing suspects in jail. American impact was modest. A few prisoners were released, and torture became less routine and severe. But in the six years since 1999, when the EU agreed to consider Turkey a candidate for EU membership, more democratic reform has taken place than took place under U.S. tutelage in the previous forty-seven. Use of the Kurdish language is legal, the military has relinquished its control of the National Security Council, and the prime minister is now forced to scramble to repair the damage whenever Turkish police forget their new instructions not to beat up protesters.

EU assistance bureaucrats speak two or three foreign languages and are culturally sensitive, but they face the same disappointments as their U.S. counterparts when they promote democracy and human rights outside Europe. The price the EU paid for effective influence on Turkey was a solemn commitment to accept Turkey as an EU member. That price now seems to many Europeans to be too high. Further expansion may well cause the EU to become dysfunctional—in 2005, with ten new members, it was already staggering. Few Europeans would take such a risk for democracy in Armenia. North Africans will never join a European democratic club. It will not be the EU that strengthens President Hamid Karzai of Afghanistan against his warlords.

Promotion of democracies that can survive more than a few years will require the creation of EU-style regional organizations in the rest of the world. The United States has routinely tried to encourage such regional integration, with mixed success. In its ill-fated Cold War pacts like the Central Treaty Organization and the Southeast Asia Treaty Organization, the U.S. paid more attention to its own domestic politics than to the nation-building priorities of the member states. Successive American governments sacrificed the welfare of the Cuban people to the goodwill of Cuban-American leaders whose commitment to democracy was at least as self-serving as Fidel Castro's commitment to communism. Misuse of the Organization of American States as a stick to shake at Cuba and Venezuela convinced many Latin Americans of U.S. hypocrisy.

In Latin America in 2005, left-leaning governments were tiptoeing toward creation of independent regional pacts, with resentment of U.S. influence a powerful argument for regional solidarity. The United States should encourage that regional integration, if necessary by denouncing it viciously. Transnational political and economic institutions will one day give central governments elected by the people the powerful ally they need against the oligarchs who otherwise monopolize their countries' wealth. The net result over time will be a gradual deepening of democracy across a whole region.

## Human Rights Promotion

Imposing democracy on skeptical foreigners is a high-stakes game the United States should play only when it knows exactly what it is doing. Human rights promotion is a game in which U.S. diplomats can afford to be more adventurous. I was the human rights officer at U.S. Embassy Athens in 1988–92.

America's best-known leverage on human rights is the annual reports to Congress on the human rights situations of every country on earth but the United States. The reports vary in quality with the embassies that prepares them and to a lesser degree with the power of the ethnic lobbies that will read them in Washington. Weak U.S. ambassadors sometimes censor critical reports or fail to edit out naive criticisms, making them unreliable for human rights comparisons between individual countries. Generally, however, the reports give a balanced account of problems states would serve their own interests by correcting. Foreign governments misread the reports wildly when they treat them purely as political documents on the health of their country's relationships with the United States.

In 1990 in Athens we had a new ambassador and new deputy chief of mission. I was home alone, cocky that I knew Greece well. I had discovered *Stochos* ("Target") newspaper, a rabid right-wing nationalist weekly that regularly leaked reports from some troglodyte in the Greek intelligence service on Greece's officially nonexistent minority of Slavic-speaking Macedonians. *Stochos* suggested that sturdy Greek patriots should go beat up the Macedonian human rights activists whose names and addresses it helpfully listed. This was the quasi-official confirmation I needed that the complaints of Greek human rights activists were correct. I was guileless, my superiors trusted me, and the Cold War was mostly over. For the first time since the 1950s, an official public document could reflect the widely known but unmentionable fact that Greece had a Slav-speaking linguistic minority with activists whose rights were denied.

One Saturday morning I walked down to my neighborhood kiosk. All the tabloids on the rack had the same banner headline: "Stabbed in the Back!" It was my human rights report. The next two weeks were stormy. The prime minister was furious with the embassy because the opposition brandished the report as proof that his party's traditionally good ties to the United States were no protection for Greek "national interests." The U.S. ambassador could not admit without losing face that he had signed off on the report without having read it carefully. Summoned to the Foreign Ministry with me sheepishly in tow, he was forced to defend America's commitment to human rights in stronger terms than short-term U.S. interests in Greece would ever have dictated. We issued a "clarification" to emphasize that the U.S. interpretation of the term "minority" differs from the legalistic interpretation of the Greek Foreign Ministry. We reassured Greeks that the United States was not endorsing Macedonian territorial claims on northern Greece but did not back down on the basic message of the report.

The United States had broken a taboo. For the first time in decades, mainstream Greek newspaper readers had to acknowledge the thousands of Greek citizens who still spoke at home a distinct language called Macedonian by linguists. No other government, certainly not one of Greece's cautious EU partners, could have been brave or foolish enough to stir up this particular anthill. The U.S. government would probably not have done it if anyone had warned them beforehand about the reaction.

Greek hysteria gradually faded away. A few years later the Macedonians had their own political party in northern Greece, with a miserable few thousand votes and no interest in becoming part of the impoverished "Former Yugoslav Republic of Macedonia." More important, Greece and the "Former Yugoslav Republic of Macedonia" had discovered the joys of doing business with one another. This would have been impossible if Greece had continued to deny fundamental human rights to those of its citizens who spoke the same language as the Macedonians.

When I returned to Athens in 2000 as political counselor, the torch had passed to a new generation. I watched with pride and delight as my Kurdish-American human rights officer took up the cudgels for the rights of trafficked foreign women. Working with local organizations, she and her successor used America's influence to do something of more potential practical benefit than anything I ever did. They shamed Greece into passing legislation protecting the foreign women and children smuggled across the border for the sex industry. Greeks recognized that on this issue America had the moral high ground. There was grumbling but no political backlash.

Human rights reporting immerses junior diplomats in the gritty details of the host country. Interceding to help dissidents, they learn firsthand the limits of American power and the unpredictable nature of the trade-offs America makes between virtue and expediency. When they do their job well, using the human rights report and the influence of their ambassador to press for reform, there is some diplomatic cost to the United States. As long as the United States does not let local groups manipulate it for their domestic political purposes, neither foreign governments nor their nationalist followers will long hold a grudge at the excessive zeal of a U.S. embassy second secretary.

America has lingering human rights problems of its own. State and local authorities routinely deny foreign diplomats any equivalent standing to enforce human rights protections on U.S. soil. It is better to overlook the hypocrisy of it all. The size and influence of the U.S. Foreign Service create opportunities for idealistic young American diplomats to help struggling people with no political power of their own. The State Department is wiser and braver than any bureaucracy has any right to be in placing that influence, once a year during Human Rights Report season, in their hands.

### Some Conclusions for Democracy Building

With benefit of my Armenian hindsight, I realize that much of the well-meaning advice the State Department gave Romanians in 1992–1994 was irrelevant to the problems facing would-be democratic politicians there. Still, Romania stumbled successfully toward democracy thanks to NATO and the EU. This success suggests that America does not really need a magic bureaucratic toolbox for democracy or even international acceptance of its self-appointed role as missionary for democracy. Countries can and will democratize themselves, provided the external incentives for following democratic rules are powerful enough. The U.S. duty, an achievable one, is to work with its partners to build a global political and economic environment in which politicians who follow democratic rules thrive better than their rivals who do not. In most countries a principled politician will need considerable outside help to deliver the good governance that generates the legitimacy to prevail over less scrupulous competitors.

The humane and effective strategy for democratization is to spare no expense in promoting the security and prosperity of democratic states. This does not mean punishing and isolating their undemocratic neighbors. Dictators may deserve punishment, but they can always hide successfully behind their starving population, like Saddam Hussein hid behind five hundred thousand suffering children. It is wiser to keep the diplomatic and economic channels of communication as wide open as modern technology permits. Exposure to prosperity fuels the demand for liberty, especially among the younger generation. When an undemocratic leader becomes illegitimate enough that his people start sacrificing their lives to throw him out, the United States can start to feel confident that alternative sources of legitimacy are being created. Then, perhaps, a firm, well-informed push from outside, backed by the opinion of a united international community, has some chance of doing more good than harm to the ordinary people democracy aims to serve.

The United States should remember, before contemplating any coup attempt or decapitation strike, that its commitment to democracy implies an election afterward. Do America and its allies indeed have the ability to guarantee that a foreign election will generate enough legitimacy for the winner to govern more effectively than the undemocratic leader the coup is about to remove? The United States and its EU partners could not meet that standard even in Armenia, a tiny, ethnically homogeneous Christian country with aspirations to belong to Europe.

It should go without saying that America's judgment of whether to accept an election or a government should not be based on whether the winner flatters the U.S. ideological perspective of the moment; that would be a betrayal of our moral principles and also dangerously stupid. America's national interests are served not by working with governments it likes but by working with governments that have the legitimacy to work effectively with it. U.S. response to an election should thus be based on U.S. and international observers' assessment of one basic issue: does this election convey enough legitimacy to the winner from his or her own people that he or she can govern the state effectively and survive the tough decisions the global environment and U.S. interests will impose?

Given the immeasurably greater difficulties in Iraq compared to Armenia, the January 2005 Iraqi elections were a triumph. But for what the United States needed those elections to produce—a parliamentary government all Iraqis would obey—they fell far short. The problems affecting many states are so intractable that America cannot even guarantee success in that most basic of moral duties: to save people from dying unnecessarily.

In terms of grand interventions for democracy, therefore, the United States would be wise to be humble. History seems to teach that a people moved by hope will demand democracy and human rights and will ultimately achieve them. A people swayed by fear will cheerfully sacrifice its freedoms. Democracy thrives in an environment of security. The United States and EU, in fostering a regional and global environment conducive to democracy, should learn to see their offer of security guarantees to struggling states not as the reward for successful democratization but as a catalyst of it.

In Africa, Asia, and South America, continents that cannot look to EU membership requirements as a source of evolutionary pressure toward democracy, the United States has a moral and practical obligation to follow George Kennan's advice to "formulate and put forward for other nations a much more positive and constructive picture of [the] sort of world we would like to see." The United States should not delude itself, however, that the American model is particularly attractive at the moment. The lapses of the U.S. political system in regulating its budget, protecting the environment, providing health care, or assuring public confidence in the rule of law makes the United States less persuasive than it should be as a global democracy purveyor.

Even now, however, when the U.S. State Department chooses its targets carefully, does its homework, and keeps its nerve, it helps make the world a freer and safer place. American diplomats contribute more to global security by building legitimate institutions than by selling F-16s. Helping incorporate a country's disgruntled minorities into the political system is a better insurance policy for U.S. interests than helping the same country pursue an equivalent army of terrorists. And when U.S. foreign service officers retire, the memories that bring them the most pride are not of the brilliant telegrams they have written but of the courageous human rights advocates they have helped to move their countries another step forward into a community of democratic states.

# 11

# ★ *Counterterrorism Lessons From Revolutionary Organization 17 November* ★

*"If," he remarked profoundly, "so sublime a principle as Justice should depend upon so fallible a thread as a single human attribute all feeling of security would be gone for ever. . . . Two persons having committed a Category One crime, two persons will automatically suffer a Category One punishment, and the Essential Equipoise of justice will thereby be painlessly maintained."*

*Ernest Brahmah Smith*, Kai Lung's Golden Hours

The U.S. national security apparatus is the most expensive and capable bureaucracy the human species has ever created. Protecting the citizens who pay for it is its sole task. With the tragic exception of 9/11, American citizens are as well protected from outside threats as any people in history. But America's national security leadership has misrepresented the nature of the terrorism problem. Their decision for military preemption instead of law and justice violated a fundamental contract between American citizens and their government.

U.S. foreign service officers have an excuse for taking the threat of terrorism personally. Two of my colleagues from my first posting in Israel, one of them briefly my boss, were murdered by al Qaeda in the Nairobi embassy truck bombing in 1998. A few weeks before I arrived in Athens in 1988, I attended the funeral of the U.S. defense attaché to Greece at Arlington National Cemetery. Capt. William Nordeen had been killed by a car bomb three blocks from his house.

The U.S. embassy in Athens calculated that it could not afford an armored car and bodyguard for every second secretary in the Political Section. My symbolic security precaution was to walk a different route every morning as I took my daughter to her bus stop. My real security depended on another ugly but accurate calculation: Revolutionary Organization 17 November (17N), Greece's deadly terror group, could not afford to murder a diplomat with his five-year-old daughter screaming at his side.

The members of 17N are safely behind bars since 2002, but murderous little groups are still targeting U.S. officials in many countries of the world. Not all of them would consider a diplomat's little girl unacceptable collateral damage.[1] Even so, taking terrorism personally is a mistake no good diplomat can afford. Terrorists advance their political aims not by killing innocent people but by making the rest of us so frightened, angry, and irrational that we do the terrorists' work for them. Terrorists count on the natural human narcissism that mislocates us at the center of the terrorists' universe as well as our own. Professional diplomats have some experience in stepping back to analyze impersonally the risks they face. Ordinary Americans, however, depend on what they are told by their elected leaders. They are still deeply frightened and angry, years after 9/11. They have been led to believe that they, personally, are terrorist targets. Americans' fear is based on a misunderstanding that bureaucrats are oddly reluctant to dispel.

## Assessing the Terrorist Threat

In twenty years I rarely saw a U.S. government employee engage in deliberate deceit. To get a security clearance, one must be an upright character. But seven years in Athens as a bit player in America's war against 17N gave me a sobering analytical baseline for threat analysis.

Every three years on average 17N would target a U.S. military service member or presumed intelligence officer for assassination. In twenty-seven years they succeeded four times. Each of those blows was devastating to the families, friends, and colleagues of the victim. Another Greek group, Revolutionary Popular Struggle (ELA), destroyed dozens of American-owned vehicles and attacked U.S. military installations. Living under the shadow of terror attacks is crippling and expensive. Shutting down 17N and ELA was, naturally, a major U.S. government priority that justified substantial resources.

Thanks to our little war against 17N, the embassy enjoyed high-level Washington attention, occasional mention in the *Washington*

*Post*, hardship pay for the embassy staff, and a huge budget relative to the limited importance of the U.S.-Greek relationship. Visiting U.S. Congress members listened raptly while the ambassador ███████ ████████ looked knowing and determined. Each briefing was a pitch for continued funding, made irresistible by letting the veil over the secret investigation slip suggestively to imply that a breakthrough against 17N was imminent. None of us volunteered that 17N was a tiny group with limited political goals, average skills, and a code of behavior that restricted its murders to a narrow group of targets, which did not include tourists and visiting members of Congress. The mere fact that Americans had been attacked was all that mattered to our audience.

Each of us at U.S. Embassy Athens would have been indignant had we been challenged for exaggerating the 17N threat and our own contribution to fighting it. But during the heat of the action, surrounded by our equally zealous peers, we often let self-interest distort the analysis we presented. Most of the massively expensive security precautions we deployed to impress visiting senators—the army of security guards, the armored motorcades with flashing lights—were to meet a threat 17N clearly did not pose. Nor did we distinguish the cost 17N attacks inflicted on U.S. interests from the costs we inflicted on ourselves. We never admitted that 17N's greatest triumph—poisoning U.S.-Greek relations—was entirely America's decision, not 17N's. In short, we failed to deal analytically with the question of how an expensive little war against 17N matched the threat the group posed to the interests of the American people.

Any prudent government pays some number of mad scientists to come up with vulnerability assessments based on a worst-case assumption that the outside world is peopled by brilliant psychopaths. The role of "Team B" is to identify holes in the nation's defenses before any enemies do, not to assess whether the world's limited stock of evil geniuses actually intends to exploit those holes. Sensible presidents recognize that ordinary people massively outnumber the psychopaths. They weigh the warnings from Team B against the more pragmatic advice of lawyers, accountants, diplomats, and public-opinion pollsters. Those wiser heads will not necessarily urge the government to bankrupt itself financially or morally in the pursuit of perfect security.

Counterterrorism planning starts with the Team B worst-case assumption that America is locked in a war to the death with a clandestine army made up of thousands of hardened Islamist fanatics, many of them experts in weapons or computers, distributed in little secret cells around the world, including sleeper cells in the United

States. These terrorists are supported by unlimited funding from a huge network of Muslim donors and mosques, money transferred through the international financial system as well as in cash. They ship weapons via a clandestine network of arms suppliers linked to hostile intelligence services.

The goal of this hypothetical army is implacable: to kill as many Americans as possible. The terrorists plan to do this by making, buying, or stealing nuclear weapons and by making poison gas and deadly bacterial toxins with recipes they share over the Internet. They will smuggle these weapons into the United States, probably by ship. Then they will poison U.S. water supplies and crash airplanes into U.S. nuclear power plants, while a coordinated computer attack takes down U.S. banks and hospitals. Millions of Americans will die. Because these hypothetical terrorists are evil fanatics who cannot be deterred, Americans have a sacred duty to seek them out around the globe and kill them first. This is total war against an inhuman enemy, and the gloves are off.

This worst-case scenario would seem to justify even more extreme measures than President Bush's decision to set aside the Geneva Conventions and make grandmothers break off the miniature nail files in their fingernail clippers before boarding airplanes. The 9/11 attacks led to an immediate rollback of twelve years of painful spending cuts. The military budget soared back to Cold War levels. The CIA doubled the number of its case officers. Police forces in every small town in American got bio-warfare kits, emergency mobile command posts, and other expensive gear their actual caseload of drug crimes and car theft did not merit. More important, the FBI and military were given open-ended new investigatory powers. Was this response indeed justified?

Security from foreigners is the only service American taxpayers will cheerfully bankrupt their grandchildren to pay for. America lost more of its citizens to Greek drivers than to Greek terrorists. But no one ever suggested it would be a legitimate use of U.S. taxpayer dollars to teach Greeks to stop at stop signs. Many Americans live comfortably with the idea that perhaps 65 million unlicensed, unregistered, concealable handguns are in circulation around them, many in the hands of hardened criminals, militant racists, or drug-addled children. They accept that twenty-nine thousand people will be killed in the United States every year by conventional firearms.[2] It is not sudden, violent death Americans mind, but only the right of unfriendly strangers to inflict it. When terrorism is invoked, ordinary calculations of cost and benefit go out the window.

If resources were infinite, the United States could treat real and theoretical threats with equal seriousness. Security is terribly expensive, however, even when the U.S. government knows exactly what to protect and from whom. Without an accurate sense of the terror risk it cannot decide how much of the national wealth should be diverted from productive investments to protecting American cities and shopping malls. More important, Americans do not know how much of their personal freedom they should sacrifice to the FBI and local sheriffs in the name of fighting terrorism. A law enforcement agency will cheerfully use any investigative or coercive powers Congress fails to withhold from it, up to and including torture.

A U.S. citizen committed to American values should weigh carefully what price to pay for security. The CIA and the Pentagon, with only limited help from Team B, massively overestimated the Soviet threat for decades and then helped the White House misread Iraq. What better incentive do our officials have now to understand the terrorist threat accurately? How credible is the evidence they have presented? Because how much Americans should pay depends on how deadly are our foes.

## *Weapons of Mass Destruction*

Since 9/11, Americans have been routinely warned that Minneapolis is in imminent danger of being annihilated by an Islamic nuclear weapon, that the water supply of Fargo will be poisoned with botulinum toxin, and that a cloud of radioactive cesium will make several square blocks of Spokane uninhabitable. Chemical, biological, and radiological ("dirty bomb") weapons are indeed possible to make or acquire. The recipes available on the Internet are mostly bogus, but a determined group can obtain the materials needed to make poisons that work. Fortunately, weapons of mass destruction (WMD) generally do not live up to their name. The fanatical anti-Muslim who mailed anthrax spores to liberal U.S. senators and journalists in 2001 managed to kill five people. Japanese end-of-the-world cult Aum Shinrikyo infected no one with its little-known anthrax attack and killed only nine people with its terrifying sarin gas attack in the Tokyo subway.

These limited results should be no surprise, once we consider the outcome of decades of U.S., Soviet, and Iraqi government research on chemical and biological weapons. Every nation in the world ultimately agreed to ban and destroy its chemical and biological warfare stockpiles, not because governments suddenly became moral in the late twentieth century but because generals and politicians concluded, in the U.S. case after producing thousands of tons of nerve gas, that the practical effectiveness of these weapons would never be decisive enough to outweigh the political cost of using them.

Terrorists face this same WMD political equation with far fewer resources than a state can manage. When Attorney General John Ashcroft unveiled Jose Padilla, a semiliterate hoodlum who allegedly dreamed of making a dirty bomb, he did not point out that Padilla was being unconstitutionally detained as an illegal combatant for a fantasy crime. High-level radioactive waste, though a hopelessly inefficient way to harm the general public, would quickly kill an untrained bomb-maker if he managed to steal any. The Justice Department finally announced in November 2005 its decision to charge Padilla for conventional crimes related to his presence in Afghanistan. The dirty bomb allegations, apparently the product of a false confession under torture, had evaporated.[3]

The alleged London ricin conspiracy, briefly trumpeted by British authorities in 2003, was based on possession of a poison recipe taken from the Internet that could not possibly have worked—the little pile of castor beans was at worst an adolescent revenge fantasy, not a serious bio-weapons threat. The pathetic little group arrested for it, apart from a zealot who managed to stab a police officer fatally during the bungled raid, was eventually convicted of seeking to commit a public nuisance.[4]

Nuclear bombs are more than a public nuisance. Given a small amount of fissile material, the physics and engineering departments of a good university could assemble a bomb small enough to fit in a rental truck and able to kill one hundred thousand Americans all at once. Ten such bombs, properly placed, would turn the world economy upside down. During the 1950s American conservatives considered such horrendous losses an acceptable price for destroying the Soviet Union, but by 2005 sensibilities had fortunately changed. The specter of nuclear devastation has rightly galvanized a massive U.S. and international campaign to prevent it.

Acquiring bomb-grade fissile material requires assistance only a state can provide. The country with the most nuclear weapons to lose, the Russian Federation, keeps its special weapons officers sober with the reminder that the Russian people would be the first victims of such a weapon in the wrong (i.e., Chechen) hands. The U.S. government has already demonstrated that, should nuclear weapons come up for sale, it will pay far more for them than any sum a group of zealots could scrape together, and with no risk of nuclear annihilation for the seller. U.S. national security pundits have not clarified what motives might persuade a North Korean or Iranian general to jeopardize his country's survival by selling a terrorist group a nuclear bomb. States, unlike individuals, have no identifiable motives for committing suicide.

## Terrorist Motives

The truly horrifying secret about terrorism is that terrorists do not need nuclear weapons, anthrax spores, or even high-explosive belts to harm the United States. With an aging .45 handgun and stolen motorcycles, 17N massively disrupted the lives of Athens businesspeople and diplomats. Any al Qaeda sympathizer can exercise his or her Second Amendment right to buy a legal firearm at Wal Mart and then start picking off passersby. Someone willing to commit suicide for a political cause has no need for the Internet recipes that turn household chemicals like acetone and hair bleach into explosives. An extremist can carry an antifreeze container full of gasoline into a rush-hour subway car and incinerate 192 people, as happened in Daegu, Korea, in 2003.[5] A handful of such suicide attacks by Islamist extremists, though meaningless militarily or economically, would provoke a horrific political backlash. A weak U.S. president might easily find himself ensnared in the "war of civilizations" Bush and every sensible mortal now rejects.

We should all wonder more than we do why it took two years for terrorists to strike London after the Iraq War began. Millions of Muslims, including in the UK and United States, had concluded from watching television that the U.S. and British governments were evil powers that needed to be punished for waging war on people like themselves. Many young people have weak ties to the society in which they live and poor prospects for winning respect by that society's rules. They could see how effectively a little terror group punished the Spanish government through the Madrid bombings of March 11, 2004. Once one's own life is expendable, it is cheap and easy to strike a blow that resounds at least within the circle of one's peers. If one-tenth of 1 percent of the world's Muslims took up their kitchen knives and gasoline cans, no Americans would be left in North Africa, Indonesia, or the Middle East. Where are the corpses?

Between 9/11 and early 2006 not a single American died in the United States as a result of terrorism. In an average year one American tourist abroad dies in a terror attack. A few U.S. military personnel, diplomats, and contractors are murdered, most of them in obvious war zones.[6] Only a handful of the dozens of overseas terrorist groups broken up by U.S. and foreign law enforcement agencies in recent years were targeting U.S. officials or businesses. No credible terror cell has been uncovered in the United States whose goal was to kill Americans at home. American civilians still live, work, and travel comfortably all over the planet.

Lack of motive, not lack of means or opportunity or even courage, sets the crucial limit on terrorist violence. This should not really surprise us. No religion encourages murder. War is acceptable and honorable, but the United States is not at war with most societies, and every society has a strong social stigma against killing defenseless people unawares. To understand and combat terrorism we should study why a certain small percentage of the human race entertains dreams of killing innocent foreigners. We should then probe what circumstances drive a tiny fraction of that percentage, very few of them competent conspirators, to undertake their own destruction by acting on that dream.

The best way to learn is to ask a terrorist. One of my jobs in Athens was to supervise and correct the embassy translation of the proclamations 17N left in a waste bin for their favorite leftist newspaper after each attack. The official motives of 17N were simple, once you got past the conspiracy theories and the bitter feuds with other leftist groups. Greek political institutions had abdicated their duty to punish certain people and groups for their crimes against Greek society. Letting criminals go unpunished was not good for society, so 17N took on the task of meting out justice on society's behalf.

Richard Welch, the CIA chief in Athens, was 17N's first victim. He was a good man, a classics major fond of Greece, not guilty of any known crime, but 17N did not draw fine personal distinctions. A crime had been committed in Greek eyes: U.S. collaboration with Greece's humiliating military dictatorship from 1967–74. And 17N provided exemplary public punishment. The second, third, and fourth 17N murders were of Greek police officers accused of torturing Greek prisoners and beating demonstrators. According to 17N's after-action proclamation, "The court system acquitted them in Chalkis and other trials, showing palpably that *there is no justice, no rule of law*" (italics mine). Each subsequent murder was followed by a similar proclamation of crimes the group claimed it avenged when the Greek state's judicial system would not.[7]

The thirst for justice is hardwired into us. After thirty-five years I can still send my heart rate up by fifty points by replaying some incident of schoolyard bullying and imagining the retribution I should have dealt out for the blow to my schoolboy honor. Most people never act out their revenge fantasies. Ideally, society punishes evildoers while we watch and enjoy from a safe distance. A society that enforces its rules by punishing violators flourishes better than one that does not. Society's official punishers often fail to do their job, however, sometimes because guilt cannot be established but often because the guilty are too well connected or the crime too widespread.

When society fails to protect its members' sense of honor or justice, most people act as mature adults, calculating that the cost to themselves and their loved ones from taking personal vengeance would outweigh the moral satisfaction revenge would bring. A few members of every society, however, would prefer to harm their own interests, on occasion even fatally, rather than see someone else go unpunished for a perceived injustice. The punisher need not have been harmed personally. Evolutionary psychologists have suggested that this perverse altruism has not been weeded out by natural selection because it has survival value for the group as a whole.

The most deadly terror groups are the ones that find the deadliest grievances to obsess over. Timothy McVeigh found no better way to "punish" a nameless, faceless U.S. government for the fiery deaths of ninety people, including young children, in Waco, Texas, than to blow up the federal building in Oklahoma City, killing 168 people, including young children. Sikh terrorists blew up two Air India 747s, killing hundreds of innocent passengers, to retaliate for the hundreds of Sikhs killed when the Indian Army stormed the Golden Temple in Amritsar in 1984 to suppress a Sikh uprising.

The International Islamic Front for Jihad, a coalition of al Qaeda and Egyptian Islamic Jihad, warned the day before bombing the U.S. embassies in Nairobi and Dar es Salaam in August 1998 that it was retaliating for the kidnapping in Albania and rendition to Egypt of five Egyptian and Sudanese militants the month before. Officially, the destruction of Pan Am 103 over Lockerby in December 1988 was retaliation for the U.S. bombing of Tripoli and Benghazi in 1986, but others insist it was the price the U.S. paid for the accidental shoot-down of an Iranian passenger plane by the U.S. Navy cruiser *Vincennes* in July 1988.[8]

This mania for justice does not exist in isolation from other motives. 17N's proclamations documented how obsessed they were with their social and intellectual standing among their leftist peers. Terrorism is also a way to earn a living. Members of 17N lived middle-class lives, complete with beach cottages, on the proceeds of their bank robberies. By playing avenger, 17N made the self-serving side of its operation seem legitimate to its friends. It also guaranteed itself a readership for political proclamations that even the staunchest of Greek leftists would otherwise have left deservedly unread in the trash.

Palestinian suicide bombers have a powerful social motive, to uphold their family's honor within a tribal society by avenging the death of a brother or cousin at Israeli hands. Terrorism sponsors in Gaza have a more pragmatic political motive. Hamas used its ability to recruit martyrs for the armed struggle against the Israeli occupation to stake its claim to greater legitimacy compared with its political rivals. The Palestinian Authority had let peaceful sources of internal legitimacy, including elections, become tainted through fraud, corruption, and manipulation by outsiders. As a tactical bonus to terrorist groups, the Israeli government retaliated for attacks by humiliating the official Palestinian leadership. Hamas terrorism tapered off as the ruling generation of the Palestine Liberation Organization (PLO) floundered after Arafat's death. The closer Hamas came to victory in its struggle for political power in Palestine, the less useful terrorism became to it.[9]

Ordinary Americans are unable to understand what motive would drive nineteen men to commit fiery suicide on 9/11 to kill twenty-eight hundred Americans they had never met. Ordinary Israelis profess equal puzzlement about motives for Palestinian terrorism against Israel. There is a social reason for this incomprehension. Successful societies do not permit their members to be punished, except by the legitimate punishment mechanisms of each society. Tit for tat, seen as moral and legitimate punishment by a society that imposes it, is rejected as immoral and illegitimate by a society that suffers it. When an outsider attacks the United States, even an outsider who announces clearly that he is retaliating for a specific U.S. action, his message violates a fundamental rule of American society and will thus be ignored.

Self-imposed incomprehension makes terrorism more frightening and thus more effective as a tactic for changing our behavior. U.S. terrorism pundits had little curiosity about the societies from which the 9/11 terrorists emerged. They understood immediately, however, how profitable it was to terrify their own society with Holocaust imagery and fantasies of genocidal, death-worshiping Muslims. But terrorists belong to a different category of human behavior than the Germans who followed orders in the Nazi death camps. Self-appointed punishers are not bound by society's official rules regarding whom to punish. They are bound by a private but still rigid moral code. When 17N accidentally killed a young Greek-Armenian passerby with a rocket aimed at a cabinet minister, it apologized profusely in repeated proclamations. The group had rejected random murder, not because its members were decent people—they were killers and thieves—but because random murder was not legitimate retaliation for any crime that might make their own crimes seem moral by comparison.

The 9/11 attackers were volunteers in a very specific war. Al Qaeda's political goal is to redeem the honor of Islam by creating a successful and virtuous state under pure Islamic law, a state centered on the Islamic holy places of Mecca, Medina, and Jerusalem.[10] To achieve this goal, al Qaeda must eliminate a corrupt Saudi royal family, secular Arab regimes, and the state of Israel. The task is impossible, and most Arabs know it. Still, al Qaeda was able to find, after years of searching and planning, twenty men willing to die for a more limited goal, to punish the U.S. government for its role as defender of the status quo in the Middle East.

Al Qaeda hoped that 9/11 would embolden the Arab masses to put aside their passive acceptance of un-Islamic regimes, but war against the American people was not the aim. The reason is simple: the self-evident impossibility of victory is not compensated by any offsetting moral necessity to attempt it. Twenty-eight hundred dead Americans were collateral damage—welcome to many Islamic fanatics, unwelcome to their more politically astute brethren—from the most spectacular attack a low-technology group could manage against two targets it obsessed over as dominant symbols of unjust American power. Bin Laden allegedly vetoed attacks on purely "civilian" targets (e.g., a football stadium). Like any political organizer he had to preserve the legitimacy of his group in the eyes of the Islamic world and maintain the flow of contributions to his struggling network of jihad fundraisers.

Strategically, 9/11 was a disaster for al Qaeda. The twenty-eight hundred ghastly deaths legitimized U.S. military retaliation and forced previously uncooperative governments around the world to launch the police and intelligence crackdowns that destroyed al Qaeda as an organized group. More important, this murder of innocent victims eased for a generation of dangerously moral young Muslims the sense that unpunished crimes of the U.S. government locked them personally into an obligation to act.

Obviously, radical groups did not run out of motives to commit murder after 9/11. Most of the militant Islamist cells uncovered in Europe and the United States in 2004–5 were recruiting martyrs for the Iraqi insurgency, not looking for assassins to murder the innocent civilians around them. Of more relevance to U.S. diplomats, terrorist groups continue to regard U.S. embassies, like the U.S. military bases in Iraq, as outposts of anti-Muslim oppression and thus a legitimate battlefield for martyrdom. Sometimes terrorists succeed. The lost lives of embassy personnel, some preventable, some not, are part of the price a superpower pays to carry out its foreign policy.

Ordinary Americans living at home in ordinary American towns and cities face no detectable threat from international terrorism, certainly none sufficient to justify sacrificing even one iota of their sacred individual liberties. A socially valid motive for strangers to travel to America to kill ordinary Americans simply does not exist. Washington, New York, and Los Angeles are cities that symbolize American political, economic, and cultural hegemony. Because of that symbolism, their residents face a genuine but—for each individual citizen—insignificant risk of terrorist violence every time they ride the subway or go to a theater. Most aspiring Saudi or Sudanese terrorists are little more capable of executing a spectacular attack on New York City than an American would be on Riyadh or Khartoum. Still, a handful of people are willing to try, as long as some group of peers offers them the moral and practical support needed to stiffen their resolution to commit suicide.

## *Whose Wars Are We Fighting?*

A dangerous bureaucratic fantasy about terrorism is that it is a chiefly American problem, one America has both a special duty and some special aptitude to solve. Whether the CIA was entitled to exemplary vengeance for the 1975 murder of its chief in Athens by 17N was a political question six successive presidents instinctively answered in the affirmative. Whether the CIA is the appropriate instrument of that vengeance is a very different question. The group that challenged the CIA was a little group of Greek leftists. They committed their crimes, mostly against fellow Greeks, on Greek soil. The Greek police ultimately caught up with them, on June 29, 2002. The next few months showed that America's twenty-seven-year war against 17N had been a fiasco.

Luck had run out for 17N, as luck always does eventually. A 17N bomber, a priest's chubby son named Savvas Xiros, attempted to blow up the ticket kiosk of an ill-famed ferry line in the port of Piraeus. Xiros used too flimsy an alarm clock, and the bomb detonated in his hands. Adequate police work, a providential tip from an old woman who recognized Xiros and his hideout, and shrewd use of psychology and a new counterterrorism law by a wise, patient prosecutor led to a chain reaction of confessions and further arrests. 17N was unmasked as an unimpressive band of narcissistic aging children ill-matched to the romantic myth that twenty-seven years of vain U.S. pursuit had inspired. A Greek court tried and convicted

17N under Greek law and sent its members to a Greek prison, the ringleaders for life. Justice was done and seen to be done.[11]

The director of the FBI came out and gave medals to the Greek police. The U.S. embassy congratulated itself on the victory as well. Dozens or hundreds of Americans—bright, dedicated, hardworking professionals from a dozen offices in at least five major U.S. government agencies—had worked decades of seventy-hour weeks toward this moment. Every efficiency report that year had some reference to the triumph. We diplomats happily recommended one another for promotions, pay raises, and honor awards. We all deserved recognition for trying hard, at least. But what exactly had we contributed to 17N's defeat?

That the past twenty-seven years had not been well spent became painfully apparent at the morning meeting of senior U.S. mission staff in the days that followed the first arrests: The ███ had been working with its Greek counterparts for a quarter century, and the FBI, with the Greek police for almost as long, but the Greek media had more information on the breaking case than embassy counterterrorism experts did. The ███████ FBI do not admit ignorance in the presence of competing agencies, but this was ignorance they could not conceal. They were dependent on whatever details the ambassador could coax each day out of the minister of public order. If the Greeks owed their success against 17N to American information, advice, equipment, training, and pressure over the years, they concealed their gratitude well. Vindication, not gratitude, was the Greeks' public attitude toward their U.S. partners. What had gone wrong?

When one of its citizens is the victim of a crime abroad, an ordinary country puts whatever diplomatic pressure it can on the host government not to rest until the guilty are punished. States have levers they can use to charm, buy, or extort an energetic investigation from local law enforcement authorities. The Greek police are a low-skill, low-technology police force not structured to investigate complex crimes. America, by contrast, is a superpower with a mystique of competence. When the secret services of a superpower involve themselves aggressively in a criminal case, the outclassed police of the country in which the crime occurred will be strongly tempted to sit back on their hands and watch the Americans flounder, fail, and backbite.

The U.S. bureaucracy has every reason not to advertise this fact, and perhaps President Bush does not know it, but American officials cannot work efficiently as criminal investigators in a foreign country. Few Americans would give a hearty welcome to heavily accented foreigners who appeared on their doorsteps to ask odd questions about neighbors and relatives. Rather than answer the questions they would probably call the police. They would certainly not hand over their life stories, business records, and telephone subscriber information.

The American counterterrorism officers sent to Athens were capable and well-trained. When they carried out tasks for which they had a competitive advantage they performed impressively. U.S. technical capabilities, for example, are unsurpassed. Americans, however, had no competitive advantage over Greek colleagues in finding Greek needles in Greek haystacks. Nor was any information they provided usable in a Greek court to convict Greek terrorists, even when the United States managed to identify them correctly.

In 1993 two of my former colleagues earned banner headlines in most Athens dailies. Tipped off by a vigilant little old lady, they were arrested by Greek police in a van full of wigs and disguises while conducting a mysterious operation against suspected terrorists. Officially, theirs was not a unilateral U.S. operation, simply a failure of communication between two Greek services, but the result was their names published for the world to see and their hasty return to the United States. The U.S. embassy experienced a substantial temporary setback to its ability to work with Greek counterparts. They in turn were forced to sweat bullets as they explained to an incredulous Parliament the circumstances under which American operatives had been allowed to violate Greece's sovereignty and the privacy of its citizens.[12]

Americans applauded when ████████████████████████ the FBI special agent crashed through the hotel door in a remote Pakistani town to seize Mir Amal Kasi, who was tried in the United States and executed for having murdered two CIA employees outside CIA headquarters in 1993. This is not a scenario that plays out very often. The CIA's quest for revenge was implacable and generously funded, and Pakistani officials prudently allowed the U.S. government to break local law to achieve it.[13] To get to the point of crashing through the door, the United States will always depend on help or at least a blind eye from local services. When U.S. services stepped beyond legal limits in a country more committed to the rule of law than Pakistan, as happened when a group of Americans kidnapped an Egyptian cleric off the streets of Milan in February 2003, the outcome was a list of indictments that may poison U.S.-Italian counterterrorism cooperation for years to come.[14]

In the battle against 17N, only the Greek authorities had the psychological affinities and the perceived legal and moral right to ask other Greeks the key questions in ways that might elicit a useful answer. Only the Greeks had enough bodies to deploy to give them a reasonable chance of being in the right place at the right time when 17N made its fatal mistake. America's correct role, the role it often played but should have played more consistently, was to make sure through training and technical support that the local authorities would be able when the breakthrough happened to build the criminal case that would put the terrorists firmly behind bars.

## *The Clash of Cultures*

Successful law enforcement depends on trust, local knowledge, and local informants. A foreigner can build trust, but it takes an agonizing amount of time. American counterterrorism experts could not afford that time. Even the "permanent" U.S. officials would stay only two or three years before moving on. They needed quick results and had little incentive to become fluent in the language and culture. Without that fluency, they routinely misunderstood the Greeks they were dealing with.

Money talks, Americans are sure, but not always and not everywhere. The State Department reward program offered $2 million for anyone who turned in 17N. That offer, which Greek journalists claim was supplemented by clandestine suitcases full of cash thrust at people on the fringes of the Athens terrorism community, attracted con men and dreamers but alienated the ideologues who were the only ones likely to have useful information about terrorist cells in their midst. Worse, each public announcement of an increase in the U.S. reward offer reconfirmed to the Greek public that 17N was an American problem, not their own. Greek authorities had announced their own reward for the 17N killers back in 1976. They soon concluded that the moral and social stigma against "Judases" was too powerful in a Greek revolutionary milieu. And so it proved. Captured terrorists sometimes admitted their own guilt, but they refused to testify against their associates for any sum.

A short-timer's bureaucratic interests are served by seeming as aggressive as possible to superiors in Washington. The U.S. government asked Greek police to take risks that would make the U.S. team heroes if they succeeded but would cost the Greeks heavily with their politicians if anything became public. A task Pakistani or Egyptian security officials would complete at U.S. request with impunity would be illegal, ineffective, or political suicide in a democratic country with human rights protections and a free press.

Given sufficient trust and respect, U.S. officials' foreign

counterparts can be persuaded to summon to police headquarters and squeeze known sympathizers or their relatives, to introduce into the radical community ███████████████████,[15] or to interview possible ideological progenitors of the 17N proclamations. The CIA and FBI achieved modest tactical successes in Greece when they were patient and sensitive to Greek legal and political realities. When they were not, the Greek response was to go limp.

Greeks are Middle Eastern enough to feel that it is impolite to utter a direct no. They sometimes resent an American's failure to take a polite hint. U.S. counterterrorism officials sometimes did not recognize even an impolite "no" when we pushed for sting operations or pressure on family members of possible suspects. When a competent and intelligent Greek bureaucrat suddenly ceased to be competent, as seemed to happen with discouraging regularity over the first twenty-five years, berating him for incompetence was usually not an effective remedy.

The CIA's formidable esprit de corps is built on genial or not-so-genial contempt for lesser breeds. So is the FBI's. When a given trail went cold, as happened frequently, one natural and prudent reaction was to blame Greek incompetence rather than admit it had been a false trail or that 17N was too small and careful for foreigners to catch. U.S. officials who disparaged the locals in closed staff meetings were polite when Greeks were in the room. Still, perceived superpower racism amplified interpersonal frictions.

Despite years of training, Greek police remained stubbornly reluctant to seize control of crime scenes from gawkers and camera crews. Right-wing politicians filled U.S. ears with scurrilous gossip about political connections between the governing Panhellenic Socialist Movement (PASOK) and international terrorists. Conservative U.S. newspapers accused PASOK of having concluded a nonaggression pact with the Abu Nidal Organization, a violent Palestinian group. It was natural to connect the dots into a grand unified theory to explain America's lack of success against 17N: senior members of the PASOK government were in league with the terrorists.

Nothing in the 17N investigation or trial ever pointed meaningfully toward PASOK. Collusion with anti-American terrorists by governing-party officials of a NATO ally was so improbable a scenario, so contrary to Greek interests, and so damaging to a fragile working relationship that it should have been aired only when no innocent explanation was possible. But many Americans were certain there was high-level collusion. My ambassador whispered the name of a senior PASOK politician in my ear. A well-placed businesswoman whispered the same name. American and Greek journalists persuaded former U.S. officials back in Washington, including ex-CIA director James Woolsey and retired U.S. diplomats, to voice these suspicions, in each case generating a firestorm of headlines and mutual recriminations between the embassy and Greek authorities.

Once one looks for signs of perfidy one finds them everywhere. Greek police were viciously politicized a century before the CIA was created. Each change of Greek government resulted in a chain of promotions, retirements, and transfers. Inevitably, U.S. agencies were drawn into the infighting in their efforts to protect Greek partners. This well-meaning support amplified native Greek paranoia. When U.S. officials' friends or trainees found themselves transferred to remote villages, they believed, predictably, that they had been punished for too-close cooperation with the Americans. In a few cases this was true. Such transfers confirmed American suspicions about Greek bad faith. Senior Greek police officers quietly concluded that catching 17N might be the end of their career.

PASOK Prime Minister Andreas Papandreou died in 1996. His replacement, Kostas Simitis, a chilly technocrat who had outgrown his childhood enthusiasm for revolutionary movements, had the good sense in 2000 to appoint a minister of public order of transparent good character. Superhuman efforts by Minister Michalis Chrysochoidis made the myth of official collusion with 17N seem increasingly implausible, and U.S.-Greek counterterrorism cooperation gradually recovered. In the end, as if by poetic justice, the Greek police chief who oversaw the 17N case to its successful conclusion was the same man the U.S. embassy had once insisted the minister fire from his position as counterterrorism chief because of his evident lack of enthusiasm for catching the group.[16]

The FBI, CIA, and State Department all made their fair share of mistakes, natural ones. The language ███████████████████ ███████████████████████████████████ ██████████████████████████████████ suggested a connection to a well-known, innocent Greek writer. The presence of this clearly innocent celebrity on the U.S. list of investigation targets was a welcome excuse for Greek officials to do nothing, especially after someone leaked the writer's name to Greek journalists.

Bureaucratic self-confidence is a useful management tool, but it is occasionally misplaced. By insisting too long and too hard on flawed theories, the American 17N team undermined the willingness of Greek authorities to follow the more promising leads U.S. services developed.[17]

One permanent source of costly tension in U.S.-Greek relations was the U.S. government's refusal to publicly disavow the idea of kidnapping suspected 17N members to bring them to America for trial. Considering the catastrophic Greek response this violation of Greek and international law would have compelled, it is thus fortunate that CIA and FBI had no realistic chance of finding 17N on their own.[18]

## *Restoring Respect for Human Life*

17N lasted so long because, unlike al Qaeda but like any illegal group that hopes to survive, it was small, cautious, and self-limiting. It did not aspire to be a mass revolutionary movement. It did not recruit new members who might be police spies. Just as Americans do not punish their politicians for the failure to stop the killing of urban youth by other urban youth, Greeks tolerated 17N's widely spaced murders as long as something distinguished the victims from themselves. Ordinary Greeks, rationally enough, judged 17N's crimes to be less dangerous to their interests than reempowering the Greek police would be.

This poor political climate for law enforcement was collateral damage from the human rights abuses of the Greek junta that collapsed in 1974. The proclamations of 17N reflected the group's determination to keep that climate poor. 17N pandered to Greek public outrage of the moment—over Iraq or Kosovo—and to Greek nationalism and fear of Turks. Its anti-U.S. rhetoric was designed to deter a counterterrorism crusade by denouncing Greek politicians and police who took part in one as tools of the United States.

The breakthrough against 17N started with the insight that the terrorists' own victims could be used to change the political climate. After the murder of British defense attaché Stephen Saunders in June 2000, his widow stood up on Greek television with her daughters. Heather Saunders was impressive in her desolation. She focused attention on the family's own suffering, rather than blustering for vengeance. At last Greeks were being asked to feel the pity and compassion every untimely death deserves.

With help from the U.S. and British embassies, family members of other 17N victims, both Greek and foreign, coalesced around Mrs. Saunders. The victims' families worked to convince Greek society that their loved ones had been human beings, not faceless targets in a revolutionary struggle for justice. The true human cost of terrorism began to hit home. 17N went on the ideological defensive with a follow-up proclamation, but it was too late. Greek public opinion would no longer sustain 17N's valuation of itself as social avengers. Saunders's murder was the last.

Prime Minister Simitis had been reluctant to offend his party's left wing with changes to the legal system that would give the police a reasonable chance of convicting 17N if the group was caught. PASOK had poached votes from the communists ten years before by promising the repeal of previous such legislation. Once the opinion polls signaled that there would be no political backlash, the prime minister sent word to his justice minister to move ahead with a cautious Greek counterpart to the Patriot Act. The new legislation gave the prosecution the legal tools it needed to prosecute the group when the lucky break came a year later.

Neither the American government nor any other bureaucracy inspires in foreigners the compassion or protectiveness they will instinctively offer a suffering individual. It was hard for our embassy to accept that official America had no useful public role to play in delegitimizing terrorism. Bureaucrats are rewarded for being proactive. Successive U.S. ambassadors had, through what Greeks perceived as self-promoting Greek bashing, infuriated Greek opinion leaders, who retaliated with rumors that 17N was a CIA invention. As the victims' group emerged, the ambassador was torn between his desire to be perceived in Washington as a tough-minded terrorism-fighter and the knowledge that his best contribution to this fragile new climate was to make himself invisible. Some Greeks complained that he was not invisible enough, with his victims' group lapel pin showing a splayed hand (a very rude gesture in Greek) and the slogan "Up to Here!" But where it counted he let the victims' families occupy center stage. They did an admirable job, and America owes them its gratitude.

The world needs frequent reminders that Americans are human beings who bleed as well as cause others to bleed. The relentless television footage of the victims was one of the reasons 9/11 is viewed with appropriate horror by most Muslims as well as most Christians. When Americans are murdered overseas, the U.S. government should gently inform their families that they have a patriotic duty not to let their loved one disappear into the grave as a nameless and faceless statistic. The Anglo-Saxon instinct to protect the privacy of the grieving families is inappropriate to collective self-defense. Local television in the country of the crime can easily be persuaded to show photos and biographies of the victims and let the families air their grief in public, because such grief is also good television.

The State Department spokesperson ritually denounces each "cowardly murder" by a suicide bomber. But this denunciation by a foreigner means nothing to the society from which the murderers sprang; their kin know the suicide bombers were ultimately not cowards, whatever else they might have been. A more persuasive tactic is reaching out to local leaders and media, who can work with the families and peers of the murderers to shape public perceptions and turn the murderers into all-too-human victims themselves—for example, the Baghdad suicide bomber with Down's syndrome in January 2005. The United States has no standing to convince foreigners to despise their local martyrs, but it can do its part to make pity rather than admiration the reaction that predominates.

Fighting and winning the war to delegitimize terrorism as a tactic requires the U.S. government to change America's rhetoric and public image to reestablish that the superpower values human life enough to go to great lengths, including risking its own citizens' lives, to save the innocent. For most U.S. soldiers this is true. Still, we kill a horrifying number of civilians in wartime, not on purpose but through overconfidence in our intelligence, reluctance to take casualties, and indifference to the complex reasons that dictate that civilians will inevitably come into the line of fire. When war is just, these civilian casualties are grieved but accepted. America has been unable to prove the justice of its recent wars.

### Reestablishing the Rule of Law

Secretary Donald Rumsfeld claimed memorably in the 2005 *U.S. National Defense Strategy* that using "international fora" and "judicial processes" is, like terrorism itself, "a strategy of the weak."[19] Rumsfeld's implied contempt for the rule of law was a bureaucratic gambit aimed at weakening his rivals in the State Department and the Department of Justice. Imposing that stance as U.S. counterterrorism policy would be a form of national suicide.

Angry Americans have the same right to demand justice that angry foreigners have, and a much better chance of getting it than most. The rule of law is everywhere slow, time consuming, and imperfect. But there are several problems with speeding up the process of justice by making the CIA or U.S. military the judge, jury, and executioner of foreigners. First is the obvious one: that the U.S. government, like every other, routinely makes horrific mistakes. Second is the problem that having a panel of U.S. government lawyers and the president sign the finding authorizing murder of a suspected terrorist does not make the murder legal in the eyes of the people whose judgment matters most, the members of the society of the person America murders.

Every society jealously guards the right of punishment. American rejection of the International Criminal Court is an extreme case, but all societies shrink from extraditing their own citizens, no matter how heinous the crime. The U.S. legal system has little legitimacy in the eyes of ordinary Greeks or Saudis to punish their fellow citizens for crimes committed against Americans, but at least the process of open trial allows society to weigh the grief of the victims' families against the character of their accused murderer. The 17N trial in Athens, conducted with weeping family members in the front row, destroyed the last shreds of popular legitimacy for 17N, and so does any trial that assigns guilt in accordance with civilized norms. When the United States commits extrajudicial murder, or even kidnapping and "extraordinary rendition" of suspects for imprisonment and torture, that action is viewed not as punishment but as another crime. As such, it makes a hero of its victim and justifies renewed punishment of the United States in turn.

The third reason for respecting the rule of law and America's human rights commitments is that torture is a shameful, even treasonable form of bureaucratic self-promotion. A tortured prisoner will confirm any plot his interrogators ask him to. They do not have to dictate the confession directly, or even be conscious that they are dictating it. By administering an electric shock to the genitals every time the story strays from what they wish to believe, they can persuade all but the bravest or stupidest prisoners to deliver up a confession that serves some useful bureaucratic purpose. But the story will not be true, and the American government will ultimately disgrace itself by acting on it as if it were true.[20]

The interrogators who rely on torture are the dim and vicious ones, those whose only hope of advancement lies in finding that one-in-a-hundred prisoner, a genuine terrorist who knows something that can be accurately tortured out of him. But a terrorist America has tortured is a terrorist no U.S. attorney can put on trial. The United States must murder the torture victim, detain him indefinitely in violation of the U.S. Constitution, pay some other state to deal with him, or let him go. Any of these outcomes is a betrayal of Americans' right and duty to see justice done.

The knowledge that the United States has sponsored torture puts American lives in danger. The U.S. war on terrorism is at its heart a war to strengthen the rule of law in societies whose citizens are themselves often helpless victims of illegitimate violence. Whether the world's population is America's ally or adversary in this quest depends on its perception of U.S. behavior. The American judicial system is capable of being a legitimate source of justice for the crimes a great power from time to time commits against foreigners. When the U.S. justice system is instead perceived as an ally in those crimes, terrorist violence gains stature as a legitimate alternative.

## Limiting the Self-Inflicted Damage

President Bush used to proclaim: "We have learned that terrorist attacks are not caused by the use of strength; they are invited by the perception of weakness." Perhaps in some parallel universe this is true, so nervous Canadians stitch American flags onto their backpacks before they set off on the grand tour. But in our universe, terrorism is a weapon aimed by the weak and irresponsible against those they perceive as strong and responsible. America's huge embassies around the world are a symbol of American power, and it is precisely for that reason that they, not Canadian or Finnish embassies, are now ringed with truck-proof concrete planter boxes. In times of tension, police buses reinforced with steel mesh provide an extra ring of protection, and in times of war an armored personnel carrier is parked alongside. The net result is ugly. So, of course, were the shattered remains of U.S. embassies in Beirut, Dar es Salaam, and Nairobi after the truck bombs.

The uglification of U.S. embassies both reflects and reinforces the uglification of America in the eyes of the world. America's official representatives are encouraged to cower behind high walls that cut them off from people who would dislike and fear Americans less if they were not cut off from them. This self-protective reaction plays into the terrorists' hands. One of their goals is to drive Americans out of the Middle Eastern marketplace of ideas and ideologies. America makes its own decision, however, whether the murder of an American official will be an effective means of silencing America's message abroad.

America's own immune system is a powerful obstacle to defeating terrorism. As a private citizen in July 2004 I could stroll freely in Ramallah and talk to Palestinians about their grievances. My foreign service colleagues at U.S. Consulate General Jerusalem were laboring under a Washington-imposed near-boycott on contacts with Palestinians. This was partly retaliation for the murder of three American security guards in Gaza, partly onerous security regulations requiring advance permission and multiple armed guards.

America sends diplomats to dangerous countries because their mission is of vital importance to U.S. national interests. Those diplomats are volunteers, encouraged by danger pay, hardship allowances, and the promise of rapid advancement. The personal risk they face goes up slightly when they do their job of speaking to local opinion leaders on those leaders' own territory. They and their superiors should be rewarded, not punished, for accepting that risk.

### *Fixing the Bureaucracy*

Identifying the real costs and benefits of counterterrorism operations is a frustrating, unrewarding exercise even in the best of times. Oversight of covert operations in a given foreign country is legally the job of the U.S. ambassador, as the president's personal representative. In Greece, ambassadors had multiple incentives to participate enthusiastically in the little war against 17N. If they had attempted to impose strict controls, it is very likely they would have been ignored.

In my arrival call on Ambassador Burns in 2000 to start my second tour in Athens, I was told that one of my jobs as political counselor was to pass messages between the ███████████████ and the ██████████████. These two officials were engaged in a bureaucratic feud so vicious that Greek journalists knew and wrote about it. Mercifully, the two protagonists left early, and their replacements did not need my services. But competing organizations cheerfully sabotage one another if allowed.

An approach to terrorism based on U.S. national interests rather than bureaucratic self-interest would not have led to ████████ distinct organizations writing ████████ reports in ██████ different formats, often based on the same Greek media reports, each time an improvised explosive device took out an automatic teller machine in Athens. Most agencies cleared the others' drafts without comment, withholding for their own report any useful tidbit a jealously guarded local source might have shared.

Individual patriots did better. One of the finest human beings I ever met pored through restricted terrorism reporting for new names for the global visa lookout list. His bureaucratic self-sacrifice led to an official commendation for ██████████████████. The names he contributed should have been shared automatically in Washington, but more than a year after 9/11 the safety of America's borders still depended on such personal devotion.

The FBI has a pathological aversion to sharing information with outsiders. This attitude harms the FBI more than its rivals. Terrorists must be brought to justice for the battle against them to succeed, and therefore the FBI and not the CIA is the natural lead agency to fight them. The FBI is a repository of relevant investigative skills and should be better than the CIA at bonding with the local police investigators and prosecutors who are America's natural allies against any terrorist group. But the FBI was far too slow in emphasizing diplomacy as a vital skill.

The verdict of the Greek talking-head establishment after the 17N trial was that the British were better law enforcement diplomats than the Americans. The British had the last victim, Brigadier Saunders, and they benefited from fresh outrage, from highest-level political support, and from the vast pile of information Greek services had already gathered and organized with the help of the FBI and CIA. But the biggest difference was that the British were not blinded by their own theories. Analyzing the huge mass of evidence, they were willing to ask questions that to a competitive American would seem a humiliating confession of ignorance after twenty-five years. Fluent Greek-speakers apparently unaffiliated with the British government took the trouble to read the books of Greek leftists. They flattered them and may even have persuaded one or two of them to talk usefully about their revolutionary past. The Americans, less patient, were allegedly rebuffed more thoroughly.

It is not at all clear whether the insights the British gained were vital to the final breakthrough. The evidence they gathered was never presented at the 17N trial. The bottom line, however, was that the British pursuit of 17N, no less dogged than America's, created no anti-British backlash in Greece. Their quest for justice for the Saunders murder was politically cost-free, because in the prevailing Greek narrative (one deeply unfair to outstanding U.S. colleagues whose patient diplomacy was forgotten), the British treated their Greek partners as partners while the Americans tried to bully them.

When fighting terrorism, the U.S. government asks for complex and expensive undercover investigations. Some of the terror suspects the United States asks foreign police to pursue are innocent, and most have not yet committed a crime a local jury would ever convict. Foreign police do not always understand why their most talented officers should drop their own work to assist U.S. colleagues. No matter how clear and positive the instructions a local service may get from its political masters, the burden of proof will always be on the U.S. side to show that cooperation is worth the time, trouble, and political risk.

The prudent response to international crime, of which terrorism is only the most obvious manifestation, is a generous long-term investment in cooperative international law enforcement. In Greece, this investment involves, for example, American help with the huge problem of Balkan organized crime. The U.S. Drug Enforcement Administration (DEA) officers I watched in Athens did an outstanding job. They were Greek-American police officers who spoke fluent

Greek and respected the culture of their hosts. They managed to inspire respect and affection not only in their police colleagues but even (amazingly) in Greek journalists who reported on their joint operations. DEA officers refused to score points off their Greek partners, shared property seizures 50-50, billed themselves humbly in the Greek media as a supporting institution, and did an unobtrusively excellent job in their doomed task of stopping the flow of heroin and cocaine to the United States.

The FBI legal attaché's office in Athens was stretched far too thin and covered too many countries to offer much support to Greek police in their own cases, even if it wanted to. The United States would do well to expand the FBI presence abroad, with qualified law enforcement diplomats, fluent speakers of the local language, stationed for long, repeated postings in many more embassies and consulates. Finding the money should not be difficult. But better funding would be counterproductive without a change in corporate culture.

Diplomacy relies on personal relationships established before one needs them. In the FBI's nativist ethos, however, personal relationships with foreigners are still a source of suspicion. The FBI team in Athens in 2001 was actually two FBI teams—one from FBI headquarters and one from the Washington field office—with overlapping missions. When the two collided, the story the victors spread was the same charge bureaucrats always use against diplomats: the losers had put good working relations with Greeks ahead of the vigorous pursuit of 17N. Until the FBI learns to prize diplomacy and respect for alien cultures as much as other skills, counterterrorism cooperation will be a dangerous gamble for the foreign partners on whom the FBI's success depends.[21]

## Extending the Lessons of 17N

I would summarize the lessons from America's unsatisfying little war against 17N as follows: First, terrorism is, in practice if not in rhetoric, local politics by other means. Terrorists are defeated when that defeat is recognized in their own political arena through a justice system their society accepts. Using Hellfire missiles to kill terror suspects together with innocent bystanders is a public confession of failure in the real battle. Second, terrorism is inherently self-limiting once we understand it properly; the victims terrorists create are a more effective weapon against them than the denunciations or cruise missiles of an angry superpower. Third, by disregarding terrorist motives when allocating security resources, bureaucrats harm the ordinary citizens they are pledged to protect. The money spent guarding train stations would be more usefully spent restoring the world's perception of American altruism. Fourth, when the United States usurps from the locals the management of local wars, it puts the interests of U.S. bureaucrats ahead of U.S. national interests.

One of the uglier bureaucratic motives for spreading the myth of freedom-hating terrorists was to persuade the president that he had no strategic duty to limit America's policies to ones ordinary decent Muslims could accept as reasonable. Americans took the word of their president that preemption of terrorism required unilateral violence and the death of innocent civilians. Those closer to the resulting rubble read the U.S. intervention as torture, kidnap, and murder. Each civilian death increases the risk that retaliatory murder of American civilians will creep into some group's moral lexicon in the way that strategic bombing of civilian targets crept into America's during World War II. America flirts with that disaster in Iraq.

Misidentifying Iraq as America's "central front in the war on terrorism" has given a generation of U.S. service members the opportunity to match their superb fighting skills against a stream of young Muslim martyrs. The contest is absorbing but not useful. Perhaps we will kill them all, but recent history suggests that a few of them will return to Saudi Arabia or southern California armed with new glamour and deadly expertise. It was a mistake to offer them a jihad their conservative societies could accept as moral and legitimate.

The struggle against terrorism is ultimately a struggle to prove that the laws and institutions of modern, secular, democratic societies like the United States offer ordinary people the guarantees of personal dignity their innate sense of justice demands. If Americans talked to more foreigners, they would feel more confident that harsh punishment and dishonor await all those who murder the innocent citizens of a benevolent and law-abiding superpower. For its own protection, America should aspire again to be that superpower.

# 12

# ★ *The Domestic Politics of Nuclear*

# *Weapons* ★

*It is well that war is so terrible, else we should grow too fond of it.*
                                                                    Gen. Robert E. Lee

New country desk officers at the State Department take an orientation visit to the country whose relationship with the United States they will be looking after. In December 1994, now the senior India desk officer in the South Asia Bureau, I made a ten-day trip to India and Pakistan, my first taste of a huge, diverse, and dangerous subcontinent. I made the rounds at the U.S. embassy in New Delhi and our consulates in Calcutta, Madras, and Bombay to get an unfiltered sense of the issues that gripped my foreign service colleagues. They were all exhausted. Frank Wisner, the U.S. ambassador, was a charismatic, gifted career diplomat who needed only four hours sleep a night. During the remaining twenty hours of the day, he drove his staff to weave as dense a web as they could of bureaucratic, commercial, and cultural relationships to bind the United States and India together.

My control officer trotted me around to meet the most interesting Indian officials, journalists, and thinkers the Political Section could muster. The embassy's unspoken goal was to convince its new desk officer that India is too large, complex, and prickly a country to leave to the tender mercies of Washington politicians and bureaucrats. At least as regarded India's nuclear arms race with Pakistan, they were fairly convincing.

I had asked to visit Kashmir, the apple of discord between India and Pakistan since 1948. The United States did not accept the Indian view that Kashmir was a purely internal Indian matter. Too much blood had been spilled for that. Terrorist attacks and cross-

217

border shelling occurred weekly across the line of control. On the Siachen glacier, at seventeen thousand feet so worthless and inaccessible an ice field that the precise line of control had never been negotiated, elite Indian and Pakistani mountain troops engaged in a bizarre and deadly slow-motion conflict to push the line forward. Kashmir was a morbidly interesting destination, but my visit was vetoed for security and political reasons. The education of a desk officer was not an adequate reason to risk embassy personnel or irritate the Indians.

My consolation prize was a drive up the Grand Truck Road from New Delhi to Chandigarh, the capital of Indian Punjab. The commerce of half of India still funneled down a two-lane strip of asphalt on a raised embankment. The fields below were full of overturned, crumpled trucks and the occasional dead bus. Watching the turbaned truck drivers as they blinked their high beams and downshifted to pass one another, I started to understand the bloody-minded stubbornness that substituted for common race, religion, language, or even roads in holding India together as a democratic state for fifty years.

In Chandigarh, I met a Sikh human rights activist who decried Indian atrocities against Sikh separatists in the Punjab. I nodded sympathetically and tried not to stare at his sword. I would not have annoyed the Indian government by talking to such dissidents if India's behavior had been impeccable. Still, neither the U.S. government nor I had any sympathy for the murderous pursuit of an independent Sikh state to be called Khalistan. Nor did we endorse an independent Assam or a Maoist paradise of workers and peasants in Bihar or the similar aspirations of any of the dozens of murderous little groups that challenged the hard-pressed Indian state's monopoly of violence. But Indian officials were deeply displeased at America's unhealthy interest in Indian internal problems. They had a difficult country to run and considered any outside intervention, even by a well-meaning superpower, a deeply unfriendly act.

Indian politicians are judged by their ability to keep the disparate populations of an ancient multiethnic empire functioning together as something that resembles a modern national state. There is no guarantee that the unique Indian model of nationalism will succeed. Some of the politicians' constituents are ferocious indeed. Sikh terrorist attacks included the assassination of an Indian prime minister, Indira Gandhi, and an Air India 747 blown out of the sky in 1985, with 331 dead. Other groups are equally deadly.

It is useful to the Indian nation-building process to believe that Pakistan is the origin of most of India's internal strife. Indians believe this unreservedly. Pakistan stoutly denies that it inspires and funds Sikh, Kashmiri, and miscellaneous Islamist extremist groups to murder Indians. In 1994 the U.S. embassy in Islamabad assessed that many of these denials were truthful. Not all, alas, but it served U.S. interests not to look too closely. Were the United States to identify Pakistan publicly as a state sponsor of terrorism, the Indian goodwill America earned would not compensate for the loss of its ability to work with the Pakistani government on crucial common interests.

Indian anger at America's selective myopia was bitter. A just superpower, India believed, would join forces with the world's largest democracy to impose order on the international criminals next door. If not, the Indian military would one day have to do the job on its own, as it had in 1965 and 1971. India, its diplomats and politicians made abundantly clear, would not shrink from any step that assured the security of its people against outside aggression or inside subversion.

I returned from India convinced that the threat from Pakistan, even if not as serious as the Indians believed, was deeply embedded in Indian domestic politics. Indian politicians were not fools—quite the contrary. They were trying to survive a brutally competitive and treacherous game of regional, tribal, and caste-based coalition politics. Any outside threat that bought them ten minutes of national unity was a precious gift. Indian governments did not want war with Pakistan, far from it. But they could seldom afford any diplomatic concession to Pakistan's own horrific domestic political problems. India wanted closer ties with the United States but would not trade away domestic political advantage simply to appease the superpower. In Indian domestic politics, as in American, security was paramount.

## The South Asia Bureau

The U.S. consulate general in Calcutta (since renamed Kolkata) had been built to house an outsized official presence, America's Cold War bastion against communist inroads in West Bengal and northeastern India. But the local communists had outlasted it. In 1994 they were still firmly in control of the Bengal state government and were wickedly polite to visiting foreign capitalists like myself. Out of old imperial habit, local gardeners still cut the consulate lawn to carpetlike perfection, apparently with fingernail scissors. The consul general bumped around in a half-empty building full of abandoned furniture even uglier than the State Department's. The cold warriors had moved on.

The State Department's Bureau of Near-Eastern Affairs (NEA) had looked after the Indian subcontinent—India, Pakistan,

Afghanistan, Nepal, and Sri Lanka—in whatever time it could spare from the Arab-Israel crisis and the Persian Gulf. Creation of my new bureaucratic home, the South Asia Bureau (SA), had been a desperate move by members of Congress in 1992 to convince the administration not to drop South Asia once the Cold War ended.

Congress was right this time. Afghanistan was unhinged and dangerous. Sri Lanka was ripped by civil war between Tamils and Sinhalese. Nepal had so-called Maoist guerillas rampaging through the countryside. Pakistan, brutally mismanaged by its oligarchs and under permanent threat of Islamist revolution, was using the Kashmir conflict with India to rally a semblance of national unity. India, meanwhile, was beginning an economic liberalization process that would turn it into a major world power over the next decade. The U.S. Indian community had begun to assert measurable political influence with Congress and the White House.

The new SA set out to attract enough favorable attention from the president and secretary of state to allow it to exert control of U.S. policy in India and Pakistan over the competing departments and agencies of the U.S. government. SA's assistant secretary, Robin Raphel, had been at Oxford with Bill Clinton before joining the Foreign Service. She would happily have dangled before her college friend the prospect of a Nobel Peace Prize for resolving the Kashmir dispute. It was easy to argue that vital U.S. national interests in India and Pakistan justified the huge commitment of diplomatic resources required.

Unfortunately, winning a Nobel Peace Prize requires coaxing at least grudging acceptance for mediation out of two warring parties. To do so presupposes a coherent U.S. position that the leaders on both sides recognize as compatible with their own political and security interests. Very few Nobel Prizes are awarded to politicians, partly because very few of them successfully persuade even their own government to take a single line on a given conflict.

The India desk officer is the State Department's first point of reference for all things Indian. No official above the desk officer has the luxury of focusing on a single country, of reading the telegrams and intelligence reports, of talking at length to Indian diplomats and visiting politicians. More often than not, the desk officer's analysis of U.S. influence is accurate. But accurate knowledge does not imply any authority to make U.S. policy. Policy, to the extent the United States has one, is hammered out in a free-flowing competitive process of senior officials from the State Department, Pentagon, National Security Council (NSC), and other departments. Senior bureaucrats are judged not by whether the policies they advocate serve U.S. interests—every bureaucrat has a different idea what those interests are—but by whether their policies prevail. Successful bureaucrats succeed by endorsing not the course that is likeliest to be effective but the course that is likeliest to be adopted. For SA, that meant studying the White House at least as carefully as we studied South Asia.

My assistant secretary was too much a realist about U.S. internal difficulties to seek bold ideas from her desk officers on how to promote relations of trust and cooperation with India. Generous gestures would not survive the interagency policy clearance process; therefore none were advocated. South Asia experts tended to confuse America's interests with those of their Indian or Pakistani clients. A few Democratic members of Congress urged embracing India as the world's largest democracy, a regional superpower, and a huge potential market. Most Republicans, however, remembered bitterly that India had played the role of moralizing neutral during the Cold War. The Indian-American community had not yet become politically powerful enough to offset their rancor. A few scoundrels—Dan Burton of Indiana was the Indian embassy's *bête noire*—hated India so viscerally that they sold their political services to Sikh and Kashmiri separatist groups. In practice, America's South Asia policy was a sterile balancing act, not so much between India and Pakistan as between warring camps of U.S. bureaucrats and politicians who dealt with South Asia.

U.S. relations with Pakistan were blighted by congressional sanctions on the Pakistani nuclear program. Unable to certify truthfully that Pakistan did not have nuclear weapons, the U.S. government was barred from delivering to Pakistan the fleet of new F-16 aircraft the Pakistanis had bought and paid for. The U.S. companies would not give the Pakistanis a refund. So the State Department wrung its hands apologetically while the Pakistanis fumed.

To preserve the strategic balance, the Pentagon and others felt the need to impose similar dysfunction on U.S. relations with India. Every proposed initiative with India was hotly contested by a vehement telegram from Embassy Islamabad pointing out the unfairness of U.S. behavior. Pakistan's allies in Washington chimed in. The U.S. and Indian governments did few things together because cooperation was bureaucratically more trouble than it was worth. U.S. internal bickering also seemed to confirm the one perception on which the entire U.S. bureaucracy and Congress could agree: Pakistan and India hated one another too much to be trusted with nuclear weapons.

With the Cold War over, the huge security and intelligence

apparatus the United States had built to contain the Russians needed new missions to justify its continued funding. No bureaucrat in his right mind could object when that apparatus launched itself at the praiseworthy goal of keeping India and Pakistan as nonnuclear states. There were enough zealots in both India and Pakistan to make it credible that each side would contemplate with equanimity the nuclear extermination of the degenerate criminals on the other side. Terrorism was another U.S. concern. Pakistan was and remains an untidy state. Despite indignant Pakistani denials, unfriendly hands might inherit the nuclear weapons if Pakistan melted down.

Before signing up for any crusade in South Asia, any aspiring American foreign policy pundit (beware the Hindi word we use) should try arguing with an Indian diplomat, preferably over a sumptuous Indian dinner. As desk officer I had that pleasure frequently. Indian officials speak English with beautiful precision and have a biting sense of humor. They are no less fiercely nationalist than Americans are. Coming from a democracy of one billion people with an ancient and rich philosophical and moral tradition, they have no disposition to accept moralizing arguments. Whenever I lectured Indian diplomats on their national security interests, it was their diplomatic duty to rip my head off.

Frequent conversations with Navdeep and Shyamala, my interlocutors at the Indian embassy in Washington, undermined any naive optimism I might have felt about America's ability to give India well-meaning advice on any issue. On nuclear nonproliferation, the issue by which my superiors would judge my performance, the United States had no moral standing in Indian eyes to say anything: America had nuclear weapons. America had used them. Until America agreed to give up its own weapons, India would insist on its own right to have them as well. Indian Hindus would wield the weapons their scientists created at least as wisely and morally as American Christians had. They dismissed our nightmare scenarios of Indo-Pakistani nuclear holocaust as paternalism or outright racism. I had little evidence to prove I knew their country better than they did.

## Cramming Genies Into Bottles

To a literal-minded person, the bureaucratic goal of a nonnuclear South Asia was a fantasy long before I arrived on the desk. India had detonated a "device" back in 1974. Indian weapons scientists had not been idle since then. In 1994, as the India desk officer, I had a "need to know." Armed with special compartmented information security clearances, I began to attend the intelligence briefings on Indian and Pakistani ballistic missile and nuclear programs.

Indians and Pakistanis were happy to sell some secrets to foreign intelligence officers, but apparently not the one the United States cared about most, the status of their nuclear programs. Satellite observations, Indian and Pakistani newspapers, and guesstimates from U.S. weapons scientists suggested to the agency that both sides already had substantial stocks of nuclear weapons their scientists desperately wanted to test and a test site that could be made ready in a matter of days.

A few months before I arrived on the desk in 1994, there had been a flurry of high-level secret U.S. diplomacy in response to increased activity at the Indian nuclear test site. Deputy Secretary of State Strobe Talbott told the Indians that the sky would fall if they tested, that the consequences for U.S.-Indian relations, though unspecified, would be very, very bad. To strengthen the U.S. argument, Congress passed new legislation later in 1994, the Glenn Amendment, that would impose sweeping economic sanctions on countries that exploded a nuclear device, with no presidential waiver possible.

Did U.S. diplomacy successfully avert a nuclear test in 1994? My Indian diplomat counterparts were skeptical that a test had been planned. Their skepticism meant little in itself. Those Indian diplomats capable of predicting the U.S. reaction to a test would not have been consulted before the test took place. Later published accounts by Indians suggest that the U.S. concern had been premature. Still, we diplomats told ourselves at the time that we had persuaded the prime minister of India, P. V. Narasimha Rao, that the harm done by U.S. sanctions would outweigh any security or political benefit from testing. Did we?

Narasimha Rao was under permanent pressure from his defense scientists to test India's nuclear arsenal. Designing a large, ugly nuclear device that will explode is easy. Miniaturizing that device to fit on a missile or in a suitcase requires very sophisticated technology indeed. The only certain proof that the calculations are correct is successful detonation. Over the decades, India had spent billions of dollars on its clandestine nuclear program and on an advanced ballistic missile program. The time had come to mate the two programs. If it did not test first, India would be taking a huge gamble as it moved to mount its nuclear deterrent on a fleet of short- and medium-range missiles.

Narasimha Rao was a politician, not a security bureaucrat. India is a democracy. The prime minister owed loyalty both to his electorate and to his reading of India's broader national interests. India has a powerful antinuclear lobby. The diverse political coalition that backed Narasimha Rao did not depend on constituents obsessed with whether he tested or not. The Congress Party, the key member of his coalition, had a public tradition of global disarmament activism under its murdered former leader, Rajiv Gandhi. It would be painful to repudiate this tradition. And Narasimha Rao himself was philosophically far from a militarist. He was also a deep enough thinker to recognize that Pakistan would test its own device immediately after India did. This would cancel out essentially all the domestic political benefit to him and his coalition from testing.

The usefulness of U.S. political pressure, of State Department threats or bribes, will never be accurately known. For self-evident nationalist reasons, no Indian politician could afford to acknowledge U.S. pressure in his calculations. Because of India's domestic political ambivalence toward nuclear weapons, Narasimha Rao had the luxury of weighing the security benefits from a nuclear test against the cost to India's other interests. The United States was not the only country threatening economic sanctions. The negative reaction of Japan and the European Union (EU) would have further undercut India's cautious economic opening to outside investment. Narasimha Rao used those economic arguments against his internal critics to defend his refusal to test.

All through my tenure on the desk, U.S. satellites monitored the Indian test site for signs of an impending nuclear test. U.S. surveillance technology was good enough to keep the U.S. government permanently nervous but not good enough to give it reliable answers. India's ballistic missile program was more public. India had tested a short-range ballistic missile, the Prithvi, and made significant progress toward a medium-range missile, the Agni. Sitting at my desk at the State Department, I strained my intellect to add persuasive arguments to the instruction cables the State Department sent Ambassador Wisner in New Delhi each time the newspapers reported that India was about to take a new step toward incorporating the Prithvi in its arsenal.

America's most compelling point for persuading India not to take the next step on ballistic missiles was the United States could not deter the Pakistanis from deploying their own missiles unless it deterred the Indians as well. I had heard the vehement Indian counterarguments by then. International law did not prohibit India's testing or deploying a missile. India had the same right to self-defense as its neighbors. I could think of no bribe or threat that would be effective to overcome India's determination, at least no threat the United States was prepared to carry out.

The telegrams my colleagues and I drafted and cleared with

our counterparts at the Defense Department and NSC were an unconvincing mixture of pious pleas and dire, vague warnings. Ambassador Wisner was instructed to deliver our talking points at the highest level of the Indian government that would agree to receive him.

I did not believe my eyes when I saw the telegram reporting the meeting. Armed with the platitudes we sent, Wisner had been amazingly persuasive. A key Indian bureaucrat had made a commitment to exercise restraint in the deployment of India's missile arsenal. There was a flurry of excitement around Washington at Wisner's diplomatic triumph. I had no doubt the Indian had said exactly what the U.S. embassy reported him as saying. And yet, I had been sure from the outset that America's was a lost cause. No Indian politician could risk the allegation of succumbing to U.S. pressure. I wondered how I had misjudged the Indians so badly on this key security issue. Was I a sober realist, as I saw myself, or simply a lazy fatalist worthy of derision?

My question was answered in the days that followed. Wisner's diplomacy had indeed been brilliant, but it had not been miraculous. As soon as the United States tried to take our new Indian promise to the bank, it got blank stares from its Indian partners. Writhing under Wisner's hypnotic gaze, the senior official had said more than he meant to. The polite, empty reassurances he was authorized to make had turned into a pledge. Rather than disgrace himself before his colleagues by confessing that he had bowed to U.S. pressure, he let his commitment quietly evaporate into the bureaucratic ether. Poetic language was employed around the Beltway to express bureaucratic solidarity with Wisner in the face of this Indian perfidy.

The Indians slowly improved their ballistic missiles. Indian officials politely made it impossible to distinguish the effect of U.S. diplomacy from the delays caused by the intrinsic difficulty of the technology, the Indian government's shortage of cash, and the refusal of major European and U.S. suppliers to sell certain specialized hardware. Militarily and politically, India was committed to developing an independent ballistic missile capability regardless of U.S. pressure. Diplomatically, India did not want that determination to be a greater source of friction than absolutely necessary.

### The Genie Reappears

As desk officer, I ran the office betting pool for the May 1996 Indian parliamentary election. The election was being fought primarily on domestic issues, but Indian political commentators, like their distant Greek cousins, loved to make dark allegations about the "foreign hand" at work. The Hindu nationalist Bharatiya Janata Party (BJP) claimed that Narasimha Rao had sacrificed India's sacred right of self-defense to U.S. pressure. Narasimha Rao's intrinsic caution made the allegations seem believable, and they hurt him. Though a colleague won the pot, I had the consolation of seeing my overall prediction borne out. The voters handed Narasimha Rao's coalition a clear defeat. The BJP emerged as largest single party, though it fell short of a majority in Parliament.

Sworn in as prime minister, BJP leader Atul Behari Vajpayee ordered the Indian defense research establishment to conduct a nuclear test as soon as possible. I learned of the order only years later, from Indian newspaper reports. If the ███████████ had picked up the information in time, my last days on the India Desk would have been a living hell as we moved heaven and earth to stop the test. As it was, we waited passively for the political situation in New Delhi to clarify itself.

The U.S. intelligence community suffered no humiliating Indian nuclear surprise in 1996. Vajpayee found himself unable to assemble a majority coalition to win a vote of confidence in Parliament. He stepped down as prime minister after thirteen days. As a responsible politician subservient to India's democratic process, he canceled the test. The weak coalition that replaced him restored Narasimha Rao's cautious nuclear policy of weapons development but no testing.[1]

Little evidence suggests that fondness for atomic bombs is a major vote-getter in India any more than in the United States. Nuclear testing, however, was a useful marker for BJP to highlight its policy differences with the government. Vajpayee routinely blasted Narasimha Rao for kowtowing to the United States and meekly accepting nuclear discrimination against India in its right to nuclear self-defense. The BJP argued, plausibly enough, that India would never achieve the respect in world affairs its size deserves without nuclear weapons. Vajpayee campaigned on a promise to induct nuclear weapons formally into the Indian arsenal. And India's nuclear high priests, major public figures thanks to this debate, were determined to hold him to his promise to test that arsenal.

Two years later, in 1998, with me now safely in Armenia, the BJP came to power again. This time it assembled a governing majority. Immediately after winning his vote of confidence Vajpayee secretly ordered tests to be carried out as soon as humanly possible. Preparations took about two weeks. On May 11 and 13, 1998, the Indians tested five bombs, including a boosted fission weapon. The U.S. acting secretary of state Strobe Talbott flew to Pakistan to beg the Pakistanis not to follow suit. The Pakistanis uttered soothing words, but privately it was clear that the Pakistani government would not survive unless it responded to India in kind. Pakistan acted on May 28 and 30, claiming to have detonated six bombs.

Vajpayee had fulfilled his campaign promise. India's bombs were apparently more effective than Pakistan's, but both sets worked well enough for domestic political purposes. Vajpayee tried to soften the blow to the United States by declaring that India had achieved its goal of minimum credible deterrence and would cease nuclear testing. The Indian parliament, however, refused to ratify the Comprehensive Test Ban Treaty, on the grounds that to do so would place an unacceptable limit on Indian sovereignty unless the United States and Pakistan agreed to bind themselves by the treaty as well.

After the tests, U.S. bureaucrats and politicians were caught in a mess largely of their own making. America had written its threats of dire consequences into U.S. law and had no flexibility. In any case, U.S. credibility, especially in the eyes of aspiring nuclear states such as Iran and North Korea, seemed to require a vigorous response. Sweeping economic sanctions were unleashed against both India and Pakistan.

Sanctions are useful as a deterrent. Once deterrence fails they become an expensive albatross around American necks. U.S. sanctions torpedoed the financing of several major investment projects and trade deals by American companies, projects worth a billion dollars. The sanctions briefly slowed the growth of the Indian economy, which was never a goal of U.S. policy, while punishing U.S. companies. Foreign competitors were free to take up the slack. The assistance programs the United States cut off, including the humanitarian ones, were designed to encourage policy reforms that served U.S. interests. Sanctions destroyed America's leverage to push for Indian economic liberalization but offered not the slightest hope of persuading India to un-invent its nuclear weapons.

After a few months, Congress meekly allowed the sanctions to be waived, and the U.S. relationship with India resumed. A year or two later the relationship was fully normal, perhaps even improved. A major political and bureaucratic rallying point for U.S. politicians and bureaucrats opposed to India for other reasons had become a losing cause. In Washington, losing causes are dropped and forgotten. In 2005 the United States announced a major new program of peaceful nuclear cooperation with India, something unthinkable when America pretended it was possible to keep India out of the ranks of nuclear weapons states.

### Some South Asian Lessons

In the mid-1990s the cost of international economic sanctions to the Indian economy was one factor Indian political leaders used privately to offset the pressure from their own bureaucrats for an Indian nuclear test. U.S. influence was significant because the domestic political balance in India for and against testing was relatively even. Unfortunately, the U.S. inability to keep its influence private handed opponents of Prime Minister Narasimha Rao a powerful weapon in India's democratic political competition. When the U.S. government is genuinely concerned about the effectiveness of its influence on any foreign leader who faces elections, it should publicly announce its lack of influence at every opportunity. Such a confession will probably be true, but if not, democratic alternation of government will make it true soon enough.

Only one diplomatic argument I used ever gave the slightest pause to my Indian interlocutors, and it was a moral rather than a rational one. The United States, I insisted, remained committed to its treaty obligation under article VI of the Nonproliferation Treaty (NPT) "to pursue negotiations in good faith on effective measures relating to cessation of the nuclear arms race at an early date and to nuclear disarmament." The United States had dramatically cut the number of weapons in its nuclear arsenal and would cut further. Not this generation, perhaps, but one day the world would be safe enough to allow America's NPT commitment to be fulfilled in its entirety. India's becoming a nuclear weapons state, I solemnly intoned, would be a grave blow to the world's shared aspiration for the total elimination of nuclear weapons. The Indians shuffled their feet uneasily. Indians' sense of superior morality makes it politically impossible for India, no matter how bellicose the government that finds itself in power a hundred years from now, to be the last nuclear weapons possessor on the planet. The United States should make diplomatic use of this Indian moral sense, not mock it through its policies.

At the time I said it, my one effective argument was not completely false. Now it would be. President Bush as commander in chief has repeatedly allowed his subordinates to assert that it is U.S. policy never to give up nuclear weapons or the legal right to test them. At every international meeting, including the 2005 UN General Assembly, a key aim of the U.S. delegation has been to strike all references to article VI of the NPT and to the Comprehensive Test Ban Treaty from the agreed text. In U.S. public documents, nuclear weapons are now presented to America's horrified partners as a permanent component of U.S. military power. For any effective nonproliferation strategy, America's nuclear posturing is an unqualified blunder.

## North Korea

President Bush made an amateur's mistake in 2001 when he came to office assuming that, unlike India, despotisms have no internal politics on which U.S. diplomacy could operate. The evidence of internal politics is everywhere, even in a closed state such as the Democratic People's Republic of Korea (DPRK). The DPRK sends out a steady stream of contradictory messages on its nuclear stance. Over the years North Koreans have bragged of their weapons, denied having them, threatened to sell them to terrorists, denied that this was possible, suggested they would trade them away for financial aid, and blustered that they would keep them forever to deter U.S. aggression. The U.S. government has embraced these contradictions as proof that the DPRK is too dangerously irrational a state to be allowed to possess nuclear weapons.

No one accused the United States of dangerous irrationality simply because President Bush contradicted Secretary Powell in March 2001 when the latter proposed resuming negotiations with North Korea from where the Clinton administration left off. When a country speaks with many voices it is generally because its leadership has not yet imposed unity on competing bureaucratic factions pursuing different agendas. Powell's agenda was a technocratic one, to reduce the threat of North Korea's nuclear program. His president's was political, to look tough and decisive to a hawkish conservative constituency by asserting a clean break with Clinton's allegedly spineless and ineffective foreign policy. In 2005, with a new U.S. secretary of state and a president no longer up for reelection, good Chinese diplomacy allowed the technocratic side to predominate in the U.S. internal policy debate.

Diverging political agendas are knowable, even in the DPRK. One goal of this or any Dear Leader is to stay in power. Kim Jong Il has selfish reasons to maintain the worship of his heroized father and cause one of his sons to inherit custody of the family mausoleum and promote the worship of himself in turn. America is the chief threat to Kim Jong Il's filial piety. Kim is perfectly rational to take seriously some U.S. officials' claim that regime change in North Korea is the U.S. goal. Watching regime change occur in Iraq, a thoughtful despot might conclude that U.S. military intervention can be deterred, if at all, through the possession of usable nuclear weapons and the ability to destroy Seoul and perhaps Tokyo.

Convincing Kim otherwise is a major diplomatic task. Kim's hold on power depends on nationalism as well as repression. Brandishing the threat of foreign invaders is as useful a tool of political mobilization for him as it has been for Fidel Castro in Cuba. Maintaining his huge, expensive military serves Kim's goal of regime survival, but only if he can keep that military loyal. Keeping that military loyal in the absence of a unifying external threat requires funding the army's special privileges better than any presumptive rival.

Legitimate sources of revenue are closed to the DPRK as long as the regime maintains despotic and destructive control over the country and its economy. North Korea has few competitive advantages, even in the heroin trade. A deal based on selling nuclear weapons is the only realistic source of enough cash to keep the regime afloat. Terrorists are not rich enough to finance the DPRK. Therefore, by necessity, the North Korean officials charged with financing their leader's appetites will speak out, whenever it seems safe to do so, in favor of trading nuclear weapons to the United States for massive economic assistance.

Dealing with the current U.S. administration is difficult and dangerous for North Korean officials. Some of them fought to revive the old Clinton-era deal—give DPRK food, oil, and money and it will forgo its right to nuclear self-defense. Their rivals told the Dear Leader that such a policy would be suicidal and that North Korea could only stave off U.S. invasion by convincing President Bush that it already had multiple nuclear weapons and was prepared to use them. A smaller group thought it could combine the two by helpfully echoing the fears of American professional doomsayers: North Korea would be willing to risk nuclear annihilation by selling nuclear weapons to terrorists if America does not pay up. And the North's ideological commitment to Korean unification is a permanent wild card.

Watching this murky debate from the outside, Americans must remember that most North Koreans had no intellectual basis for understanding the United States and its motives.[2] Intelligence services are rewarded for confirming the hopes and fears of their political bosses. Few leaders are mature enough to demand nuanced analysis of the domestic political balances that shape U.S. policy toward the Korean peninsula when they can read lurid and frightening gossip instead. What the United States says publicly about its intentions is of vital importance to counterbalance such voices.

Diplomatic strategy toward North Korea during the first four years of the George W. Bush administration was blighted by John

Bolton, then the rabidly militarist undersecretary for arms control. On a visit to Seoul Bolton publicly insulted the North Korean leadership, calling it a dictatorship that needed to be overthrown. The undersecretary's motives were obscure; perhaps he genuinely hoped for a military solution in North Korea. As a result of his comments, the undersecretary basked in the admiration of his neoconservative friends in Washington, while the North Korean officials who favored a deal with the United States were castrated bureaucratically. With Bolton's threat seen as a statement of official U.S. policy, no DPRK official in his right mind would suggest to the Dear Leader that North Korea could afford to trade away its nuclear deterrent. The discussion dried up.

Chinese mediation eventually allowed direct dialogue between U.S. and North Korean politicians and diplomats to resume. The United States demanded and received the political cover of a six-nation negotiating process. These talks were the necessary antidote to the fear-mongering of the security bureaucrats on both sides. One of America's most competent, reasonable, and modest diplomats, Assistant Secretary for East Asian Affairs Chris Hill, took on that task in August 2005. A breakthrough seemed impossible. The official U.S. and North Korean positions were incompatible, and neither delegation could stray far from the lines drawn by their capitals in the first round. Still, the talks helped erase years of dangerous mutual demonizing.

A breakthrough occurred on the last day of the second round of talks, in September 2005. Ambassador Hill, with Chinese help, convinced the U.S. government that it had no choice but to back away from its absolute rejection of North Korea's right to build a light water nuclear reactor (one less usable for weapons production) sometime in the future. A successful U.S. nonproliferation strategy will continue this diplomatic dialogue with the aim of gradually shifting the North Korean internal political balance to favor economic prosperity over regime security. This is a diplomatic service almost any country would find valuable. Perhaps China's newly energized diplomacy can convince even America's own government.

History suggests that the best way to remove the United States as a convenient prop for the North Korean regime is to normalize relations as fully as possible. The U.S. political system is strong enough to survive the loss of a convenient enemy. The North Korean system may not be. By reducing the North Korean sense of crisis through binding security guarantees, the United States can speed up the process of opening North Korea to the outside world. Under the evolutionary pressure of the world economy, North

Korea will turn in a decade or two into something unrecognizable to its current ideologues and America's own.

## *Iran*

It was an enlightening experience as a U.S. diplomat to stare across the Iranian border from Armenia. Armenians and Persians are distant cousins whose fates are intertwined. Armenians know that Iran is a status-quo empire. Iranians have no burning irredentist issues to match North Korea's ideological obsession with Korean unification. The flurry of Islamic revolutionary proselytizing that followed the 1979 Iranian revolution faded away ingloriously. Iran's Revolutionary Guard corps still murdered Iranian dissidents and Bahais in the name of religion, but left other infidels pretty much alone. When Armenia earned its independence from the USSR, there were more working Armenian Christian churches in Iran than in Armenia. A French diplomatic colleague returned to Yerevan from a road trip grumbling that Iranians saw southern California as the promised land.

Americans assume that the Iranian government has been pursuing nuclear weapons for decades. It probably has been. Locked in a brutal war with Iraq during the 1980s, Iran presumably wanted to deter Saddam Hussein's use of chemical or nuclear weapons. Russia, a neighbor and former predator, was armed to the teeth. Pakistan, another neighbor, was proliferating apace. But the hard evidence of Iranian nuclear weapons never surfaced. At nonproliferation threat assessment meetings I attended in 1996, an analyst would insist that Iran was a few scant years away from possessing a nuclear arsenal. My colleagues from the Department of Energy and the Arms Control and Disarmament Agency (since dissolved into the State Department) would ask politely for the intelligence to document the assertion. Silence. Whatever the analyst thought he knew would not withstand expert scrutiny.

After the Iraq weapons of mass destruction fiasco it behooves the United States to be skeptical of the information and disinformation provided by Iranian exiles and Israel. In 2003, by the time I resigned, the evidence of Iranian weapons programs available at the ordinary secret level was no more specific than it had been in 1996. In 2005 the judgment of the U.S. intelligence community, at least as leaked to the press, was that it would still take Iran another five to ten years to have a bomb, unless the international community intervened one way or another. Russia (which sold Iran its nuclear reactor at Bushehr) and Pakistan (which secretly sold

Iran uranium enrichment centrifuge technology) are oddly complacent about a nuclear-armed Shiite theocracy on their doorsteps.

With the Russian empire truncated and Iraq in ruins, it would be reasonable for Iranian politicians to conclude that nuclear weapons are too expensive a luxury to be justified by the security threats Iran now faces. Such rationality, however, presupposes Iranian recognition that the United States is a status-quo power as well. At the moment this requires a leap of faith.

Iranian politicians find the "Great Satan" irresistible for domestic political purposes. Iranians are told that the United States and Israel are nuclear-armed and avowedly hostile states that pose an implacable threat to their pious experiment in Islamic governance. In foreign policy, however, Iranian officials are often surprisingly pragmatic. The low-key Iranian response to the massive U.S. troop presence just across its borders in Iraq and Afghanistan is a useful corrective to the U.S. view that Iran is always and everywhere hostile. Iran has more at stake than the United States in its concern for the overall stability of its neighborhood.

Recognizing its demonized role in Iranian domestic politics, the United States wisely agreed in 2004 to cede control of nonproliferation negotiations with Iran to the EU. Extensive trade ties give the EU leverage with the Iranian commercial constituencies that fund the political world. And Iranian politicians cannot turn against the EU the reflexive outrage that greets U.S. diplomatic pressure. Senior French, British, and German officials spent many frustrating hours negotiating with their Iranian counterparts. Iranian leaders refused to sign away Iran's right to enrich uranium for nuclear power generation. This was America's nonnegotiable precondition for sweetening the deal with security and economic guarantees of its own.

Iran's domestic politics are as bitterly divided, nationalistic, and competitive as any other state's. Their tone has hardened under President Mahmoud Ahmadinejad, but even his moderate predecessor insisted that Iran keep its right to a full nuclear fuel cycle, under international safeguards no more onerous than those every other state accepts. Islamic republics, like secular democracies, do not allow their politicians to give away to outsiders any sovereign right. They will rent out such rights on a long-term basis, when the price is right, but such concessions must be shrouded in diplomatic ambiguity. Tehran, however, like Washington, is full of people opportunistically poised to denounce diplomatic ambiguity as proof of incompetence or treason on the part of their rivals.

In the end, it is very difficult for any democratic or semidemocratic state to negotiate a nonproliferation agreement that will be politically acceptable to the United States. As a safely remote superpower, the United States has the luxury of rejecting any deal that does not fulfill all the domestic political aspirations of the administration currently in power. It is safer bureaucratically for U.S. officials to accuse the EU of weakness and the Iranians of intransigence than it is to accept a flawed deal.

The difficulty of negotiations does not mean that Iran is doomed to become a nuclear weapons state. Iran is bound by its own Islamic version of superior morality. In President Ahmadinejad's speech to the UN General Assembly in September 2005, he insisted that use of nuclear weapons was contrary to the moral tenets of Islam. So far, competing Iranian politicians, unlike their Indian counterparts in the 1990s, have refused to link Iran's national security explicitly to the acquisition of nuclear weapons.

The ambiguity of this nuclear stance gives Iranian politicians a relatively free hand at home to embrace or reject nuclear weapons, depending on the international political climate. Iran's leaders currently pay no detectable domestic political price for paying at least lip service to their NPT commitment and, like Japan or Germany, keeping nuclear weapons research on the back burner. That moral sense can be nurtured by the UN and the International Atomic Energy Agency (IAEA) if not by the United States. The threat of U.S. invasion, should it become credible, would make nuclear weapons a political duty for even the most moralistic mullah.

### *Learning to Love the Bomb*

Ronald Reagan horrified his nuclear priesthood at the Reykjavik summit in 1986 by revealing to General Secretary Mikhail Gorbachev that he found the doctrine of mutual assured destruction immoral. Reagan's modern acolytes show few of their hero's moral reservations about using the threat of tens of millions of deaths as political leverage. Instead they bitterly resent the fact that nuclear weapons in the hands of foreigners limit America's freedom of military action. If deterrence works, then it is possible to exclude as laughably unrealistic about 95 percent of the military scenarios used to justify America's spending as much on defense as the rest of the world put together.

The strategic logic of nuclear deterrence is ugly, but the United States has flourished reasonably well under it. Nuclear-armed states do not directly wage war on other nuclear-armed states because the cost-benefit ratio of nuclear war is even worse than it is for ordinary war. Saddam Hussein, who still had a massive chemical weapons arsenal in early 1991, was successfully deterred from using that arsenal against the troops of Desert Storm by the certainty of massive U.S. retaliation, possibly nuclear. As long as one state is not perceived as trying to lock in an unanswerable first-strike advantage over its rivals, nuclear weapons exert a calming effect.

There was an odd sigh of relief in Washington after India and Pakistan detonated their bombs in 1998. Ordinary Americans did not feel any closer to ground zero the day after those tests than they had the day before. In fact, Americans and the world were temporarily slightly safer. First, a source of strategic miscalculation had been eliminated from the Indian subcontinent. Second, the United States could drop the dangerous fantasy of counterproliferation, of shutting down Pakistan's nuclear program by military force. Once Pakistan tested, U.S. pundits stopped proclaiming pompously that the United States would never permit a Muslim country to acquire nuclear weapons.

Security is an unquenchable thirst. When the Pentagon acts out its dream of eliminating every theoretical threat America or its allies might conceivably face, it generates real threats. Canada has enough weapons-grade uranium to assemble at least a half-dozen nuclear weapons in a matter of days and can produce any amount of plutonium it chooses. Yet no one suggests that the United States launch a preemptive strike on Canada's nuclear facilities simply because of the theoretical possibility that Canada could annihilate six major U.S. cities tomorrow in a truck-borne nuclear surprise attack. But if the United States were insane enough to threaten Canada with preemptive attack in the way Vice President Cheney threatened Iran in his January 2005 MSNBC television interview, it would change Canada's security calculation. The threat would create a powerful Canadian political movement to build a credible nuclear deterrent to U.S. aggression.

In 2003 the United States established with absolute certainty that Iraq did not pose a nuclear weapons threat and would not pose one in the next decade or more. The United States paid a trillion dollars for that luxury.[3]

The Turks have an unambitious but useful proverb: "May the snake that does not bite me live a thousand years." Poisonous snakes are still part of the international ecosystem because they are smart enough not to attack humans except when cornered. The United States can sometimes pay snakes to defang themselves, as happened with Libya. The United States also has the option of leaving snakes alone. It will not be the end of the world for the United States if its nonproliferation efforts fail. North Korea probably has nuclear weapons, and the diplomatic minuet goes on. If Iran or Japan or even Venezuela were to acquire nuclear weapons, the United States would adapt in the same calm way it adapted to Pakistan's crossing the nuclear threshold. Suicidal stupidity is rarer than Americans' Hollywood-inflamed imagination suggests, and with competent diplomacy it can generally be deterred at negligible cost.

Deterrence buys time and helps calmer heads prevail in times of crisis. Deterrence, however, is not a solution Americans are satisfied with. Nor should they be. The U.S. government routinely miscalculates. Many foreign governments are less wise, less brave, and more paranoid than America's. As long as deadly weapons exist, there is a real possibility that they will be used. If the U.S. government is serious about making the American people and the planet safe from mass murder, it should be searching frantically for effective arguments to tip the balance in the domestic political debate of aspiring nuclear states. It should also recognize that America's is not currently the voice that can make those arguments credibly to foreigners.

### Nonproliferation Diplomacy and the Double Standard

The Rumsfeld Defense Department is uniquely perverse in publicly rejecting even anodyne limitations on when and how nuclear weapons might be used. The sales pitch for one planned new U.S. nuclear weapon, a deep-earth penetrator for use against underground bunkers, was that the blast would produce so little fallout that the bomb would be usable in enemy cities during an otherwise conventional war. America's ballistic missile defense program (Star Wars) was another attempt to make nuclear weapons seem usable, by reducing the risk of retaliation in kind.

If all states shared the Bush administration view that nuclear weapons are too useful not to brandish, then nonproliferation diplomacy would be a waste of time. But most countries have ratified the NPT and firmly renounced nuclear weapons. These are not only those countries too small and poor to aspire to them. Germany, Japan, and South Korea, like Canada, could assemble nuclear bombs in a matter of weeks. Their politicians, however, respect the power of the domestic constituencies that recoil at such weapons. The U.S. nuclear umbrella helps silence the competing pro-nuclear security arguments, but Japanese and Canadians do not credit U.S. security guarantees for their self-restraint.

Brazil and South Africa both launched ambitious nuclear weapons programs under repressive governments. Now both are regional superpowers with no nuclear security umbrella or perceived need for one. Their new democratic leaders gave them up, recognizing that the bomb and its attendant costs did not serve the security needs of their people. In Brazil's case, a secret nuclear weapons program was fatally discredited by its origin under a cruel, corrupt dictatorship.

When the Soviet Union collapsed, Ukraine, Kazakhstan, and Belarus had weak domestic political constituencies pressing to keep their inherited nuclear arsenals. They were overruled thanks to generous promises of assistance from the international community. Libyan leader Muammar al Qaddafi had never made nuclear weapons part of his political platform. He had a free hand to trade Libya's fledgling uranium enrichment program and nuclear weapon design, purchased from Pakistan, for the end of U.S. sanctions and international isolation.

Nuclear disarmament is perfectly defensible as the rational outcome of a political process, even in countries where the domestic security debate is more irrational than America's own. Americans should understand, however, that in rationally renouncing nuclear weapons no politician on the planet renounces the moral right to have them on an equal basis with the United States and every other sovereign state. This would be a betrayal of the national dignity. On a more practical level, no nuclear state will disarm itself unless any deadly foes do the same. India points to Chinese nuclear weapons as an excuse not to conclude a bilateral nuclear disarmament pact with Pakistan. A globally bellicose United States inserts its own nuclear arsenal unhelpfully into each potential nuclear state's security equation.

The nuclear policies of the Bush administration during 2001–2004 were insanely counterproductive in terms of U.S. national interests. Faced with Rumsfeld's unapologetic double standard, Iranians, North Koreans, and nuclear proliferators yet unborn will find it politically unrewarding to make an accurate cost-benefit analysis of their own nuclear arsenals. The architects of America's policies are brilliant bureaucrats. The prudent conclusion is not that they are incompetent but that Washington's claimed interest in nuclear nonproliferation during President Bush's first term was an exercise in bureaucratic self-promotion that had nothing to do with making Americans safer.

A key test of U.S. sincerity will be the willingness of U.S. bureaucrats to cede the credit for good diplomacy—though not the responsibility—to foreign partners, hiding the U.S. role behind international organizations such as the 2005 Nobel Peace Prize winner, the IAEA. The UN has legitimacy only when it is seen not as a U.S. surrogate but as the united voice of the international community, conveying norms of international behavior accepted by all, including the United States, as binding limits on their freedom of action. At the moment, without a comprehensive test ban treaty or other universally binding nuclear limits, the UN has few tools with which to influence the internal political debate in Iran or North Korea.

America is not currently a useful nuclear target for any of the handful of states with both the means and motive to obtain a nuclear weapon. But the U.S. government cannot use America's relative security to justify nuclear policy incompetence indefinitely. The price of rolling back nuclear weapons is affordable: security guarantees, generous U.S. foreign aid, including for peaceful nuclear programs, and acceptance that nuclear limits apply to all.[4] The diplomatic attention paid to North Korea through revived diplomacy in 2005 is a hopeful sign. The American public would do well to signal that it will no longer tolerate any administration that treats nonproliferation policy simply as bureaucratic self-promotion by other means.

# 13

## ★ The Diplomatic Cost of Clandestine Intelligence ★

*From time to time, God causes men to be born—and thou art one of them—who have a lust to go abroad at the risk of their lives and discover news—today it may be of far-off things, to-morrow of some hidden mountains, and the next day of some nearby men who have done a foolishness against the state. These souls are very few; and of these few, not more than ten are of the best. Among these ten I count the babu, and that is curious. How great, therefore, and desirable must be a business that brazens the heart of a Bengali!*

*Rudyard Kipling*, Kim

Diplomacy and espionage live together in tense symbiosis. Twenty years after the fact I still feel guilty about "Ahmed," the idealistic young university student I found pacing with his lecture notes in the circle of light under the streetlamp outside our raw new villa in Casablanca. Ahmed lived in two rooms with parents and multiple noisy siblings. He was a devout Muslim who had earned entrance to the state university in Arabic philology despite his lack of family connections. Ahmed was determined to make his way in Morocco as a teacher or intellectual. The odds of his success were terribly poor, but he was cramming for his exams in the only clean, well-lighted place he could find.

I ended up inviting Ahmed inside for mint tea and to take the weight off his feet. My French was as bad as his, and my wife and young daughter were a reassuring presence. That evening, and in a handful of chance encounters in the following months, he told me about the rigors of university life, the Muslim brotherhoods, the state imams and Libyan missionaries, and the pervasive campus police

239

informers called AWACS (for Boeing's Airborne Warning and
Control System, a grim little student joke with an anti-U.S. sting in
its tail). This was scarcely "actionable intelligence," but it was for me
a window into an important world.

Decades before 9/11, the State Department and the CIA knew
perfectly well that Muslim anger was something to watch carefully.
New generations of unemployed, semieducated university students
were ticking time bombs throughout the Middle East and North
Africa. One of the secondary goals of the economic reporting officer position in Casablanca in 1985 was to keep an eye on student
politics.

Morocco is a comparatively closed society. In this, my first posting as a real diplomat, I was clueless on how to proceed. My formal
meetings with professors and rectors and the official student organization got me nothing but the emptiest of polite platitudes. But
my conversations with Ahmed were useful information, the core of
a vivid reporting telegram on student politics. The NEA Bureau at
the State Department sent a nice message to encourage more such
reporting, and our ambassador in Rabat praised my work in the
weekly Country Team meeting.

I had "recruited" a useful source. But all I had to offer Ahmed
was tea and sympathy. He conjured up his own hope that this random connection with a U.S. diplomat would somehow help him
find a job. He asked, finally, one day when he was particularly desperate, if there was not some small temporary paid work he could
do for the consulate, translations from Arabic to French, little analy-
ses, or the like. And of course there was not, at least nothing that
could be arranged by a junior officer in a modest consulate in a
State Department that was permanently short of cash. But I was soft-
hearted and did not want to dash his hopes completely. Information
such as his was worth a few dollars to the U.S. government, and I
understood that Ahmed was flirting with the idea of such a
transaction.

I had a quiet talk with a colleague whose organization has cash
it can spend for information. I explained to him that here was an
idealistic young man, a mainstream Muslim semiactivist, hard up
and willing to be of service. Though Ahmed would never be a spy, if
we could find him any plausible chores to do for $40 a month, his
conscience would permit him to provide a flow of general information about the climate of student activism at the university.

A meeting was arranged, and it proved disastrous. Ahmed appeared at my door one last time, angry and shaking, to say that I had
betrayed our friendship. He complained bitterly that this American

friend of mine had asked dangerous political questions that had nothing to do with what we had talked about. I replied that I was sure there had been a terrible misunderstanding. Both Ahmed and I knew that there had not been.

I had been naive. Ahmed's information was of a kind valuable to a political officer trying to understand the overseas political environment. That understanding is a key goal of State Department diplomats and the intelligence analysts back home. Intelligence officers overseas aren't paid to look at the fuzzy big picture. They chase more specific and urgent intelligence targets.

In the course of the interview, Ahmed would have made clear that he had no interest in ratting on any Islamic militant acquaintances, nor did he have access to important political, military, economic, or intelligence circles. An unwitting source like Ahmed is no more than a tiny insurance policy. Intelligence gathering and agent management are agonizingly labor intensive. America's intelligence services are spread too thin to justify, simply for insurance, the case officer time and mandatory security vetting even the most innocuous intelligence relationship requires.

My working relationship with Ahmed need not have been destroyed in the process of rejecting his services. A good-faith interviewer could have reached the negative conclusion quickly and painlessly, and he or I could have given the bad news to Ahmed that he hadn't made the cut for a consulate job. Losing Ahmed as a friend and source was my first hint that I had been fooling myself that my intelligence colleagues saw me as a member of the same team.

## Diplomats and Spies

The pundits on Fox News who begrudge U.S. diplomats their privileged life of cocktail parties assign too much value to free alcohol. Tired political officers who drag themselves to the Latvian National Day get much useful business done. They also help the wider U.S. national security establishment build the personal relationships that allow it to do its work overseas.

The line between a diplomat's overt intelligence collection and the secret intelligence gathering of their evil twins is a blurry one. The demands of World War II convinced Congress and the White House that the world was too interesting and dangerous to leave to diplomats and military attachés. ████████████████████████

The CIA censors ruthlessly any discussion of the "diplomatic cover" that allows intelligence officers to operate safely in foreign countries. Suffice it to say that U.S. intelligence officers are highly dedicated professionals. Their commitment to secrecy is absolute. Still, as a retired CIA officer told the *Chicago Tribune* regarding Valerie Plame's diplomatic service in Athens, it is prudent to assume that the host government has a pretty good idea who most intelligence officers are.[1] A great deal of intelligence work is liaison with host-country intelligence services. U.S. spies talk to local spies, bartering information and cooperating against intelligence targets of mutual interest.

A friendly government keeps track of U.S. government employees with a light hand. Even when intelligence gathering is detected, it is often left unchallenged, partly out of good manners toward the sole superpower and partly because sensible intelligence services would rather not reveal how much they know. They prefer to keep careful tabs rather than expel anyone and then have to absorb the relocation expenses for the inevitable retaliatory expulsion of their equivalent spy in Washington.

A spy case that becomes public knowledge creates a much greater domestic political problem for the host government than it does for the United States. It is practically impossible to craft a response tough enough to satisfy public opinion but mild enough not to sabotage valuable intelligence liaison relationships. Governments understand that it is good politics to ignore the behavior of errant diplomats in all but the most public and embarrassing circumstances.

## Policy and Image

Any sophisticated foreigner meeting an American (or Russian, British, French, Chinese, or Israeli) diplomat for the first time will always wonder whom he is actually meeting. In Greece in the 1980s, members of the conservative opposition party liked to believe that "real" U.S. policy was made by the CIA and that talking to State Department functionaries was a waste of time. Some diplomats adapted smoothly to this.

More often this assumption worked to a diplomat's detriment. The Panhellenic Socialist Movement (PASOK) of Andreas Papandreou had sprung out of leftist resistance to the Greek military dictatorship of 1967–74. The resistance movement, some of whose members became cabinet ministers in the PASOK government, was convinced that the CIA had actively aided the junta in persecuting them and was now attempting to thwart their dreams of a socialist paradise in Greece.

This belief made PASOK a harder nut for U.S. diplomats to crack. Prime Minister and PASOK leader Papandreou, a former U.S.

citizen himself, used fear of the CIA bogeyman as one of his ways to keep his party's relations with the Americans under his tight personal control. In my efforts to cultivate other PASOK voices, indiscriminate anti-Americanism was less a problem than suspicion about my employer. Occasionally, as well, journalists and diplomats punish real or imagined slights by spreading spy rumors. Contacts then turn mysteriously cold. ████████████████████████████

## *The Information Market*

"A secret kept is a secret wasted," said Oscar Wilde, and of course he was right. Information is a commodity that can be traded for cash or influence or at least other information. The trading value of information is determined by scarcity and novelty more than truth. There is a strong incentive to make everything secret simply to increase that value. Hoarded secrets are an important part of any country's diplomatic capital.

Secrets age badly, however. A few months or years strip most secrets of their power to help or harm. Secrets also tend to be shared by people who cannot fully trust one another. The first divulger of a given secret generally gets the bulk of the benefit. There is thus an incentive to disclose secrets, preferably to the person who values them most.

One of the virtues of having grown up in Silicon Valley as it was being created was to see firsthand that information, unlike other commodities, multiplies in volume and quality by being shared without immediate payment. This is a useful doctrine for the State Department, whose permanent poverty does not give it the option of paying cash for information.

Like any diplomat, I spent a substantial part of my time trying to persuade people that the world would profit from their sharing their information with me for free, or at worst for the price of lunch at a decent restaurant. Being articulate and sensitive got me a discount sometimes, especially with the intelligent and embittered women civil servants who do the bulk of the actual work at most Greek public sector institutions. Usually, however, I would have to trade information of my own. A pithy factoid or two from an unclassified State Department cable cobbled together with the latest from the *International Herald Tribune* would often be good enough. Still, access to seriously useful information would dry up if I were not an informed and informative interlocutor, willing to say more than the State Department was prepared to announce publicly.

I did well as an information gatherer and analyst by being relatively open and honest with my foreign interlocutors about U.S.

policy. The appearance of indiscretion ("sunshine in government" was Clinton's gentler term) encourages indiscretion on the other side. Diplomats succeed by appealing to the better side of human nature, to shared interests and values, and to shared culture and humanity, and shared pseudo-secrets are an excellent way to break the ice.

Intelligence officers, however, look for human weakness rather than human strength. On a planet swarming with underpaid bureaucrats, finding vulnerable officials with vices too costly for their income is not too hard. The ability to offer cash, however, supports a zero-sum, dysfunctional logic in which even the most innocent and mutually beneficial fact comes with a price tag attached.

I cannot claim that I ever learned the identity of a single clandestine source. Unlike one colleague, I never had a good contact bought away from me. I came to realize, however, slowly over years of oblique conversations, that the fact that some people pay money for secret information made it more difficult for me to coax even the most harmless information out of foreigners for free.

### Covert Operations and the Uncertainty Principle

If the only price Americans paid for U.S. clandestine intelligence collection efforts was a classified number of billions of dollars per year and minor inconvenience to State Department employees, this chapter would have no business being written. Diplomats and intelligence officers are on the same team, America's team. Plenty of people in the CIA are convinced, like plenty of people in the State Department, that diplomacy and intelligence are interdependent partners in defending America's interests around the globe. In an urgent crisis interagency teamwork can be exhilarating indeed.

In the absence of a unifying crisis, however, U.S. embassies reflect the competition that marks the interagency bureaucratic process back in Washington. There is a permanent quiet struggle for resources and headlines and influence. The CIA survives and thrives by convincing the U.S. president that, even when its answers are dead wrong, they meet the political needs of the White House better than the State Department's answers.

Greeks tell a joke: Spying is pointless in two countries, China and Greece; in China because no one talks and in Greece because everyone does. Romanians and Indians tell this same joke on themselves, Arabs gossip incessantly about politics, and I'm not sure that even the Chinese fully live up to their taciturn reputation. Diplomats can discover an amazing percentage of what they need to know simply by asking two or three people sympathetic questions based on a careful reading of the morning newspaper.

The CIA felt in 1990 (and with luck still feels) under strong competitive pressure to justify its budget by producing information that is both secret and useful to U.S. interests. Competition between diplomats and intelligence-gatherers is healthy. It is a fine thing to have two groups of bright people look at the same problem from different angles and see who calls the situation most accurately. As a young political officer in Athens, I gloated when I called three successive Greek parliamentary elections better than my rivals.

A clandestine source can tell—at best—only what he knows. During those elections, the CIA was victimized by wishful thinking. Its Greek sources cared deeply who won, believed their side was going to win, and made a point of signaling to Washington that Greek-U.S. intelligence cooperation would be easier once they came to power and fired all the obstructionist bastards from the previous government. Only a couple of no-hope monarchists ever bothered to promise me anything similar.

Getting the Greek elections wrong was a mistake that had no practical implications for U.S. interests. Occasional reminders that the CIA is not omniscient and omnipresent actually helped U.S.-Greek relations. There would have been a hefty foreign policy cost for the United States, however, if the CIA had felt its stake in getting the elections right was urgent enough to cause it to intervene directly in the Greek political process.

One mantra of the management gurus is "the only way to predict the future is to create it." The only certain way of monitoring the activities of a terrorist group is by becoming a terrorist oneself. Only by playing an active role in a country's internal political or bureaucratic struggles can an intelligence service assure its ability to predict events correctly.

Even by the late 1980s information had come into the public domain about CIA covert interventions in European domestic politics in the 1950s and 1960s. The U.S. goal, shared by European rightists, was to reduce the risk that leftist parties would come to power through democratic elections and then unveil a hidden devotion to Moscow. Twenty years after these interventions, many Greeks, Italians, and others still firmly believed that briefcases full of cash backed CIA election predictions. Democratic legitimacy is a scarce commodity, scarcer than cash. If Greek political parties took money from foreigners (and I have no information to that effect), I would not be surprised if they lost more than they gained.

Greeks prefer to believe the myth that their disastrous 1967–74 military dictatorship was imposed on them by the United States. In the process of embarrassing their country internationally and giving anticommunism a bad name, the Greek junta handed Turkey a perfect excuse to invade and partition Cyprus in 1974. Still unresolved, the Cyprus conflict has blighted the faith in humankind of almost everyone unfortunate enough to have to deal with it. It is now a major barrier to Turkey's hopes of joining the European Union, hopes the United States sees as strongly in America's interests.

Perhaps the CIA did not realize that its work of keeping an eye on Greek military conspiracies would be interpreted erroneously as a signal that the U.S. government favored a coup. Declassified documents show that by 1966 U.S. clandestine services were well aware of the instability of the Greek political situation and had identified participants of a "military conspiratorial group." In 1967 members of that group overthrew the government and formed a military junta.[2]

But toleration of a military coup was not U.S. government policy in Greece. When the coup finally came, the U.S. embassy in Athens, the State Department, and the White House were caught flat-footed. Most (though not all) of the U.S. government recognized that the communist menace to Greece was not urgent enough to justify having handed the Soviet Union such a propaganda gift. The United States defended its damaged reputation by imposing a strategically costly arms embargo on Greece.

Over the next six years ▮▮▮▮▮ and U.S. military argued strongly that relations with the dictatorship ought to be normalized. President Richard Nixon and Henry Kissinger were so much the prisoners of their Cold War logic, so intent on strengthening military and intelligence alliances, that they happily sacrificed America's image in Greece for the next twenty-five years. Gen. Dimitris Ioannidis, the last and dumbest of the ruling junta, was misled by the silence (or worse) of his ▮▮▮▮▮ contacts into believing he had America's authorization to intervene on the island of Cyprus and topple Archbishop Makarios III, the elected president. President Clinton finally apologized to Greece in 1999 for U.S. cooperation with the junta.

▮▮▮▮▮▮▮▮▮▮▮▮▮▮▮▮▮▮▮▮▮▮▮▮▮▮▮▮▮▮▮▮▮

▮▮▮▮▮▮▮▮▮▮▮▮▮▮

Subatomic particles do not take on a single quantum state until that state is measured. At a human scale as well, the questions asked influence the answers. Worming out information about the intentions of foreign powers is difficult, because the motives of most politicians and bureaucrats are mixed and obscure even to themselves. Politicians study the shifting balances of interests within their country up until the last possible moment, when a parliamentary deadline, a media leak, an official visitor, or a pointed question from the representative of a superpower triggers a decision.

Diplomats and other intelligence collectors insert themselves, subtly or otherwise, into foreign decision-making processes. When a given issue is hopelessly deadlocked within a bureaucracy, perceived U.S. pressure in a given direction can be a decisive factor, one way or another. The State Department is mandated to make sure *all* U.S. interests are taken into account in deciding U.S. policy. Ideally, questions of a foreign government are asked with full sensitivity to the impact the process of asking will have on U.S. interests. The CIA's interest is often more limited and selfish; it is to provide the director of central intelligence with something juicy to tell the president. When a clandestine service makes policy by the manner in which it gathers that intelligence, America's broader national interests can be (and in Greece certainly were) harmed.

### *Private Wars*

The fact that the CIA is clandestine does not protect the United States when covert operations violate America's founding principles of freedom, democracy, human rights, and justice for all. Conservative ideologues have justified the presence of American officials as spectators or worse in the torture chambers of dictators from countries from Argentina to Uzbekistan by stressing the idea that torture is a necessary concession to America's wars with communism or "Islamo-fascist" terrorism. In my experience, however, such wars should not be America's.

I described in chapter 11 the CIA's war against the Greek terrorist group 17 November. The CIA's pursuit of vengeance for the murder of its Athens chief in 1975 was a source of bilateral friction for two decades. The CIA's zeal does not necessarily track with America's broader security needs.

When I came to the Romania Desk of the State Department in 1992 and began reading CIA intelligence reports on Romania, I suddenly began to wonder whether the CIA was worth paying for at all. The small amount of intelligence disseminated on Romania was a litany of treachery and corruption. According to CIA sources, key politicians were in Russian pockets and Romania, despite its desperate denials, was concealing chemical weapons. Compared against U.S. embassy reports, information from Romanian diplomats, and Romania's overarching self-interest in winning Western guarantees of its independence from Moscow, the CIA reports made no sense.

I gradually concluded that the CIA had unwittingly been recruited as an agent of influence of Romanian opposition political parties determined to oust the current Romanian President Ion Iliescu. I speculate that this was the result of case officers' misplaced loyalty to clandestine sources who had risked execution during the Ceausescu period. Romania's domestic political battle was not America's war, however, and the CIA had no business taking sides in it. Events were to prove that the CIA had been misinformed. Iliescu, returned to power by the voters four years after losing a fair election to the opposition, was the "crypto-communist" who brought Romania into NATO and offered his country as a willing and eager base for U.S. military operations.

Today in Afghanistan, U.S. policy, as represented by the U.S. embassy in Kabul, is to strengthen Afghan president Hamid Karzai's control over the whole country. America's national interests there include security, democracy, and eradication of opium poppies. The CIA's covert mission, however, works at cross-purposes to these national interests. CIA case officers arm, pay, and train local warlords to pursue Bin Laden and the Taliban. The goal of the warlords is to protect their hard-won independence and revenues from the Karzai government, not to deepen their blood feuds with fellow Afghans by fighting as America's proxies. The contradiction between CIA tactical convenience and the long-term strategy of unifying Afghanistan is ultimately too brutal to ignore.

For forty years the CIA failed catastrophically at the principal task of its struggle with the USSR: to accurately estimate Soviet intentions and capabilities. The collapse of the Soviet Union made clear how massively the CIA had exaggerated Soviet power and how poorly it had read Soviet intentions. The Soviet Union was admittedly a hard target. Individual CIA analysts got various pieces of the puzzle right. Overall, however, the performance of the U.S. intelligence community made sense only if the goal was not containing the Soviet threat but rather supporting the Pentagon and the defense contractors in their war to secure funding for the most ornate and expensive new weapons systems imaginable.

What is heartening is how tiny a role intelligence victories and defeats actually play in most conflicts. The United States uncovered a steady trickle of American traitors who had sold precious information about U.S. military and intelligence capabilities to the Soviets, the Hungarians, the Israelis, and even the Greeks. In 1990 two U.S. Army sergeants were arrested for having, over the past several years, passed to the Hungarian secret services many of NATO's most precious secrets, including its war plans and the location of U.S. nuclear weapons. If the Soviets had been planning war, this stolen information would have given them a massive advantage.

Whether the CIA had ever stolen material of offsetting defensive value is unclear. The shadow world in which spies battle one another is so self-contained, so irrelevant to the real arena in which the United States and Soviet Union jousted for influence, that it seems to have made no practical difference that the KGB frequently bested the U.S. intelligence agencies in espionage. Thanks to Aldrich Ames (CIA) and Robert Hanssen (FBI), who sold their services to the KGB for cash and remained undetected all through the 1980s, the KGB was able to shut down the CIA's Soviet spy networks almost completely. Yet this made no difference to the outcome of the Cold War.

### Reducing the Cost of Intelligence

In an age of global threats and problems, the United States needs close, effective liaison with intelligence services around the world, by Americans who can build personal relationships with capable foreign spies based on sharing the unique corporate culture of the clandestine intelligence world. Rarely, more rarely than it believes, the United States needs its own covert operations to make up for the incapacity or unwillingness of America's foreign partners.

It would be a disaster to hand any more responsibility for intelligence collection to the Pentagon. The Pentagon has plenty of private wars of its own to blinker its analytical capabilities and lead it into quicksand. One of the catastrophic consequences of Secretary Rumsfeld's attempted expansion of Defense Department human intelligence collection would be destruction of the weak safety net that now protects against foreign relations fiascos: the authority given the U.S. ambassador in each country to oversee intelligence operations as the president's designated representative.

I have met CIA officers, particularly from a generation now retired, who were incredibly smart, charming, and well briefed, as diplomatic as the best U.S. diplomats. On average, however, real diplomats tend to be more attuned to the fine points of U.S. foreign policy and more aware of the cost to U.S. interests when Americans act badly. The CIA recruits officers with a clear, sometimes religious, sense of the battle between good and evil. This mind-set makes them less than ideal as official mouthpieces of U.S. policy. I still wince at the many stupid things I have said to foreigners over the years in the process of trying to learn my diplomatic trade. But I wince as well when I think how many foreigners have heard superficial and schematic views of U.S. foreign policy. To the extent that America's image in the world is shaped by U.S. officials abroad rather than the president and secretary of state at home, let that image be of a well-informed superpower able to enunciate and defend its policies with logic, nuance, and eloquence.

The best way to encourage the CIA to be a disciplined instrument of a single, coordinated U.S. foreign policy is to rebuild the CIA with fewer secrets but better ones. The State Department and CIA do not work effectively together now except on the basis of individual relations of trust. Given my depiction of the CIA, it may sound paradoxical to urge reducing the sharp intellectual and bureaucratic separation between intelligence and diplomacy. Only bold reform, however, will reduce the institutional contempt of the spies for the "cookie pushers" and enforce a culture of communication and mutual benefit.

The boldest step of such reform would be to integrate the recruitment and personnel systems of State and CIA into a combined Foreign Service system. Diplomacy and intelligence collection draw from closely overlapping talent pools. The current role of the CIA as a counterinsurgency force in Afghanistan paints a misleading picture of the spectrum of skills required. The CIA needs hard-headed idealists with cultural sensitivity, political savvy, foreign languages, and people skills. So does the State Department. Those with analytic and writing skills should be political and economic officers, and those with a taste for manipulation and nifty hardware should join the dark side.

If State and CIA recruits had their initial training together, each would learn greater respect for their shared mission. Their corporate cultures would become less incompatible. This would allow greater functional integration overseas, including harmonization of reporting formats, source-protection standards, and classification/declassification procedures to make sure information is distributed based on its utility to policy makers, not its bureaucratic origin.

With more cross-postings between Langley and Foggy Bottom, intelligence officers would get a better idea of what U.S. policy really is. Any diplomat bound for ambassadorial rank would do well to experience from inside the triumphs and otherwise of the covert world.

The work of the CIA Directorate of Intelligence and the analysts in State's Bureau of Intelligence and Research (INR) overlap enormously. A fraction the size, INR won itself glory in 2002 by being less wrong than the other intelligence agencies on Iraqi weapons of mass destruction. This reflects the realist institutional biases of the State Department but also the fact that INR is often the parking place for foreign service officers whose analytical skills are better than their bureaucratic ones. If bureaucratic rivalries were reduced, INR could be abolished in favor of housing those same officers at CIA headquarters. The goal, wherever they sit, is to protect U.S. foreign policy from the illusion that secret intelligence has the best answers.

### Listening to Ahmed

Successive U.S. presidents have found their cooperation with the kings of Morocco quite useful. Much of that cooperation used to happen through intelligence channels established as far back as the 1950s by famous cold warriors like Vernon Walters. Such officers found it easy and pleasant to drink mint tea in the palaces of Rabat and Casablanca, trade lurid Middle Eastern political gossip (the Saudi princes who pass through Casablanca looking for virgins to debauch are an endless source), and dismiss as trivial the price America pays for Moroccan support of the Middle East peace process and counterterrorism cooperation.

In 1979 in Iran, Americans were horrified to discover the true cost of U.S. friendship with the shah. When he was overthrown, America became the "Great Satan" to two generations of Iranians. Mohammed VI of Morocco is not the shah. With luck his careful reforms will succeed. Very likely the U.S. relationship with His Sherifian Majesty benefits the Moroccan population and U.S. national interests. I believed this when I served in Morocco under Mohammed VI's father, and I hope it is true today. Weighing the costs and benefits of cooperation with an autocratic regime is the hardest judgment a diplomat can make. Without listening to the Ahmeds of the world, diplomats cannot know the true terms of their devil's bargains.

Talking to Ahmed is far more difficult now than it was in 1986. In the current security climate, my replacement in Casablanca would be scolded by the post security officer for venturing into conversation with a young Islamic male loitering outside his house. The Moroccan police would drag Ahmed to the police station for photographs, fingerprinting, and an ungentle interrogation before cautioning him to find a safer streetlight to study under. What idealistic Ahmed, with Abu Ghraib prison fresh in his mind, would consent to be drawn into conversation about Islamic politics with a representative of the U.S. crusaders? I would find it safer to assume now that such an earnest young man was either a plant of an intelligence service or else a watcher for a terrorist group.

A melancholy lesson, one of the hardest for a soft-hearted diplomat, is that the U.S. government is not in the business of helping foreigners. The assistance America gives is designed to serve U.S. interests, and helping others is only a happy byproduct. If I wanted to help Ahmed, I was on my own. I should have paid him to teach me Arabic, but I should never have entangled him, however briefly and innocently, in the cruel, expensive world of secret intelligence.

# 14

## ★ *Diplomatic Skepticism and the Lessons of Iraq* ★

*Remember, when the nuns tell you to beware of the deceptions of men who make love to you, that the mind of man is on the whole less tortuous when he is love-making than at any other time. It is when he speaks of governments and armies that he utters strange and dangerous nonsense to please the bats at the back of his soul.*
*Rebecca West*, Black Lamb and Grey Falcon

I came to dread the distinctive telephone voice of Warren Medoff, my Florida con man—knowledgeable, insinuating, patient, but somehow with a hint of menace. I played an educational bit part in one of his business deals back in 1993. Medoff had set his sights on the Romanian government. This fledgling democracy was trying to persuade international banks to lend it money to prop up an economy that had collapsed with the fall of the Soviet Union. Failing that, it wanted to be annexed as the fifty-first U.S. state. Any friendly American in a well-tailored suit could fleece the Romanians in a heartbeat.

Medoff introduced his thrilling Balkan tale by dropping names of alleged CIA contacts in Florida. According to secret but very highly placed Romanian sources, Romania was not as poor as it seemed. The late dictator Nicolae Ceausescu had squirreled away billions of dollars in Swiss banks before he was ousted and executed in 1990, and his fortune was not lost forever. The bad news was that corrupt officials high up in the Romanian government controlled the secret accounts. Such corruption would be enough to bring down the whole state, if revealed. Still, Medoff could get at Ceausescu's billions without causing a scandal. The hidden fortune could be used to obtain

"prime bank guarantees," on the basis of which Romania could bor-
row the billions it needed. Absolute secrecy was vital.

These days anyone with an e-mail account encounters a similar
scenario about once a week courtesy of the heirs of some defunct
Nigerian official. Back then, my economic colleague Alec and I
breathlessly wrote up Medoff's claim in a secret/no distribution
memorandum to the assistant secretary and a telegram to the U.S.
ambassador to Romania. Among the names Medoff had dropped
were two the U.S. embassy in Bucharest knew pretty well, and parts
of the story could be checked. We were also alert enough to recognize that Medoff's line about "prime bank guarantees" echoed a
financial scam the *Washington Post* had reported.

The fraud expert at the Federal Reserve Bank confirmed that
Medoff's spiel was that of a con man, not a financier. We sent a memo
through State Department liaison to the Department of Justice. But
it was unclear what crime Medoff was trying to commit. If Ceausescu's
fortune didn't exist, he couldn't steal it. Nor could he hope to bilk
an impoverished State Department out of much more than my lunch
money.

Accusing fellow Romanians of corruption is a Romanian national sport, not an exercise in civic virtue, and Medoff's alleged
sources were hardly trustworthy. Still, to protect U.S. policy, which
was to lock Romania firmly into the Western alliance before Russia
could recover and drag the Romanians back, Alec and I had every
incentive to keep this affair secret. Not everyone in Washington
agreed with this policy. Energetic Romanian exiles eager to keep
their right to political asylum in America had predisposed Congress
and others to believe any scurrilous gossip. The Appropriations
Committee would cut the Romanian government off without a dime
if word of a potential scandal leaked out. Valuable time was lost before we dared take the CIA and the Romanian embassy economic
chief into our confidence. The CIA told us nothing useful, but our
Romanian embassy ally Mihai called friends in Bucharest and pieced
together the story. He was a few hours too late.

Medoff lured a Romanian deputy finance minister to the United
States with promises of a huge bank loan. From a hotel room in New
York, Medoff placed a call to me at the State Department. When he
handed the phone to the poor Romanian gentleman, I should have
hung up. Instead I told him as slowly and clearly as I could that
Romania was involved in negotiations with the World Bank and IMF,
that Romania could not afford to make any mistakes, and that he
should authorize everything with the World Bank before he signed
anything. The jet-lagged deputy minister understood even less

English than he spoke, and his interpreter, if he had one, must have been one of Medoff's confederates. He also knew what he wanted to believe. He signed.

The Romanian embassy got a copy of the contract the next day. All the talk of prime bank guarantees and hidden fortunes had evaporated. The government of Romania had just hired Medoff as a consultant, for a fee of $250,000, to use his "best efforts" to secure foreign bank loans for Romania. The kicker was a clause according to which, should the Romanian government actually land any loans from any source, Medoff would get a percentage of the proceeds. Their embassy spent the remainder of its operating budget to hire a lawyer, who concluded it would be cheaper to pay Medoff to go away than to advertise a deputy minister's stupidity to the Romanian public and the international financial community. This, alas, is behavior con men can count on.

Part of the State Department's work is to encourage foreign governments to employ U.S. businesses, some of which provide services a moral person might find more distasteful than Medoff's foray into international finance. By prevailing business standards in Washington, Medoff had earned his quarter million. I disagree with these standards, and not only out of wounded vanity for being Medoff's stage prop or even because I have a liberal's distaste for fleecing the innocent. The United States had accepted Romania as an ally rather hesitantly. Ten years later, lumbering toward Iraq, Americans discovered what a wise decision that had been. Robbing loyal allies is a stupid strategy.

But there is a more basic reason not to be an accessory to fraud. Romanians are not the only people who are gullible. Medoff went on to entrap White House Chief of Staff Harold Ickes in a campaign fund-raising scandal. Ickes ended up calling Medoff his "personal favorite" of all the scoundrels that plagued the Clinton White House.[1] A prudent superpower would take its swindlers off the streets.

### School for Swindle

The United States is a magnet for confidence men from all around the planet. First, Washington is where much of the world's money and decision making are concentrated. Second, Americans elevate their prejudices and preferences to the mythic stature of "American common sense," and this inflated self-assurance is a tempting target. Third, the sheer size of the U.S. government implies that the system can't share information quickly or reliably, even when the rules of U.S. bureaucratic competition permit it. And fourth, the United States is an open society with a praiseworthy desire to be

loved by all and a political system that rewards foreigners who profess that love.

A U.S. diplomat's life is routinely enlivened by heavily accented
attempts to enlist the United States in dubious schemes. Fortunately,
diplomats are not thrust helpless onto the diplomatic circuit. Our
training in skepticism starts at the nonimmigrant visa window of
U.S. embassies and consulates around the world. Brand new U.S.
vice consuls spend six or more hours a day listening to foreigners
who have spent weeks concocting the story that will convince America
to give them a visa. Some of the applicants are brilliant. Some are
simply demented. But after a few months of hearing what foreigners
think the United States wants to hear, new diplomats catch on that
people do not always tell the truth to American officials.

I was too fortunate in some respects. After five months on the
visa line at U.S. Embassy Tel Aviv I was kicked upstairs to be the
ambassador's aide. Therefore, I was no longer in the visa section to
blush when the first blue sheets came back from the Immigration
and Naturalization Service to tell me that some Israeli to whom I
had issued a tourist visa to visit Disney World had just applied for
permanent residence to rejoin the wife, children and taxicab he
hadn't mentioned during the interview. But the knowledge that I
could be fooled, and fooled pretty easily, is a useful corrective to the
intellectual vanity with which aspiring young diplomats emerge from
graduate school.

In 1993 I failed to prevent a Florida con man from bilking the
government of Romania out of $250,000. It would have been an act
of megalomania in 2003 to think that as a mid-level foreign service
officer in Athens I could have persuaded Washington that invading
Iraq would be a similar, equally avoidable swindle. The most senior
officials in the U.S. government, men and women far smarter and
tougher than I, were in the process of showing a horrified but
secretly gratified world that a wealthy superpower, with the largest
intelligence service in the world, is no less vulnerable to being flim-
flammed by con men, Iraqi exiles in this case, than my Romanians.

### Preemptive War

The United States opened the war with Iraq on March 19, 2003,
two days earlier than planned, with a fiendish barrage of Tomahawk
missiles and bunker-busting bombs on the Dora Farms compound
near Baghdad. The reason for jumping the gun was a major U.S.
intelligence coup. The CIA had penetrated Saddam Hussein's security and pinpointed his location in real time for a "decapitation"
strike. Hopes were high. Even if Saddam survived in his buried bun-

ker, he was in no shape to give orders. A month after the strike, journalists interviewed the U.S. officer in charge of finding Saddam's DNA in the wreckage. Not only was there no dead Saddam in the bunker, there was no bunker. The CIA had been misinformed.[2]

American soldiers are brave. They were reasonably confident that Saddam Hussein did not have nuclear weapons. Still, U.S. troops *knew* that Iraq had bunkers full of artillery shells loaded with nerve gas and botulinum toxin. As they sweltered in their chem-bio protective suits, U.S. troops fully expected that the Iraqis would unleash a deadly barrage once the main defensive line around Baghdad had been breached. But that barrage never came. The weapons of mass destruction (WMD) bunkers had been empty for over a decade, the key facilities destroyed or under UN seal. U.S. troops had been misinformed.

President Bush is a patriotic Methodist. American politicians do not launch wars for domestic political benefit or to give oil contracts to their friends. But America is not a charity either. Bush would not have launched a war costing tens of thousands of lives, hundreds of billions of dollars, and the blackening of America's global reputation merely to rid the Iraqi people of an intermittently murderous tyrant. Nor would the U.S. Congress have authorized the use of force without the conviction that Saddam's Iraq constituted an urgent threat to America's security and the peace of the world.

The U.S. political consensus for the Iraq War (neatly stated at appendix B) was clear and public. It depended on three premises: First, Saddam Hussein still had WMD, even though the UN inspectors could not find them. Second, Saddam was a madman motivated by irrational hatred of the United States intense enough to risk suicide by using WMD against U.S. interests. And third, legitimate leadership alternatives were waiting in exile, so no long U.S. military occupation of Iraq would be required. President Bush believed all three so firmly that he did not even bother to ask his experts in the intelligence community about them until months after he had made his decision for war. He was misinformed.

At the heart of the war was a decade's worth of misinformation provided to the U.S. government by an Iraqi exile named Ahmed Chalabi and his associates. By fabricating evidence of Saddam's continuing violations of UN Security Council (UNSC) resolutions regarding WMD, Chalabi made the war seem legal in U.S. eyes. By persuading Vice President Cheney that the Iraqi National Congress would be accepted as a legitimate replacement to Saddam, Chalabi made postwar occupation and reconstruction seem affordable. He persuaded naive Jewish neoconservatives that he would make post-

Saddam Iraq a pro-Israel democracy, with an oil pipeline to Haifa. He reassured rabid anti-UN zealots that the UN weapons inspection process had failed, when in fact it had succeeded. He handed Rumsfeld and the Pentagon an apparently well-placed intelligence capacity to outflank its CIA rivals. He promised military bases in Iraq to replace America's politically unsustainable presence in Saudi Arabia. He promised oil to the oil companies, reconstruction contracts to the businesspeople, and democracy to the human rights organizations. Most important, he promised President Bush a glorious victory in his otherwise inconclusive war on terrorism.

I wonder how sheltered a life Vice President Cheney and Defense Secretary Rumsfeld must have lived to have been so easily manipulated by an indicted embezzler who had already been written off by both the CIA and the State Department as a swindler. I like to think that, if Cheney had been forced to interview desperate Palestinian student visa applicants from Gaza or had been humiliated by Warren Medoff, he would have been more suspicious of Chalabi and others with such a gift for figuring out what he wanted to hear.

### Iraq as a Legacy of Past Mistakes

America's mistakes on the Iraq issue predated the Bush administration. The American zealots who dominated the multinational UN weapons inspection process since 1991 gravely misled President Clinton. Their first, most basic analytical blunder was to rigidly assume what they were trying to prove: that weapons stockpiles and labs continued to exist after the dismantling of the main programs and arsenals in 1991. This assumption was a necessary hypothesis for designing an intrusive inspection program and an excellent rhetorical strategy for squeezing the Iraqi government for information. It was catastrophic, however, as an analytical tool for judging the reliability of Iraqi sources of information. In practice, any truthful Iraqi who contradicted the inspectors' preconceptions by telling them that Iraq had disarmed itself was automatically invalidated as a source. Only gifted and persistent liars stood any chance of being believed.

Technically very competent indeed, the UN inspectors relentlessly unearthed information the Iraqis had tried to conceal about the extent of the WMD programs Saddam had ordered destroyed. This information was accepted as proof of Saddam's cunning and evil intentions but rejected as proof of his current compliance. It did not occur to these tough-minded realists that a political leader might sacrifice military capabilities that cost him draconian economic sanctions and anyway were too dangerous to use.

Second, the United States destroyed the political legitimacy of the inspection process when President Clinton and Secretary of State Madeleine Albright made clear to Saddam Hussein and the world that the United States would not permit UN sanctions to be lifted no matter how complete Saddam's compliance with the UNSC resolutions on WMD. Driven by congressional conservatives and misleading intelligence, the Clinton administration embraced the goal of Saddam's ouster, though this was not what the UNSC had agreed to when it imposed sanctions. This misuse of the sanctions regime left the United States open to damaging charges of murdering Iraqi babies by denying them milk and medicines.[3] It also left the fear of invasion as Saddam's only incentive for full cooperation with the UN inspectors.

Third, the inspectors forgot who they were. Halfway through the inspection process, elements of the UN team loyally took on the incompatible parallel mission of overthrowing Saddam Hussein in accordance with the wishes of the U.S. Congress and Mr. Chalabi. Neither Clinton nor Bush focused on the small but crucial distinction between Saddam's grudging willingness to comply with the letter of UNSC resolutions and his absolute refusal to be a party to his own non-UN-mandated overthrow.[4]

Fourth, the United States had no diplomatic presence in Baghdad that could talk to Saddam or his people and figure out what drove their superficially puzzling behavior. The United States did not factor in the exaggerated appreciation of U.S. intelligence capabilities that most foreigners maintained until the Iraq WMD debacle. Saddam could not have imagined that the U.S. government was unaware that his stockpiles were gone. Saddam's own son-in-law Hussein Kamel had defected to Jordan in 1995 to carry that very message. Saddam was behaving in accordance with his logical conclusion that the UN inspection process was undertaken in bad faith to humiliate him publicly and to probe Iraq's military defenses for a U.S. push to topple him.

President Clinton unfortunately believed his intelligence community's assessment that Saddam's behavior was that of a madman with much to hide. The Iraqi dictator threatened to shut down the inspections but always backed off under U.S. military threats. In the end, as President Bush forgot, Saddam Hussein did not expel the UN weapons inspectors; rather President Clinton did. Clinton's 1998 cruise missile strike, pointless because there was no valid policy objective it could achieve in Iraq, helped convince Bush that only an invasion would suffice.

## *Living in the Shadow World*

It is human nature to trust our own sources more than someone else's and to value information we buy or steal more highly than information we are given for free. The widespread belief that there is a "real" story out there, one only spies can uncover, shows a fundamental misunderstanding of the information universe we inhabit.

George W. Bush admitted once in an interview that he rarely reads newspapers. He relies on his morning intelligence briefing and what his aides tell him for his information. The *President's Daily Brief* contains a dazzling variety of amazing and titillating secret information, material far too sensitive for U.S. diplomats to see. But trying to direct U.S. foreign policy on the basis of information in the brief is like asking Mayor Michael Bloomberg to run New York City on the basis of FBI wiretaps of the major mafia families. Such information is colorful and interesting and much of it is true, but underworld gossip dangerously understates the less disagreeable side of the politicians with whom the mayor does business. So does U.S. intelligence community gossip.

At least 95 percent of human activity occurs on the surface. People have certain wants and needs and certain ways of fulfilling them, most of which cannot be hidden from the people around them. Most of the time, like ordinary people, politicians do pretty much what they say publicly they are going to do, for reasons that may not be identical to but certainly are inseparable from the reasons they give publicly. Their lives are dictated by the morning's headlines and what they must say on television this evening. A seamy and corrupt underside exists, yes, but politicians cannot afford to spend very much time there. Nor can they be madmen or even amoral sociopaths. Their rise to power rests on their ability to operate successfully within human society, at least until they attain so much power that society no longer can punish them.

The CIA and the National Security Agency (NSA) are not paid to report information that can be found in the newspapers or by talking openly to journalists and politicians and academics. That job belongs to the diplomats of the State Department. The CIA talks to corrupt businesspeople, suborned officials, and defectors motivated by hatred of the regime they left. When the NSA eavesdrops on telephone conversations, what it chooses to pass on to policymakers is not the 99.9 percent that consists of harmless chitchat or repetitions of stories from CNN but rather the lurid and interesting indications of evil schemes and evil motives. Those who rely on secret intelligence for their knowledge of the world will perceive the planet as terrifyingly dangerous, full of corrupt, heavily armed, bloodthirsty psychopaths. This mistake is known to statisticians as systematic sampling error.[5]

The Saddam Hussein who emerged blinking from his spider hole in December 2003 was not the madman that George W. Bush had fantasized on the basis of his briefing books. As one might have expected from America's long history of doing business with the dictator, Saddam turned out to have been a rational politician. He was the comprehensible product of a brutal, dysfunctional, but comprehensible state and society. In his early days he did much to modernize Iraqi society. He was savage in suppressing the chronic tribal strife that has plagued Iraq throughout its history. As an Iraqi patriot as well as a scoundrel, he tried desperately to persuade the UN to lift sanctions against his country, even while letting his friends profit handsomely from circumventing those sanctions.

Iraq was a closed society, with nothing published in the newspapers but what the arbitrary, brutal, and dishonest regime permitted. Even there, however, the foreign diplomats based in Baghdad were able to glean from the city's newspapers, from public statements of the Iraqi government itself, from gossip, from academics, from the published reports of the UN weapons inspectors, and from a commonsense analysis of Saddam Hussein's personal and political self-interest, a more accurate and useful picture of Saddam's Iraq than all the secrets the CIA and NSA provided U.S. policymakers.

The United States had no diplomatic presence in Baghdad. This was a serious lapse, the triumph of domestic posturing over good sense. America was represented there by a Polish diplomat memorable to his diplomatic colleagues mostly for his inability to recognize them at receptions. He must have had some compensating virtues, but as I confirmed later with the Turkish *chargé d'affaires* who served in Baghdad in the run-up to the invasion, the United States displayed absolutely no official curiosity to compare notes with the diplomats of NATO allies about a country it was planning to disarm and democratize.[6]

Information gathering from diplomatic allies would have been a job for the State Department. Bureaucratically, however, the State Department was excluded from any share in the coming military triumph. State had disqualified itself as a player by letting its Iraq experts raise awkward questions in Iraq War planning meetings at the Defense Department. Cheney's office disinvited State from the meetings in favor of academic specialists on Israel and Turkey, whose contempt for Arabs and lack of Iraq knowledge made them a better fit with the political agenda of the Bush administration.[7]

Another reason the United States did not take counsel with more of its allies was that it did not trust their motives. The countries with a diplomatic mission in Baghdad were presumed to have sacrificed their integrity to sordid commercial interests. The populist charge that France and Russia resisted the war in hopes of protecting their vested interests in Iraq has some truth, about as much as the charge that America invaded Iraq for oil. Business constituencies influence the foreign policy decision-making process in every country of the world strongly but not decisively. The business strategy of Halliburton, like that of its French rival Elf, was to position itself to be indispensable to government contracting officers whatever political current prevailed.

Saddam Hussein had few foreign defenders. The world was happy to see him ousted and Iraq restored to the community of civilized states. The basic reservation was cost, including the cost to the fragile concept of international legality as a constraint on U.S. or any other military hegemony.[8]

Clandestine intelligence betrayed America in Iraq and will always betray the superpower—and not only when it is wrong—because it illuminates only a small part of a much larger picture of how the world operates. If President Bush had read foreign diplomatic reports, or even the *Financial Times*, he could have realized that the costs of even a brilliantly conducted war would be much higher than advertised. With those costs in mind, he might have asked for a more balanced assessment of Saddam's rationality. That in turn would have led him to pay closer attention to Iraqis' repeated insistence, confirmed by high-level defectors, that they had destroyed Iraq's WMD in 1991. He certainly would have questioned the motives of those insisting that Saddam aspired to commit regime suicide by consorting with terrorists or using chemical weapons against U.S. interests.

## *Too Good to Be True*

Diplomats learn that if a story sounds too good to be true, it is. Consider the business world, where thousands of brilliant minds are struggling to be the first to discover the next way to take momentary advantage of arcane U.S. financial markets and an intricate tax code. Only the most childish of narcissists would believe that some stranger would entrust to him a precious, short-lived method for easy wealth when Goldman Sachs would pay millions and deploy it immediately had it the slightest chance of working. This goes for Medoff's billions of dollars in Swiss banks. It goes double for intelligence windfalls. Only a naive United States of America would have such faith in the kindness of strangers to believe Chalabi when his agents came up, time and again, with exactly the secret reporting politicians demanded from the intelligence community regarding Iraqi WMD.

Mobile biological weapons labs were a peculiar answer to Saddam's security problems. The U.S. military, with the most advanced stationary labs on the planet, had struggled for decades to turn bacteria into weapons it could imagine using. It ultimately agreed without much anguish to give them up under the Biological Weapons Convention. Even if Saddam's generals were more tolerant of slow, haphazard slaughter than America's, bio-weapons are not something like wet cement or Krispy Kreme donuts that need to be driven fresh to the battlefield. Putting them in trucks would offer little advantage in concealment to compensate for the hugely expanded risk of accidental toxic release.

Iraqi mobile laboratories were, however, the perfect solution to a dire U.S. political problem. UN inspectors had uniformly failed to find prohibited weapons or programs in the places the United States told them to inspect, and skeptics were beginning to conclude that U.S. intelligence was worthless. Invading Iraq without international acquiescence would dramatically raise the political cost of a war to the United States and its allies. Secretary Powell would not knowingly lie to the world about WMD but was desperate to make his president's policy as affordable as possible to the American people. Mobile labs were a threat that could not be disproved, a threat reported by multiple, ostensibly independent sources. America could make a case for war, weak though it was, secure that no one could disprove it.

One of the less distinguished moments in the history of the *New York Times* occurred in the early days of the Iraq invasion. The WMD were nowhere to be found, and the administration was beginning to get nervous. Judith Miller of the *Times* had blighted her professional reputation with her role as passive conduit for Chalabi's forged intelligence. Chalabi was going to save her and the credibility of the U.S. government. He led Miller to a defector, and she, as documented in a devastating *Washington Post* article by Howard Kurtz, introduced the defector to a U.S. Army WMD search team floundering in the Iraqi desert with no intelligence support.

Nerve gas had indeed been concealed in Iraq, the defector claimed, but it had been shipped to Syria just before the war. Rumsfeld, Cheney, and even Powell breathed a sigh of relief and went on television to suggest that they were on the verge of invading Syria. But alas, elementary fact-checking revealed that the informant was a fabricator. He had nothing to show the search teams but a few drums of insecticide, and the story quietly evaporated. It was too good to be true, and luckily, this time someone bothered to verify the information before launching a war.[9]

## Consider Your Source

Diplomats do not judge information without judging its source at the same time. The more valuable the information provided, the more certain it is that the person who provided it has some selfish motive for doing so. Anyone reading the current book must weigh the validity of its contents against the presumed motives of an un-employed diplomat, which include earning a living. Anyone listening to an exiled politician should remember his goal of being restored to his palaces at U.S. expense. Clandestine sources stand to gain more from their handlers if they exaggerate threats than if they describe them honestly. They also have more to gain from fooling the United States than any given American bureaucrat has to gain by preventing them. Selfish motives do not make information invalid, but they are a crucial part of the analytical framework that makes information usable.

Intelligence operatives in the field prefer not to identify their sources to the analysts who use the information provided. First, sometimes even the CIA is leaky. The Directorate of Intelligence (DI) is quite discreet, but it does not have the same mystical devotion as the Directorate of Operation (DO) to its secret sources and routinely engages in intelligence sharing with outsiders. An unintentional slip could get a source killed or worse. Second, a known source is easier to discredit than an unknown source, and the DO makes its living by preserving its mystique. A third reason for the "firewall" between collection and analysis is protection of the independent judgment of intelligence analysts from the strong personalities and policy biases of the covert branch.

The key source on Iraq's mobile biological weapons labs, a crucial data point for Saddam's alleged aspirations, turned out to be living in a German refugee camp. The German intelligence service was delighted to bring his story to the attention of the CIA. It did not, however, reveal that its source was the relative of a Chalabi aide or allow direct interrogation. Not knowing the source, the U.S. government overvalued the information, to the embarrassment of Colin Powell, who used it in good faith at the UN.

In Athens in late 2002 I played a bit part in the process by which Iraqi defectors fed the U.S. government with information. In response to a phone call from a Greek opposition political party contact, I dutifully trotted over to be briefed on the existence of an Iraqi military officer who, sitting unhappily in his refugee camp on a Greek island, had been unable to interest the Greek authorities in the story he had to tell. A colleague passed the details to the appropriate Greek authorities to investigate.

I have no idea what story the defector told the Greeks. Iraqi defectors and their interrogators took part in a Darwinian selection process. If defectors told the truth (i.e., that Iraq had indeed, as it repeatedly insisted, destroyed all its WMD in 1991) or an easily checkable falsehood they would remain in their grim camp. Only if they told exactly the right falsehood, one politically useful but also not disprovable, would they stand any chance of a new life in Southern California.

According to the *New York Times* of February 13, 2004, CIA director George Tenet responded to the Iraq WMD intelligence fiasco by reducing the firewall between source and content. Henceforth, the analysts might be given some indication that, for example, the person supplying information had been plucked by the Iraqi National Congress from a refugee camp and carefully briefed by experienced operatives on what story might win him and his family a new home. Details like this are useful for an analyst to have.

## *Compare Notes*

It generally takes a diplomat about twenty years and a top-secret/codeword security clearance to reach the disappointing realization that most of the information the United States uses for making policy either is not secret or else should not be. America's proper secrets are its intelligence sources and methods, its military vulnerabilities, and information that could damage the ability of U.S. allies to continue cooperating with it. These secrets the U.S. government protects reasonably well and so do most foreign governments. Everything else will come out in the papers tomorrow. Most of it should have come out yesterday.

Most secrets are classified not to keep them from unfriendly foreigners but rather to keep them out of the hands of political and bureaucratic rivals. The most famous example of this use of information classification was Henry Kissinger's "secret war" in Laos and Cambodia. The Cambodians knew perfectly well that they were being bombed and had a shrewd guess by whom. It was Congress and the skeptics in the State Department that needed to be kept ignorant of U.S. foreign policy. Such internal bureaucratic and political rivalries are the swindler's best friend. Medoff bought time and maneuvering room by exploiting my desire to protect Romania's fragile reputation from U.S. bureaucratic foes.

Chalabi swindled the U.S. government the first time, in the mid-1990s, by exploiting Republican hard-liners' desire to embarrass President Clinton by portraying him as ineffectual on Iraq. With a steady flow of congressionally mandated money to spend, the ███ dutifully listened to Chalabi and sent a credulous Iraqi resistance into the waiting machine guns in 1996. The foredoomed coup had been secret from the American public but not from Saddam Hussein. Impervious to past failures, Congress passed the Iraq Liberation Act in 1998, continuing to fund Chalabi's activities with reckless disregard for America's ability to protect the Kurds and Shiites the United States enlisted to fight his battles.

Chalabi swindled us so easily the second time around because the Office of the Secretary of Defense (OSD) put its ideological and bureaucratic convenience above U.S. national interests. Painfully over fifty years, the U.S. government has developed procedures to prevent officials from manipulating the president and vice president by feeding them raw intelligence of dubious value. OSD intentionally sabotaged the information-vetting mechanisms, creating its own intelligence office to feed self-serving information from Chalabi's organization directly to friends at the White House. Wiser heads in the CIA and State Department found themselves silenced because they were not asked for their input until the president's prejudices were so firmly established that Tenet and Powell would not venture to contradict them. The result was international humiliation when the information on Iraq WMD and ties to 9/11 proved patently untrue.

Medoff's lies were so grandiose, their consequences so damaging if true, that his interlocutors did not dare compare notes properly. The names he dropped were difficult to challenge. Medoff would have been defanged immediately if the United States had enough faith in the Romanian government to share the con man's story about Ceausescu's hidden fortune and allegedly corrupt aides. The risk of a leak to the newspapers was real but manageable: the story would have died quickly once journalists discovered Medoff's duplicity. In the unlikely event he was telling the truth, long-term U.S. commitment to Romanian democracy would be better served by having the Romanian people learn the bad news early on.

Chalabi had Medoff's skill on an even grander scale. In July 2004, the *Washington Times* reported that Chalabi had told the Iranian intelligence chief in Baghdad that the United States had the ability to read the encrypted message traffic of the Iranian Ministry of Information and Security. If the story is true, Chalabi's leak had destroyed an important tool of U.S. intelligence-gathering. Two years later, Chalabi still enjoyed high office in Iraq. Some people make themselves too prominent to punish.[10]

The U.S. war with Iraq might have taken a different turn if Congress and the American people had insisted in advance on a detailed look at the intelligence information. The authenticity of the famous forged Niger yellowcake documents did not withstand a ten-minute Google search once the documents were shared with International Atomic Energy Agency experts. Nor would the U.S. government have chased so long down the blind alley of Iraq's imported aluminum tubes—missile casings we now know—had the information been shared early on with missile experts as well as specialists in centrifuge technology.

When information is shared quickly, the risks to U.S. national interests drop dramatically. If it is true, it will become known eventually in any case, and the people who failed to make it known in a timely way will pay a price. If it is false, only rapid dissemination will allow the United States to discover its falseness immediately.

## *Easy Does It*

A superpower bull in the global china shop should aspire to belong, like Oscar Wilde, "to a school which regards all sudden movements as ill-bred." Swindlers always try to force the pace, to make us move before we think. The United States should be immune to this ploy. One of the charms of sharing a remote and well-endowed continent with two weak and reasonably friendly neighbors is that the United States generally has ample time to study foreign policy disasters as they approach. The United States is powerful enough and rich enough that it can afford to take a little extra time, spend a little more money, and accept the risk of minor embarrassment to examine all its options.

When the U.S. government develops a sense of urgency, it is generally in response to some self-imposed political deadline, not actual impending doom. The March timing of the Iraq War was driven by the difficulty of wearing chem-bio protective suits in the summer sun and the reluctance to keep hundreds of thousands of U.S. troops deployed in the Persian Gulf for longer than necessary. Secretary Rumsfeld had reversed the normal decision-making process by signing deployment orders months before the intelligence community was asked (by Congress, not the president!) to give its definitive assessment of the Iraqi WMD threat. A stronger president would not have allowed his policy options to be so constrained by a subordinate's decision.

## Choose Your Friends

It is a mistake to do business with anyone, anywhere in the world, who makes a point of his intelligence connections. Medoff's ostentatious familiarity with the CIA should have been my automatic tip-off of trouble. Outside the Washington beltway, the only people who discourse knowledgeably about the CIA are con men, psychotics, dreamers, ideological journalists, and aging émigré politicians looking for U.S. help in reclaiming their lands and serfs. This is not to imply that the CIA associates only with such folk, just that the true friends of the CIA do not advertise their association.

When in Washington, much wisdom may be gained from talking to the CIA analysts responsible for a given issue. Beware of their bosses, however, and their bosses' middlemen. Beyond a certain level in any intelligence bureaucracy, stubborn insistence on the rules of evidence becomes a disqualifying psychological disorder. Spies exist in happy symbiosis with naive congressional staffers and newspaper columnists who delight in being manipulated by selective sharing of CIA or Mossad "secrets." These spy buffs often seem harmless enough, and their gossip is lurid and seductive. Influence, not U.S. national interests, is their addiction, however, and they have no interest in being cured.

## Learning From Mistakes

I thought I was tough-minded in being suspicious of Medoff. Vice President Cheney is justly celebrated by fellow conservatives for his tough-mindedness. Mere tough-mindedness, it turns out, is no protection for the national interest. Stalin was at least as tough-minded as Cheney, yet he preferred to believe his intuition regarding Hitler rather than his experts' warnings that the Germans were about to invade. As a result, the USSR was caught flat-footed in 1941, and millions of Russians died who might have been saved.

Unlike Stalin's subjects, U.S. voters have the right to hold their politicians accountable when they blunder by ignoring their experts. Alas, politicians seldom learn from any mistakes but their own. The reelection of President Bush allows him to profit from the expensive lesson Chalabi taught. The president should ask himself what I asked myself after my brush with Medoff: Which of my weaknesses did he play on? What did he tell me that I wanted to believe? What motives kept me listening despite my skepticism and good intentions?

Pending a golden age of presidential self-knowledge, the only

protection for ordinary Americans is to take the foreign policy decision process out of the vice president's office or any other narrow
cabal of senior officials and put it back into the formal bureaucratic
channels that have evolved since 1948 to present decision options
to the president and then convey the decision he makes to the U.S.
government and people. The existence of an unclassified, or soon
to be declassified, paper trail, with the names of the drafters and
decision makers prominently affixed, is the best guarantee Americans will ever have that someone will be held accountable for each
mistake. Secrecy's role in the U.S. government is to protect senior
officials from learning from their mistakes. A responsible superpower
cannot afford that seeming luxury.

U.S. diplomats would do well to ponder the consequences of
failing to wield their diplomatic skepticism more effectively before
the Iraq War became inevitable. In 2005 several hundred of them
were living in Baghdad's Green Zone, working feverishly to rebuild
Iraq while avoiding incoming mortar rounds. Diplomats are trained
to recognize more quickly than their compatriots how America's
interests differ from those of an émigré politician. Their happiness
as well as their career depends on the existence of a transparent,
flexible, nonpunitive bureaucratic system for turning a diplomat's
precious knowledge of the outside world into good U.S. policy. It is
their duty to fight for such a system.

# 15

# ★ *A Look Toward the Future* ★

*"For myself," said Faramir, "I would see the White Tree in flower
again in the courts of the kings, and the Silver Crown return,
and Minas Tirith in peace: Minas Anor again as of old, full of
light, high and fair, beautiful as a queen among other queens:
not a mistress of many slaves, nay, not even a kind mistress of
willing slaves. War must be, while we defend our lives against a
destroyer who would devour all; but I do not love the bright sword
for its sharpness, nor the arrow for its swiftness, nor the warrior
for his glory. I love only that which they defend: the city of the
Men of Númenor; and I would have her loved for her memory,
her ancientry, her beauty, and her present wisdom. Not feared,
save as men may fear the dignity of a man, old and wise."*
                                    J. R. R. *Tolkien*, The Two Towers

The struggle for the soul of U.S. diplomacy is fundamentally
an argument about human nature. One of my duties as I wrote this
book was not to write off as knaves and fools the intelligent, deeply
patriotic Americans who led their country into Iraq and ill-repute.
The diplomat's charitable explanation is probably true: the nationalist blinders that made President Bush and his associates so effective on
the American political stage made them incompetent to evaluate information about the world outside. But nationalism is not in itself
immoral. It inspires the bravest human behavior as well as the deadliest.

During the Cold War, both the United States and Soviet Union
struggled to preserve the clear, ennobling division of the world that
prevailed during World War II. Both states embraced the illusion
that they could reliably discern good from evil in human hearts by
whether foreign politicians chose to flatter Washington or Moscow.
This clear moral line, once drawn, allowed both sides to sustain incredible national burdens. It encouraged interludes of unselfishness

271

during which America built up an incredibly rich and useful web of international relationships. It also sanctified—in the decision-making process if not in the eyes of its victims—practically any means an ambitious bureaucrat cared to propose. Many innocent people died cruelly and unnecessarily in the name of U.S. national security. Still, future ancient historians are likely to judge the outcome of the Cold War charitably. I felt enormous pride to be an instrument of the vague but benevolent "New World Order" that George H. W. Bush recognized in the U.S.-led, UN-flagged liberation of Kuwait in 1991.

The "global war on terror" launched after 9/11 was a failed reprise of the illusory moral clarity of the Cold War. With so paltry and shadowy an adversary, the price Americans paid for moral clarity was to unwittingly make the United States the most frightening entity on the planet. To their credit, few Americans relished their newfound status of unloved superpower. Officials quickly recognized that fighting tiny groups of terrorists dispersed around the globe would require at least as dense a web of intelligence and law enforcement relationships as the United States had maintained during the Cold War. Being unloved was not an advantage in building such relationships.

Foreigners no less than Americans are moved by deeply moral as well as rational impulses. Conscience is a nuisance, but it survives as a constraint on human behavior because individuals and societies that ignore it ultimately destroy themselves in ugly ways. Because everyone has an almost infinite capacity to distort the world to make perceived self-interest compatible with their moral code, cherished words like "good" and "evil" turn out to be worthless for a diplomat's effective understanding of the planet. Everyone is capable of terrible crimes or inconceivable magnanimity. The greatest gift a superpower or anyone else can offer is the opportunity to behave decently and incur no disadvantage from doing so. This is the moral center of effective superpower diplomacy.

## The Challenge to U.S. Hegemony

Until 9/11, Americans could blithely congratulate themselves on how well their system had fared since the U.S. government leapt onto the diplomatic stage in 1905 with the Treaty of Portsmouth that made peace between Japan and Russia. One reasonably rational conservative scholar, Francis Fukuyama, published a book in 1992 entitled *The End of History*. He thought liberal Western democracy was the foreordained peaceful endpoint to human evolution. If Fukuyama had studied biology, archaeology, or even economics, he would have shaken his head at any notion of evolutionary endpoints.

A stable international system, even a stable ideological basis for one, is a short-term illusion, as is stability in any other ecosystem. The ecological niches humans occupy are subject to constant transformation. The more successful a given survival strategy is in a specific environment, the more pressure a growing population places on that environment. Competitors, predators, and parasites evolve to shrink a given niche or bleed away the competitive advantages of its occupants.

The physiologist-geographer Jared Diamond published a book in 2004 entitled *Collapse: How Societies Choose to Fail or Succeed.* Describing the collapse of civilizations such as the Anasazi in the American Southwest, he argued that societies could fail catastrophically if their institutions were not strong enough to protect a fragile ecosystem from population pressure. The book struck chords in my own experience. As a junior economic officer in Morocco, I watched huge coastal fish stocks disappear over a decade because of overfishing. In Greece, cowardly governments still pay cotton and citrus farmers to pump ancient aquifers dry. American institutions are more effective, sometimes.

The planet is scarier than even the unloveliest superpower. Unprecedented population densities mean that traditional environmental challenges—tsunamis, earthquakes, hurricanes, climate variation, and the evolution of epidemic diseases—now routinely overwhelm national borders and capabilities. The nationalism that has dominated human political behavior over the past century can mobilize resources against human rivals but not against rising sea levels or price increases for fossil fuels. Relatively small environmental changes are likely to slam shut, or at least shift across once-firm national borders, ecological niches that have until now supported hundreds of millions of human beings.[1]

Humans are not lemmings, foredoomed to periodic population booms and die-offs. Improved technology and evolving human institutions make it possible to imagine keeping alive indefinitely a global population of 9 billion people, the level the world population is supposed to reach in 2050.[2] Survival of so large a population presupposes lifestyle changes to double the efficiency of current use of scarce water, energy, and arable land. Without that social evolution, even the sustainability of earth's current 6.5 billion people is open to question.

Historically, the proven strategies for coping with the local mismatch between man and his environment were migration and war. America's grand strategy during the previous century was a braver and better one, to foster the evolution of an international political and economic system strong, flexible, and efficient enough to make worldwide economic growth the antidote to each local drought or flood. Americans recognized then that they were condemned either to cooperate with foreigners to maintain an international system of states with fixed, sacred borders, or else to suffer like everyone else the changes caused by the failure of that system. In many countries around the world, particularly in Africa, states have become too weak to assure the basic welfare of their citizens.

The power of the EU, particularly regarding human rights and environmental protection, is an illustration that transnational legitimacy can under certain circumstances substitute for nationalism in organizing human societies to meet the basic needs of their members. The EU experiment was made possible by sixty years of peace and stability in Europe, an interlude the United States partly subsidized with NATO and the Marshall Plan. In terms of quality of life, a number of EU countries and Singapore have pulled ahead of the United States.[3] Cooperative societies can allocate scarce resources more efficiently than competitive ones.

Expert opinion is divided on whether the deadly mirage of the nation-state is an evolutionary stage that can be bypassed. The political success of the EU depends on memories of bloody national history that are beginning to fade. Can Africa avoid similar bloodshed and build peaceful multiethnic states? I do not know. More ambitious transnationalism, however, is unlikely. No country I have ever visited would countenance "world federalism" or a major transfer of additional sovereignty to the UN or any other global body. National attitudes would change, history suggests, only after a new world war or comparable global calamity.

A conservative school of thought in the United States says national competition, like economic competition, is indispensable to the health of society. One price paid for reduced nationalism is less legitimate national governments, with leaders afraid to ask sacrifices from their citizens. The pessimistic view would turn transnationalism into an evolutionary dead end. If so, the EU will find itself, thirty years down the road, a fat, hopelessly sluggish zebra among the hungry lions.

This is not an academic question. The instinct to reward successful violence is built into us. Fragile political systems cope with their inability to allocate scarce resources equitably by regularly reinventing violent nationalism. U.S. diplomacy and military power have provided adequate excuses for avoiding armed hostilities countless times in the world's recent history, but it is soberingly difficult to point to an international conflict that ever really ended. The beneficial rules now limiting international competition to the economic and cultural sphere would quickly collapse without continued U.S. determination to put its power behind the international institutions that enforce them.

The first administration of George W. Bush saw conservative ideologues successfully argue that previous U.S. strategy did not allow America to profit from its overwhelming military supremacy. The United States had power to reshape the global environment, and it would use it. The initial experiments in U.S. unilateralism grotesquely underestimated the strength of foreign nationalism and overestimated U.S. ability to change the rules of local political competition. This failure has already changed the global political environment to make foreign partners more suspicious of U.S. political hegemony. Meanwhile, a huge share of the world's population has quietly adopted energy-intensive Western lifestyles and fluency in English as indispensable markers of social standing. Demand for scarce resources is growing. For the first time in human history, economic competition is genuinely global.

America's ability to support its lifestyle by attracting foreign capital has allowed U.S. policymakers to postpone recognition that America as a nation is no longer a clear beneficiary of the rules of international economic competition it imposed fifty years ago as the world's dominant economic as well as military power. Temporarily sheltered from evolutionary pressure, the United States watched other hungrier states like China evolve to exploit the rules of free trade better than the superpower could. America's vaunted dominance in global management and financial services is already disappearing, along with the dominance of American brands. Indian and Chinese MBAs will soon prefer to keep in their home countries the huge share of the world's wealth now tamely ceded to a U.S.-based corporate management elite. After studying America's unbalanced national accounts, even the most junior economic diplomat would conclude that a new economic model must be found if America is to remain the land of opportunity for an acceptable percentage of its own people.

Let us remember the life cycle of empires. The transnational EU is no grounds for believing that nationalism will soon burn itself out in any of the world's major energy exporters. Iraq should tell us there can be no wave of profitable U.S. imperialism to correct America's balance of payments problem or guarantee the flow of unlimited crude oil to its shores. Nor will the United States find an enemy sufficiently frightening to its allies to justify their subsidizing an unchanged American lifestyle. Fear of terrorism is an unsustainable basis for a protection racket, unless the United States intends to make self-fulfilling the evangelical Christian prophecies of a war of extermination against Muslim fellow-citizens. Americans have no appetite for the slaughter of innocents such a course would demand.

U.S. preeminence in the international system requires a sustainable basis for American prosperity. No military strategy, not even one backed by brilliant U.S. diplomacy, will maintain the lifestyles of ordinary Americans on so crowded, competitive, and irritable a planet as the one they currently inhabit. Nor can Americans hope to keep inventing new pyramid schemes—real estate bubbles, Internet stock crazes—to keep the world's surplus capital flowing toward them. Technological and social evolution to reduce U.S. national dependence on the kindness of strangers is the only honorable course. Building a healthy U.S. economy—that is to say, an environmentally sustainable one with a narrowing gap between rich and poor—will require political leadership brave enough to make the environmental, social, and other hidden costs of the American lifestyle an integral part of calculating the economic bottom line.

The Iraq debacle and budget constraints have driven the U.S. government back toward realist diplomacy that focuses on economic issues. Realism will probably require America at some point to level the economic playing field by using the threat of tariff barriers to force market-based environmental standards—carbon taxes being the easiest, but also charges for maritime pollution and the other hidden costs of international trade—on emerging industrial competitors as well as itself. In the long run, both Americans and the rest of the world will benefit if exports are no longer subsidized by massive environmental degradation.

As the multiyear deadlock in the World Trade Organization over agricultural subsidies and industrial access illustrates, the process of renegotiating the terms of economic competition is slow and politically perilous for all concerned. America's most vital diplomatic mission is not to preemptively destroy a few hundred hypothetical suicide bombers but rather to build, step by painful step, the political basis for U.S.-led global economic reforms.

Since 2005 there have been diligent efforts to demonstrate around the world that America is a benevolent, competent superpower. A wealthy, legitimate superpower routinely sacrifices certain bureaucratic conveniences to buy the consent of poorer, less legitimate governments around the planet. When the United States improves its international image, it lowers the price it must pay for that consent. When the United States yields some of its freedom of action to international organizations, it regains its ability to demand concessions no nation would grant any rival. When the United States promotes local and regional security and prosperity, even to the short-term benefit of tyrannical regimes, it creates the soil in which democracy can grow. But success depends on respecting domestic politics in other states as well as our own. Those politics ultimately compel America to embrace the rule of law—internationally as well as nationally—as the basic principle of effective diplomacy.

Between 2001 and 2004 the United States squandered much of its diplomatic capital to pursue an irresponsible war in Iraq. The U.S. president lost his title of "the leader of the free world." Many former friends wrote America off as an amoral, superstitious empire in decline. The damage is reparable because the United States still has enormous power for good and because no sensible person is comfortable with the power vacuum America's retreat to isolationism would create.

America's most precious diplomatic capital is other peoples' faith that the interests of a justice-loving America are compatible with their own. To make it politically possible to rebuild that capital, it helps to embrace the optimistic side of the diplomat's cynical worldview: morality and self-interest are inseparable, provided we persuade our politicians to take a long enough view of those interests. In the long run, security cannot be purchased at the expense of justice. Good diplomacy situates U.S. interests in the shared, humane values of the rational Enlightenment. Those values, as articulated by the Founding Fathers, once made the United States the acknowledged, admired leader of progress-minded people all around the world. Those values will make America a respected superpower again.

# ★ *Appendix A* ★

*Embassy of the United States of America*

Athens, Greece
February 24, 2003

The Honorable Colin Powell
Secretary of State
Washington, D.C.

Dear Mr. Secretary:

I am writing you to submit my resignation from the Foreign Service of the United States and from my position as Political Counselor in U.S. Embassy Athens, effective March 7. I do so with a heavy heart. The baggage of my upbringing included a felt obligation to give something back to my country. Service as a U.S. diplomat was a dream job. I was paid to understand foreign languages and cultures, to seek out diplomats, politicians, scholars and journalists, and to persuade them that U.S. interests and theirs fundamentally coincided. My faith in my country and its values was the most powerful weapon in my diplomatic arsenal.

It is inevitable that during twenty years with the State Department I would become more sophisticated and cynical about the narrow and selfish bureaucratic motives that sometimes shaped our policies. Human nature is what it is, and I was rewarded and promoted for understanding human nature. But until this Administration it had been possible to believe that by upholding the policies of my president I was also upholding the interests of the American people and the world. I believe it no longer.

The policies we are now asked to advance are incompatible not only with American values but also with American interests. Our fervent pursuit of war with Iraq is driving us to squander the international legitimacy that has been America's most potent weapon of both offense and defense since the days of Woodrow Wilson. We have begun to dismantle the largest and most effective web of international relationships the world has ever known. Our current course will bring instability and danger, not security.

The sacrifice of global interests to domestic politics and to bureaucratic self-interest is nothing new, and it is certainly not a uniquely American problem. Still, we have not seen such systematic distortion of intelligence, such systematic manipulation of American opinion, since the war in Vietnam. The September 11 tragedy left us stronger than before, rallying around us a vast international coalition to cooperate for the first time in a systematic way against the threat of terrorism. But rather than take credit for those successes and build on them, this Administration has chosen to make terrorism a domestic political tool, enlisting a scattered and largely defeated Al Qaeda as its bureaucratic ally. We spread disproportionate terror and confusion in the public mind, arbitrarily linking the unrelated problems of terrorism and Iraq. The result, and perhaps the motive, is to justify a vast misallocation of shrinking public wealth to the military and to weaken the safeguards that protect American citizens from the heavy hand of government. September 11 did not do as much damage to the fabric of American society as we seem determined to so to ourselves. Is the Russia of the late Romanovs really our model, a selfish, superstitious empire thrashing toward self-destruction in the name of a doomed status quo?

We should ask ourselves why we have failed to persuade more of the world that a war with Iraq is necessary. We have over the past two years done too much to assert to our world partners that narrow and mercenary U.S. interests override the cherished values of our partners. Even where our aims were not in question, our consistency is at issue. The model of Afghanistan is little comfort to allies wondering on what basis we plan to rebuild the Middle East, and in whose image and interests. Have we indeed become blind, as Russia is blind in Chechnya, as Israel is blind in the Occupied Territories, to our own advice, that overwhelming military power is not the answer to terrorism? After the shambles of post-war Iraq joins the shambles in Grozny and Ramallah, it will be a brave foreigner who forms ranks with Micronesia to follow where we lead.

We have a coalition still, a good one. The loyalty of many of our friends is impressive, a tribute to American moral capital built up over a century. But our closest allies are persuaded less that war is justified than that it would be perilous to allow the U.S. to drift into complete solipsism. Loyalty should be reciprocal. Why does our President condone the swaggering and contemptuous approach to our friends and allies this Administration is fostering, including among its most senior officials. Has "oderint dum metuant" really become our motto?

I urge you to listen to America's friends around the world. Even here in Greece, purported hotbed of European anti-Americanism, we have more and closer friends than the American newspaper reader can possibly imagine. Even when they complain about American arrogance, Greeks know that the world is a difficult and dangerous place, and they want a strong international system, with the U.S. and EU in close partnership. When our friends are afraid of us rather than for us, it is time to worry. And now they are afraid. Who will tell them convincingly that the United States is as it was, a beacon of liberty, security, and justice for the planet?

Mr. Secretary, I have enormous respect for your character and ability. You have preserved more international credibility for us than our policy deserves, and salvaged something positive from the excesses of an ideological and self-serving Administration. But your loyalty to the President goes too far. We are straining beyond its limits an international system we built with such toil and treasure, a web of laws, treaties, organizations, and shared values that sets limits on our foes far more effectively than it ever constrained America's ability to defend its interests.

I am resigning because I have tried and failed to reconcile my conscience with my ability to represent the current U.S. Administration. I have confidence that our democratic process is ultimately self-correcting, and hope that in a small way I can contribute from outside to shaping policies that better serve the security and prosperity of the American people and the world we share.

Sincerely,

John Brady Kiesling
U.S. Embassy Athens

# ★ *Appendix B* ★

DEPARTMENT OF STATE
DIRECTOR, POLICY PLANNING STAFF
WASHINGTON

DISSENT CHANNEL

March 17, 2003

SENSITIVE BUT UNCLASSIFIED

TO:        John Brady Kiesling

FROM:      S/P - Richard N. Haass

SUBJECT:   Your Dissent Channel Message Regarding U.S.
           Policy Toward Iraq

    I am writing in response to your Dissent Channel
message, in which you informed the Secretary of your
resignation from the Foreign Service and expressed your
concerns about the conduct of American foreign policy.  I
wish to convey the Department's regret over your decision,
but to express our appreciation of the depth of conviction
that led to it.  Thank you for your past service, and for
the informed dissent in your message, which has been
reviewed in depth by the Secretary and other senior
policymakers, per Foreign Affairs Manual regulations.

    While I respect your views and your right to express
them, I must take exception with a number of the ways in
which you characterize U.S. policies and motives with
respect to Iraq.  Our actions on Iraq are fully compatible
both with American values and American interests.  They
reflect our goal of protecting the American people and the
international community from the growing threat of weapons
of mass destruction held by the Iraqi regime.  For more
than a decade, Iraq has defied the United Nations and

283

maintained a biological and chemical weapons capability. As Secretary Powell demonstrated to the U.N. Security Council on February 5, Iraq continues to hide evidence and dangerous weapons, muzzle its scientists, pursue nuclear weapons capabilities, and maintain ties with terrorists. In particular, it has failed to account for thousands of liters of anthrax and botulinum toxin, 5000 tons of sarin, mustard and VX nerve agent, and thousands of munitions to deliver chemical agents.

We are also facing in Iraq a regime that flouts the basic norms of civilized behavior. It has brutally repressed its people, launched wars of aggression against its neighbors, murdered members of ethnic and religious groups, used chemical weapons against its neighbors and its own people, and diverted humanitarian aid intended to feed and house its citizens. Working with the United Nations and our friends and allies, we must ensure that a regime with such destructive intentions as Iraq does not possess the means to blackmail the world, attack innocent people, or support terrorists. We seek an Iraq that is democratic, unified, and peaceful, and that has no weapons of mass destruction and no links to terrorists.

I must take exception as well to your characterization of American policy towards Iraq as a "fervent pursuit of war." Indeed, under President Bush's leadership, the United States has stated consistently that military action is the last resort. We have worked diligently in the United Nations to build an international consensus for a unified stance in the face of Iraqi non-compliance with more than a dozen resolutions over more than a decade. On September 12, 2002, the President went to the United Nations to reaffirm our commitment to the peaceful disarmament of Iraq, and we worked over the next seven weeks tirelessly to pass unanimously on November 8 United Nations Security Council Resolution 1441 giving Iraq one last chance to avoid war. Iraq has failed to take the final opportunity afforded by Resolution 1441; instead, it has sought to divide and distract the international community, doing just enough to reduce international pressure. Still, even at this late hour, Iraq has the opportunity to avoid conflict if it shifts its stance and fully disarms.

I do not share your portrayal of our presentation of evidence before the international community as a "systematic distortion of intelligence." On the contrary, the United States has taken extraordinary steps to share with the U.N. weapons inspectors and with the U.N. Security Council a wide variety of highly credible intelligence information generated from sensitive sources. We have done so precisely because we want the world to see clearly the kind of leader and regime we are dealing with: one that does not hesitate to lie to the international community about his WMD programs, torture and intimidate its own citizens, and consort with terrorists.

I assure you that we will continue to do all we can to pursue a policy in Iraq that is consistent with our national interests and values, and to ensure, as you so eloquently put it, that the United States remains a beacon of liberty, security and justice.

# ★ *Notes* ★

## *Obligatory Disclaimer and Note on Secrecy*

*The opinions and characterizations in this book are those of the author and do not necessarily represent official positions of the United States government.*

To obtain my State Department security clearance I signed an agreement that I would not publish a book on my experiences without submitting it to the State Department for a security review. I complied. My reviewer, always helpful and courteous, was able to persuade the agencies involved to disgorge my manuscript after five months.

More often than not, secrecy is a cloak for incompetence. Perhaps this is why the current U.S. administration is the most secretive in recent history. Four agencies generated a list of some seventy-two requested deletions, many of them prudent but others based on the misconception that foreigners would read my book but not their own newspapers.

Pretending that covert operations can be kept secret from their victims indefinitely is wishful thinking or worse. Retired CIA officials talk pretty freely to journalists and write self-glamorizing memoirs.

I made a good-faith effort to respect my obligations without undermining the utility of the book to the U.S. public. Where the requested deletions were legitimate I made them without noting them in the text. I also rewrote key episodes to replace arguably sensitive examples with information available to any newspaper reader. Where words or paragraphs are blacked out in the text, it is a plea to readers to be skeptical of their government's desire to keep them in the dark.

## *Note on Sources*

This book is an ex-practitioner's attempt to make practical sense of the human landscape in which U.S. foreign policy must operate, not an academic work with a scholarly bibliography. The literature on international relations is now so huge that no mortal could cope with it.

My ideas, scavenged from a career of diplomatic conversations and un-systematic reading, are recombined in ways their originators might find unrecognizable even if I could identify them. The notes that follow point to worthy books and articles I have read or skimmed and to ready-to-hand sources for the more obscure assertions I make. Defending my assertions more formally would require several books this same size. No one would read them.

## Chapter 1: A Diplomat's Rebellion

1. My moral education, one I still recommend to any aspiring super-power official, was C. S. Lewis's *Chronicles of Narnia* and J. R. R. Tolkien's *Lord of the Rings*. They are, of course, works of fantasy. I swallowed their elitist message of duty as more real and true than anything I heard in catechism or civics class.

2. Many diplomatic services have special academies with two-year programs. Their trainee diplomats learn international law, inter-national relations, trade promotion, public speaking, and other excellent skills. America's diplomats learn to bluff and improvise. On balance the U.S. way is better.

3. In 1983 Central America was a region to avoid. The State Depart-ment found other postings for idealistic and/or squeamish junior officers, and ambassadors did not rub their noses in America's guilty knowledge of the death squads.

4. Nick Burns went on to serve as U.S. permanent representative to NATO and then returned to Washington in 2005 as "P," Secretary Rice's undersecretary for political affairs. This is the most senior position a career U.S. diplomat can aspire to.

5. A Greek journalist, Manolis Vasilakis, published a book entitled *Kala na Pathoun* (*It Serves Them Right*) (Athens: Gnoseis, 2002) to document for the historical record the ugly satisfaction over 9/11 many Greek intellectuals and journalists had expressed in print. With such encouragement, ordinary Greeks found it easy to reach the somewhat less indefensible conclusion that 9/11 had been predictable retaliation for U.S. arrogance.

6. More charitably, the Navy might have been prepositioning itself for the Iraq War, assuming that one of its tasks would be to block the secret export of Saddam's nonexistent WMD through Syrian ports. This is not what the Pentagon told U.S. embassies.

7. Charles J. Hanley, "Bolton Said to Orchestrate Unlawful Firing," *Associated Press*, June 4, 2005; and Joseph Cirincione, "The Hunt for El Baradei," *Foreign Policy*, May 2005.

8. An article by Walter Pincus, "Prewar Findings Worried Analysts," *Washington Post*, May 22, 2005, A26, documents growing CIA rec-

ognition that Powell's star Iraqi defector, Curveball, was a fabricator, even before the crucial UN speech.

9.  David L. Phillips, *Losing Iraq: Inside the Postwar Reconstruction Fiasco* (New York: Westview, 2004) describes how the Pentagon killed the State Department's Future of Iraq project. If implemented from the outset, in the first wave of U.S. dominance, the federal solution envisaged by the State Department would have postponed the bloodshed. The Pentagon had nothing comparable for Gen. Jay Garner to use when he arrived, clueless, to administer Iraq.

10. The reply to my Dissent Channel message came a month later, in the form of a memorandum signed by Richard Haass, then-director of the State Department Policy Planning Staff, who shortly afterward left to head the prestigious but servile Council on Foreign Relations. Haass's staff had prudently reproduced the State Department's official talking points on Iraqi WMD, the ones I had used to so little effect on incredulous Greeks. See appendix B.

## *Chapter 2: Understanding Foreign Nationalism*

1.  When the first draft of this book was almost finished, a Greek bibliophile in Washington introduced me to the diplomat-theoretician-historian Edward Hallett Carr. Armed with a classical education like mine and the analytical eye of a professional outsider, Carr served for twenty years as a British diplomat. He resigned from the Foreign Office in 1936 and wrote *The Twenty Years' Crisis, 1919–1939* (New York: Harper Torchbooks, 1964), an unsentimental dissection of realism and utopianism that still serves as an introductory textbook in the international relations courses I never took. Carr's work, based on an unostentatiously moral sense that keeping the peace requires an accurate understanding of the workings of power, is easy to misread as an endorsement of brutality. Read carefully, it is a superb inoculation against wishful thinking. I follow timidly in his footsteps.

2.  The burgeoning academic disciplines of evolutionary psychology and neuroscience seem well on the way to making human behavior as intelligible as that of other animals. Close diplomatic observation seems to support the scientific insight that the outsized human brain is an evolutionary counterpart to the outsized tail of the peacock, more useful for attracting mates than for averting nuclear holocaust. See Geoffrey Miller, *The Mating Mind* (New York: Anchor, 2001). We should view Henry Kissinger's aphorism that "power is the ultimate aphrodisiac" in that context, though it would sound less sinister if it had been uttered by one of the women he dated. Ordinary male diplomats enjoy reasonable reproductive

success. Perhaps a true science of diplomacy will one day be possible on the basis of such insights.

3.  Niall Ferguson, *Colossus: The Price of America's Empire* (New York: Penguin, 2004); Max Boot, "American Imperialism? No Need to Run Away From Label," *USA Today*, May 5, 2003, http://www.usatoday.com/news/opinion/editorials/2003-05-05-boot_x.htm; Boot, *The Savage Wars of Peace: Small Wars and the Rise of American Power* (New York: Basic Books, 2002). Both of these gentlemen would do well to read Brig. Nigel Aylwin-Foster, "Changing the Army for Counterinsurgency Operations," *Military Review*, November–December 2005. A British military officer, Aylwin-Foster documents for U.S. readers how the U.S. Army is unsuited, by force structure, training, doctrine, and ethos, to the role of enforcer of a profitable imperial protection racket, whether in Iraq or anywhere else.

## Chapter 3: The Sources of U.S. Legitimacy

1.  Fear of the Russians was America's best tool of occupation and reconstruction in both Germany and Japan. The Russians cooperated to legitimize the U.S. occupation by carving off pieces of Germany and seizing islands seen by all Japanese as integral parts of their nation. Soviet greed and cynicism enlisted both the nobler and nastier elements of Japanese and German nationalism firmly on the U.S. side.

2.  Any apprentice warmonger should read Shimon Tzabar, *The White Flag Principle: How to Lose a War (and Why)* (New York: Four Walls Eight Windows, 2002). Between irony and satire, Tzabar brutally reminds us how far divorced military victory is from the purposes for which wars are fought. A more serious, equally salutary work is Gwynne Dyer, *War: The Lethal Custom* (New York: Carroll and Graf, 2005).

3.  Joseph S. Nye, *Soft Power: The Means to Success in World Politics* (New York: Public Affairs, 2004).

4.  Legitimacy in Korea derived from aiding Korea's liberation from Japanese occupation. One of the eeriest moments in Errol Morris's 2003 documentary film, *Fog of War*, was ex-Secretary of Defense Robert McNamara's realization, decades after the U.S. defeat in Vietnam, that the North Vietnamese saw themselves as fighting a war of national liberation against a foreign occupier, the United States, rather than a war between the communist and capitalist blocs. That such a fundamental recognition of the nature of the war he was fighting escaped this brilliant analyst is a reminder of the blinding power of ideology.

5.  I had only weak grounds to criticize the Greeks for their misun-

derstanding of human rights. The Reagan administration embraced human rights as a tool for discrediting Soviet rule in Eastern Europe but had no interest in human rights in Central
America, where close U.S. scrutiny would undermine the willingness of Congress to fund counterinsurgency death squads. America
does better now, but not enough.

6. This is a delicate tightrope to walk. Kosovar Albanians and Serbs
alike misunderstand the 1999 NATO intervention in Kosovo. U.S.
military personnel are welcome in the streets of Pristina because
Kosovars misperceive America's grudging and temporary peacekeeping presence as an alliance with them against the Serbs.

7. Carr, *Twenty Years' Crisis,* 181–192.

## Chapter 4: Some Rules of the Game

1. The surprise U.S. decision to recognize the Republic of Macedonia
by that name, in November 2004, was an excellent example of a
decision that, while perfectly defensible as U.S. policy, cut the
embassy's Greek ministry colleagues off at the knees. See chapter
6 for more details.

2. Clinton-era budget cuts to the Foreign Service brought to a premature end a number of solid careers. The positive side was that,
when George W. Bush allowed the U.S. government to balloon
again, Powell had "headroom" to hire an impressive group of new
junior foreign service officers, many of whom were dropped still
dripping wet into jobs formerly occupied by hardened and cynical diplomats. With luck, their accelerated education in Iraq and
elsewhere will be the basis for a renaissance of moderate, skeptical U.S. diplomacy.

3. Every officer must draw some line. I had no problem talking to
communists. The extreme nationalist, anti-Semitic party was un-
represented in the Greek parliament, and I could ignore it with a
clear conscience. Similarly bigoted Islamist parties are, alas, too
influential and dangerous to shun these days, and likewise are
the European hard-right anti-immigrant parties.

## Chapter 5: Diplomatic Character and the Art of Curiosity

1. Monteagle Stearns, *Talking to Strangers: Improving American Diplomacy at Home and Abroad* (Princeton, NJ: Princeton University Press,
1989) is a fine, concise introduction to U.S. diplomacy by one of
its best practitioners. Henry Kissinger, *Diplomacy* (New York: Simon
& Schuster, 1994), a by-product of a life spent treating human
beings as pieces on a chessboard, is useless as a guide to diplomacy.

## Chapter 6: Bureaucratic Fantasy and the Duty of Dissent

1.  The bureaucratic shortcomings I describe are probably universal, though they became more visible after 2001 under a president whose instinctive ability to exploit the weaknesses of his own citizenry failed him with foreigners. For an eerie example of deja vu, see the classic essay on flawed decision making: James C. Thomson Jr., "How Could Vietnam Happen?" *The Atlantic*, April 1968. I am grateful to Mark H. O'Donoghue for the reference.

2.  For information on Bernard Lewis's role, see Michael Hirsh, "Bernard Lewis Revisited: What If Islam Isn't an Obstacle to Democracy in the Middle East, but the Secret to Achieving It?" *Washington Monthly*, November 2004, http://www.findarticles.com/p/articles/mi_m1316/is_11_36/ai_n7070000. For Victor Davis Hanson, see Evan Thomas, "The 12-Year Itch," *Newsweek*, March 31, 2003, http://msnbc.msn.com/id/3068684/. A former classics professor at Fresno State, Hanson made himself famous and rich by wrenching appropriate gobbets of history out of context to flatter the prejudices of fellow conservatives. In his glorification of the redemptive power of war, Hanson placed himself in a rich pseudo-classical tradition that includes Friedrich Nietzsche's celebration of German "will" and Enoch Powell's British fascism.

    For more on the removal of the Iraq expert from the Iraq planning process, see chapter 14.

3.  Secretary of State Colin Powell's chief of staff, Lt. Col. Lawrence Wilkerson, let rip on the subject of a Cheney-Rumsfeld "cabal" in a talk at the New America Foundation on October 19, 2005, http://www.thewashingtonnote.com/archives/001020.html, summarized in "The White House Cabal," op-ed, *Los Angeles Times*, October 25, 2005.

4.  In the felicitous phrase of George Finlay's indispensable *History of the Greek Revolution* (n.p., 1877), 5.

5.  Steve Lalas, a Greek-American diplomatic communications technician at the embassy, was surreptitiously photocopying secret telegrams and sharing them with the Greek government. If Mitsotakis and the small group of Greek officials with access to the Lalas intelligence read my Dissent Channel cable, they swallowed their bile. It was not a message Mitsotakis wanted read.

6.  Sanctions are an excellent business opportunity. At least one major Greek shipowner allegedly got his start smuggling oil to the former Rhodesia in violation of the UN embargo.

7.  Michael R. Gordon, "12 in State Dept. Ask Military Move Against the Serbs," *New York Times*, April 23, 1993, 1. We all swore innocence of the leak. At the time I believed my colleagues unquestioningly. That belief, however, has no scientific basis.

8.  Nancy Soderberg, *The Superpower Myth: The Use and Misuse of Ameri-*

*can Might* (Hoboken, NJ: Wiley, 2005), 21–31, gives a serviceable account of the NSC side of the policy debate over Bosnia.

9.  The less dire and inaccurate assessments of Iraq's nuclear program offered by skeptical experts in the State Department's Bureau of Intelligence and Research were buried in footnotes no president would read.

10. Albert O. Hirschman, *Exit, Voice, and Loyalty: Responses to Decline in Firms, Organizations, and States* (Cambridge: Harvard University Press, 1970) is a classic work on bureaucratic resignation.

11. Daniel Ellsberg, *Secrets: A Memoir of Vietnam and the Pentagon Papers* (New York: Viking, 2002). The Plumbers were the little group of clandestine operatives that brought down President Richard Nixon through excessive zeal. In an attempt to discredit Pentagon Papers leaker Ellsberg, they burgled his psychiatrist's office. Then they burgled Democratic Party headquarters at the Watergate to plant listening devices. It was not their "third-rate burglary" but the White House's attempted cover-up that ultimately forced Nixon to resign.

12. It is a sad commentary on the disconnect between government and politics that Libby and Rove could come up with no more damning way to discredit Ambassador Wilson's information with the Republican Party's "conservative base" than the fact that he and it were tainted by association with the CIA. Liberals fond of conspiracy theorizing about the CIA should stop to consider that Vice President Cheney and his friends see the CIA as almost as treasonably liberal and ineffective as the State Department.

## *Chapter 7: The Cost of U.S. Unpopularity*

1.  London was, as a one-time card-carrying member of the American Socialist Party, one of the few U.S. writers whose works were widely available in Soviet Armenia. Children's librarians from different cultures draw widely diverging ideological lessons from a book like *Call of the Wild.*

2.  For statistics on attitudes toward the United States, see Pew Global Attitudes Project, "U.S. Image Up Slightly, but Still Negative," June 23, 2005, http://pewglobal.org/reports/. For Middle Eastern attitudes, see Zogby International/University of Maryland, "Arab Nations Deeply Suspicious of U.S. Motive—Poll," Reuters Alertnet, December 2, 2005, http://www.alertnet.org/thenews/ newsdesk/N02305592.htm. In some places, of course, the U.S. image never stopped being rosy. The Statue of Liberty adorning the Hotel Victory in Pristina, the capital of Kosovo, signals that the ethnic Albanian Kosovars still cherish Americans as the comrades in arms who freed them from Serbian rule in 1999. Gratitude for U.S. support for independence will keep America's star

somewhat shiny in the former Warsaw Pact for a time, but not indefinitely.

3. Hutchings's body has never been found. The courage, persistence, and devotion of Jane Schelly, Hutchings's wife, inspired me deeply. Her efforts to mobilize the U.S., Indian, and Pakistani governments and public deserved a better outcome. Her story is told by Ann Hagedorn, *RANSOM: The Untold Story of International Kidnapping* (New York: Henry Holt, 1998).

4. In twenty years of diplomatic service I was burgled twice in Tel Aviv, pick-pocketed in Tetouan in Morocco, and robbed at knifepoint in Yerevan, about what I could have expected living in San Francisco on a federal employee's salary during those years. Unquestionably, street crime is more dangerous abroad than at home because at home we are less distracted and also know what neighborhoods to avoid.

5. U.S. Department of State, *Patterns of Global Terrorism 2003* (Washington, DC: Department of State, 2004).

6. "U.S. Brands Learning to Fly the Flag Subtly," *International Herald Tribune*, February 14, 2004, 13. The article cites U.S. corporate branding specialist Nick Wreden, who notes that U.S. companies do not admit back in the United States that they are downplaying their U.S. connections overseas.

7. Institute of International Education, "Open Doors 2004: International Students in the U.S.," November 2004, http://opendoors.iienetwork.org/?p=50137. The decline in student numbers from the Middle East was steepest, a bad omen given the importance of that region to U.S. policy goals.

8. In Turkey, the Republican People's Party (CHP) leader Deniz Baykal did exactly that on January 24, 2005, claiming the United States was supporting his rival so that the CHP would not thwart the impending U.S. invasions of Iran and Syria.

## *Chapter 8: Public Diplomacy and the Limits of Persuasiveness*

1. Lady Mary Wortley Montague, *The Turkish Embassy Letters* (London: Virago, 1994), 129. Her splendid letters are an early and precious example of how an energetic, curious, socially gifted diplomatic wife could help bridge massive gulfs of culture, language, and religion, in this case between eighteenth-century England and the Ottoman Empire. Describing the huge contribution of diplomatic spouses to U.S. national interests is beyond the scope of this book, and modern gender politics anyway make the task perilous. But thanks are due.

2. I never saw the report that resulted. Perhaps the recommendations were, like those of the infamous Defense Science Review

Board's September 2004 report on strategic communication, unpalatable. Or perhaps the unraveling of 17N in July 2002 made the State Department lose interest in Greek attitudes.

3.  See, for example, Victor Davis Hanson's "Islamists Hate Us for What We Are . . . " January 2005, http://www.victorhanson.com/articles/hanson011805.html.

4.  Various U.S. ambassadors to Greece made it a personal goal to persuade the sponsors that a fair-minded assessment of history does not justify that the U.S. embassy be the target of the annual November 17 march, which commemorates the junta's suppression with U.S.-built tanks of a 1973 student protest at the Athens Polytechneion. The effort is doomed by the lack of any other unifying symbol for the marchers.

5.  Quoted in Edward H. Carr, *What Is History* (New York: Vintage Books, 1961), 8, a stimulating set of lectures.

6.  President Bush made this bizarre statement on July 14, 2003, following a meeting at the White House with Kofi Annan. Press Spokesman Scott McClellan made a feeble attempt to dismiss the statement at the next day's press briefing, http://www.whitehouse.gov/news/releases/2003/07/20030715-2.html.

7.  By most accounts, U.S. ambassador to Greece Nick Burns played a crucial role in giving visiting President Clinton the speech he needed to regain a measure of Greek goodwill in 1999 after Kosovo. A gifted politician, armed with a speech crafted to the historical understanding of its audience, can do wonders.

8.  For a recent confirmation of this draconian policy, see Peter Baker, "From Amsterdam to the White House," *Washington Post*, October 12, 2005, A15.

9.  Hughes seems to have recognized the need to use her access to President Bush. See Glenn Kessler, "Hughes Spurred Bush-Palestinian Meeting," *Washington Post*, October 12, 2005, for a sensible intervention to convince Palestinians of the seriousness of U.S. engagement in their cause.

10. Inuit spokespeople, backed by enterprising lawyers, announced that they would seek a ruling from the Inter-American Commission on Human Rights that U.S. global warming policies were threatening their existence as a people. Richard Black, "Inuit Sue US Over Climate Policy," *BBC News*, December 8, 2005, http://news.bbc.co.uk/1/low/sci/tech/4511556.stm.

11. Since 1994 the overall number of high school student exchange visits to the United States dropped by over half, from 62,000 to only 27,700 in the 2003–4 school year. State Department statistics show a 36 percent drop in high school student exchange visas between 1999–2000 and 2002–3. "(Student) Exchange Rate Falls," *Times–Trenton*, February 12, 2005.

12. The Senate hearings on the nomination of John Bolton as U.S. permanent representative to the UN made public that the telephone conversations of American diplomats with foreign officials are subject to eavesdropping (Charles Babington and Jim VandeHei, "Democrats Block Vote on Bolton," *Washington Post*, June 21, 2005, A01, http://www.washingtonpost.com/wp-dyn/content/article/2005/06/20/AR2005062000402_pf.html; and Wayne Madsen, "NSA Intercepts for Bolton Masked as 'Training Missions,'" *Online Journal*, April 25, 2005, http://www.onlinejournal.org/Special_Reports/042505Madsen/042505madsen.html). Over the course of their careers, U.S. diplomats gradually realize that the higher they rise in rank the more likely it is that any unconventional remarks they make will become the subject of lively discussion between (e.g.) Ambassador Bolton and the vice president's office. Congress, in debating the widely publicized illegal monitoring of U.S. citizens by the NSA in the wake of 9/11, should ask itself whether the practice of sharing such intercepts with senior bureaucrats in rival agencies really encourages U.S. diplomats to exercise their full powers of persuasion with foreign interlocutors.

## Chapter 9: Diplomats and Journalists

1. "Envoy Calls '82 Mideast Plan Ill-Timed," *New York Times*, October 31, 1984, A8.

2. Alerted by the operations center to (for example) a terrorist kidnapping in India, the Office of the Press Spokesman would e-mail a tasking for press guidance to the India desk officer, with a 10:00 AM deadline. I would craft a customized condemnation designed to encourage U.S.-India counterterrorism cooperation and allow the spokesman to pronounce the names correctly. I would hand-carry it to the regional specialist in the Counterterrorism Office who would eliminate language that failed to correspond with condemnations of other groups the United States detested similarly. This result would be e-mailed to the India-watcher in the Office of the Undersecretary for Political Affairs in case a political nuance had been missed. Then, it would be cleared through my office director, the deputy assistant secretary, and finally the assistant secretary for South Asia. She would delete any language that might be seen by her interagency peers as an attempt to make policy. The result would be presented triumphantly to Public Affairs, which would shorten it further. If a journalist were naive enough to ask, the spokesman would paraphrase the maimed relic, reconfirming America's generic distaste for terrorism. If not, the text would be cabled off to New Delhi in case the embassy had any doubts.

3.  Peer-driven evenhandedness is not the same as journalistic integrity. The journalistic ethics of the *New York Times* or the *Economist* are looked at bemusedly outside the United States and the UK. The Greek government made a quixotic attempt at the beginning of 2005 to bring to public attention the ethical and political problems of a system in which Greek journalists see no conflict of interest between working simultaneously for two or three different media outlets, a government press office at which they appear only on paydays, and a public relations consulting company. I was taken aback the first time a full-time journalist approached me in her capacity of press adviser to a deputy minister. Her employer wanted foreign press play. I suggested various newsworthy initiatives that might attract the interest of the *Financial Times*. She was fishing for my personal introduction to the *FT* correspondent.

4.  I showed a Greek journalist friend a supportive handwritten note from ex-President Clinton after my resignation. His editor made it the banner headline on the front page of a major Greek newspaper (Takis Michas, "Clinton Against Bush," *Eleftherotypia*, July 29, 2003, 1) spinning the note as documentary proof that Clinton had opposed the Iraq War. I need not have bothered to apologize to Clinton's office in Harlem for this misuse of his private correspondence. No U.S. journalist noticed the story.

## Chapter 10: Democratizing an Oligarchic Planet

1.  Farid Zakaria, *The Future of Freedom: Illiberal Democracy at Home and Abroad* (New York: Norton, 2004) is an indispensable work for any American committed to the idea that democracy is a program to be advanced, not simply a slogan to be chanted.

2.  The OSCE mission to the 2004 U.S. presidential elections caused outrage in the U.S. nativist community. Conservative newspapers in the United States denounced the presence of foreign observers as an affront to American democracy and violation of U.S. sovereignty. A Bush-Cheney campaign office in Orlando, Florida, generated headlines in Europe by barring a visit by OSCE election observers ("Finnish MP Reports Election Observers Turned Away from Florida Republican Office," *Helsingin Sanomat*, November 2, 2004, http://www.hs.fi/english/article/print/1076154411442). Armenian nationalists were not brave enough to violate treaty commitments, but their sentiments were similarly hostile. In Florida, visiting OSCE observers were embraced by Democratic Party activists as official confirmation that the Republican Party had vote fraud in mind. OSCE observers cannot prevent this unbalanced use of their presence, though they try, but the aid and comfort they give the opposition is a tiny counterweight

to a sitting government's decisive advantage in controlling the levers of patronage and fraud.

3. President Bush's favorite theoretician of democracy, former Russian dissident, now Israeli Knesset member Natan Sharansky, in his book *The Case for Democracy* (New York: Public Affairs, 2004), did not dispel the impression created by his Knesset votes that he loves democracy all the more when it is an excuse not to restore the West Bank to Palestinian control.

## Chapter 11: Counterterrorism Lessons From Revolutionary Organization 17 November

1. Monte Melkonian preceded me as an archaeology student at U.C. Berkeley by a few years. His pathological sense of duty turned him into a terrorist assassin for the Armenian Secret Army for the Liberation of Armenia (ASALA). In the process of murdering Turkish embassy administrative attaché Galip Özmen in July 1980, he also shot and killed Özmen's fourteen-year-old daughter, Neslihan. Murdering the child haunted Melkonian, however (Markar Melkonian, *My Brother's Road: An American's Fateful Journey to Armenia* [London: I. B. Tauris, 2005], 85). Melkonian redeemed some of his lost honor restraining fellow Armenians from similar atrocities as an Armenian military commander fighting the Azerbaijani army in Nagorno Karabakh. He was killed in action in 1993. Markar's biography illuminates usefully, partly at firsthand, how moral sensibilities play a crucial role in even the slimiest and most corrupt terrorist groups.

2. For handgun statistics, see National Institute of Justice, "Guns in America," http://www.ncjrs.org/txtfiles/165476.txt. For recent U.S. firearms death figures, see Centers for Disease Control, "Deaths: Preliminary Data for 2003," National Vital Statistics Reports, February 28, 2005, 18, http://www.cdc.gov/nchs/data/nvsr/nvsr53/nvsr53_15.pdf.

3. For more on Padilla, see Lewis Z. Koch, "Dirty Bomber? Dirty Justice," *Bulletin of the Atomic Scientists* 60:1 (January–February 2004): 59–68, http://www.thebulletin.org/article.php?art_ofn=jf04koch; and Jamie Wilson, "Torture Claims 'Force U.S. to Cut Terror Charges,'" *Guardian*, November 25, 2005.

4. George Smith, "UK Terror Trial Finds No Terror," National Security Notes, *GlobalSecurity.org*, http://www.globalsecurity.org/org/nsn/nsn-050411.htm.

5. Both criminals and law enforcement err expensively when they emphasize exotic weaponry at the expense of common sense. 17N stole a hundred light antitank rockets (LAW) from Greek military arsenal. Trying to show off by using the LAW in urban warfare for

which it was not designed, they killed a bystander, wounded one of their own members (leaving DNA-laden bloodstains behind), and missed their targets consistently.

6. A determined FBI search for terror cells in the United States, involving paid informers, entrapment, and substantial violations of the privacy and convenience of ordinary Americans, has turned up bigoted Muslim preachers and Hamas fund-raisers, a corrupt arms dealer, and a few dozen romantics in Northern Virginia and elsewhere play-acting with paint guns. The jihad they preached was not against their American neighbors.

7. 17 November, *Hoi prokeryxeis, 1975–2000: hola ta keimena tes organoses (The Proclamations)*, (Athens: Kaktos, 2002). This collection gives the full text in Greek of all the known 17N proclamations and includes a useful name index. In a subsequent letter to Kaktos, 17N member Dimitris Koufodinas disavowed a few of the proclamations as forgeries. "Koufodinas: 6 Proclamations Work of the Secret Services," *Eleftherotypia* (Athens), December 12, 2002. English translations of the proclamations were prepared, usually within a couple of days of original Greek publication, by the Foreign Broadcast Information Service, available at major research libraries. For the physiology of revenge, see the suggestive article, Will Knight, "Brain Scans Reveal Men's Pleasure in Revenge," *NewScientist.com*, January 18, 2006, http://www.newscientist.com/article.ns?id=dn8605.

8. Libya was fingered as the culprit for the Pan Am 103 attack, but the legal case against the two accused Libyan intelligence officers was frustratingly weak, leading the Scottish court to one conviction and one "not proven" verdict. The Libyan foreign minister implied, in a public statement a more cynical diplomat would have avoided as counterproductive, that the compensation Libya paid to end sanctions was blackmail to serve U.S. domestic political requirements. We will never know for sure.

9. For a sensitive view of Hamas suicide bombers by a social scientist, see Scott Atran, "Tuning out Hell's Harpists" (update of paper presented to the Permanent Monitoring Panel on Terrorism, World Federation of Scientists, Geneva, November 2004), http://jeannicod.ccsd.cnrs.fr/documents/disk0/00/00/05/64/ijn_00000564_00/ijn_00000564_00.pdf.

10. Anyone interested in the problem of terrorist motives must read the July 2005 letter allegedly written by Ayman al Zawahiri, the key al Qaeda commander in Afghanistan, to Abu Musab al Zarqawi, http://www.weeklystandard.com/Content/Public/Articles/000/000/006/203gpuul.asp?pg=1. Whether genuine or not, the letter situates terrorism firmly in an overall strategic context that makes

it intelligible. Zawahiri's reminder that terrorists suffer personal losses with the same all-too-human emotions as the rest of us is a useful one.

11. As political counselor in Athens I had no formal "need to know" the details of CIA and FBI operations against 17N. Much of what I knew derived from the vain attempts of Greek journalists to get me to confirm operations that they had learned about from Greek sources, information I was not privy to. Those hints became leverage by which I could often confirm the substance if not the spin with better-placed official colleagues. My confidence in my analysis of the 17N campaign is strengthened by personal interviews I conducted in 2004 and 2006 with key Greek figures such as counterterrorism prosecutor Ioannis Diotis, former Greek Intelligence Service director Pavlos Apostolidis, and Greek counterterrorism journalist Tassos Telloglou. The fullest published account of the pursuit and capture of 17N, in Greek, is Alexis Papachelas and Tassos Telloglou, *17: Phakelos 17 Noemvre (File 17 November)* (Athens: Vivliopoleio tis Estias, 2002). These two journalists were in regular contact with Minister of Public Order Michalis Chrysochoidis, senior police officials, and successive U.S. ambassadors. They give far more operational detail than I could, and the American public would benefit from being able to read in English their sometimes painful conclusions. The critique of their book by Ios ("Virus"), "One, Two, Many Gerard de Villiers," *Eleftherotypia* (Athens), January 26, 2003, http://www.iospress.gr//ios2003/ios20030126b.htm, offers useful cautions and corrections. The refusal of 17N's convicted mastermind Alexandros Giotopoulos to admit his role leaves a substantial hole in the overall picture of the group.

12. Papachelas and Telloglou, *17*, 173.

13. Steve Coll, *Ghost Wars* (New York: Penguin, 2004), 5–6, 371–375, brilliantly documents the single-mindedness of CIA efforts in Afghanistan and Pakistan to bring Kasi to justice. The CIA's obsession with private vengeance should give us pause.

14. In June 2005 this scandal blew up in Italy as Italian authorities handed down indictments against thirteen named CIA officers for having kidnapped and handed over to Egyptian authorities an Islamic cleric living in Milan. "'The kidnapping of Abu Omar was not only a serious crime against Italian sovereignty and human rights, but it also seriously damaged counterterrorism efforts in Italy and Europe,' said Armando Spataro, the lead prosecutor in Milan. 'In fact, if Abu Omar had not been kidnapped, he would now be in prison, subject to a regular trial, and we would have probably identified his other accomplices.'" Craig Whitlock, "CIA

Ruse Is Said to Have Damaged Probe in Milan," *Washington Post*, December 6, 2005, A01, http://www.washingtonpost.com/wp-dyn/content/article/2005/12/04/AR2005120400885.html. The trail of luxury hotel bills the CIA left behind damned the exercise as an out-of-control bureaucratic junket worthy of Jack Abramoff. No information has surfaced to suggest that the United States benefited in any way from the CIA's Italian holiday or from providing the Egyptians a fresh Muslim militant to torture. Tracy Wilkinson, "CIA Said to Leave Trail in Abduction," *Los Angeles Times*, June 26, 2005, A3.

15. Papachelas and Telloglou, *17*, 183.
16. Gen. Fotis Nasiakos was retired in 2004. An article in Athens daily newspaper, V. G. Lambropoulos, "EL.AS.: The End of the Nasiakos Era," *To Vima* (Athens), October 10, 2004, A38, in Greek, documents U.S. pressure, such as a demand to take into custody two men the United States erroneously claimed were 17N members.
17. Papachelas and Telloglou, *17*, 179. I first heard the name from a Greek journalist. My embassy colleagues, including one protagonist of the discredited theory, later confirmed it.
18. 17N leader Giotopoulos was apparently terrified that he would be kidnapped and taken to Guantanamo (Ibid., 260–261). The U.S. embassy hoped that the threat of extradition to the United States, left deliberately undenied, would be helpful in squeezing out the first 17N confessions. Greek newspapers headlined this legally and politically impossible threat to outrage the Greek public and thereby increase their sales.
19. U.S. Department of Defense, *The National Defense Strategy of the United States of America* (March 2005), 9, http://www.defenselink.mil/news/Mar2005/d20050318nds1.pdf.
20. Former U.S. ambassador to the USSR Jack Matlock tells a horrifying tale in his book *Reagan and Gorbachev* (New York: Random House, 2004) about how the Naval Investigative Service coerced a young Marine security guard at Embassy Moscow into a false confession about letting the KGB into secure areas of the embassy. The U.S. government seized on the confession because the alternative was to admit that the KGB had penetrated both the CIA and FBI—via Aldrich Ames and Robert Hannsen as it turned out.
21. Bassem Youssef, an FBI officer of Middle Eastern extraction, sued the FBI in 2005 citing discrimination in promotion. The FBI attracted headlines (e.g., "Terror Expertise Not a Priority at FBI," *USA Today/AP*, June 19, 2005) by denying that Youssef's undisputed counterterrorism and cross-cultural expertise was relevant to senior jobs combating Islamic terrorism.

## Chapter 12: The Domestic Politics of Nuclear Weapons

1. The *Nuclear Threat Initiative* website maintains an excellent, detailed chronology of nuclear proliferation activities. For a detailed timeline of proliferation in India in 1996, see http://www.nti.org/ e_research/profiles/India/Nuclear/2296_2891.html.

2. For a superb illustration of the difficulty of communicating effectively with North Korean officials, see Tong Kim, "You Say Okjeryok, I Say Deterrent," *Washington Post*, September 25, 2005, http://www.washingtonpost.com/wp-dyn/content/article/2005/09/24/AR2005092400004.html. The accompanying piece by Glenn Kessler in the same issue, "What That Accord Really Says," http://www.washingtonpost.com/wp-dyn/content/article/2005/09/24/AR2005092400009.html, is remarkable in offering readers the detailed background of the negotiations in a balanced, intelligible way.

3. Linda Bilmes and Joseph E. Stiglitz, "The Economic Costs of the Iraq War" (paper presented to AASA, January 2006), http://www2.gsb.columbia.edu/faculty/jstiglitz/Cost_of_War_in_Iraq.pdf.

   For a short, extremely sensible discussion of how poorly the pseudo-alternative of targeted strikes on nuclear facilities fulfills its purported goal, see Joseph Cirincione, "No Military Option," *Proliferation News*, January 19, 2006, http://www.carnegie endowment.org/npp/publications/index.cfm?fa=view&id=17922.

4. The nonproliferation specialists at the Carnegie Endowment for International Peace, led by George Perkovich, produced a comprehensive set of proposals in 2005, published as *Universal Compliance: A Strategy for Nuclear Security*, http://www.carnegie endowment.org/publications/index.cfm?fa=view&id=16593. This is an excellent blueprint for any government serious about keeping its citizens alive to follow.

## Chapter 13: The Diplomatic Cost of Clandestine Intelligence

1. U.S. diplomats have not contributed as much as they ought to the vast, heavily romanticized literature on secret intelligence. One set of essays that takes a useful look at the practical costs and benefits of intelligence is Craig Eisendrath, ed., *National Insecurity: U.S. Intelligence After the Cold War* (Philadelphia: Temple University Press, 2000). For recent revelations by retired CIA officers, see for example John Crewdson, "Secrecy of Plame's CIA work at issue," *Chicago Tribune*, March 11, 2006.

2. Key documentation has been assembled in James Miller, ed., *Foreign Relations of the United States 1964–1968: Cyprus, Greece, Turkey* (Washington, DC: U.S. Government Printing Office, 2001), Vol. 16, docs. 225–272, on-line at http://www.state.gov/r/pa/ho/frus/

johnsonlb/xvi/. See especially report 225. A valuable book on the CIA and the Greek junta, derived primarily from U.S. official documents and testimony, is unfortunately not yet available in English: Alexis Papachelas, *Ho Viasmos tës Hellenikës Demokratias: Ho Amerikanikos Paragon, 1947–1967* ( *The Rape of Greek Democracy: The American Factor, 1947–1967*) (Athens: Vivliopoleia tis Estias, 2000). This has just been updated by a fine new study, Mogens Pelt, *Tying Greece to the West,* (Copenhagen: Museum Tusculanum Press, 2006).

## Chapter 14: Diplomatic Skepticism and the Lessons of Iraq

1.  For the White House troubles with Warren Medoff, see for example: Harold Ickes, "Public Service in the Theater of the Absurd" (remarks to the Forum at the Wagner School of Public Service's Taub Urban Research Center, New York University, New York, March 5, 1998), http://urban.nyu.edu/calendar/ickes.htm; and House Committee on Government Reform and Oversight, *Campaign Finance Improprieties and Possible Violations of Law,* 105th Cong., 1st sess., 1997, http://commdocs.house.gov/committees/gro/hgo281.000/hgo281_0.HTM.

2.  CBS news broke the Dora Farms story on May 28, 2003. See "At Saddam's Bombed Palace," *CBSNews.com,* May 28, 2003, http://www.cbsnews.com/stories/2003/05/28/eveningnews/main555948.shtml; and "Dora Farms," *GlobalSecurity.com,* http://www.globalsecurity.org/military/world/iraq/dora.htm.

3.  For a convenient, brief summary of U.S. statements on Iraq sanctions, see Glen Rangwala, "The Myth That All Iraq Needs to Do to Lift Sanctions Is Comply With Weapons Inspectors," *Middle East Reference,* http://middleeastreference.org.uk/mythoflifting.html.

    On May 12, 1996, Lesley Stahl of *Sixty Minutes* asked Secretary of State Madeleine Albright, "We have heard that a half million children have died. I mean, that's more children than died in Hiroshima. And, you know, is the price worth it?" Albright replied, "I think this is a very hard choice, but the price—we think the price is worth it." Though she certainly did not mean to sound so callous, Albright's diplomatic blunder helped equate the United States with Saddam Hussein in the minds of anyone who saw the welfare of the Iraqi people as the sole moral basis for international intervention. Murderously incurious U.S. sanctions policy guaranteed that the Arab world would reject U.S. good intentions and also guaranteed that Iraq would be an expensive basket case by the time the United States moved in to disarm and/or democratize it.

4.  William Rivers Pitt, *War on Iraq,* with Scott Ritter (New York:

Context Books, 2002); Scott Ritter, *Iraq Confidential: The Untold Story of the Intelligence Conspiracy to Undermine the UN and Overthrow Saddam Hussein* (New York: Nation Books, 2005). Ritter's trajectory from fervent UN Special Commission inspector to merciless critic of the Iraq War deserved more sympathetic attention than U.S. media gave him, not least because he proved more correct than they on Iraqi WMD.

5. In fairness one must distinguish between the CIA analysts of the Directorate of Intelligence, who do read foreign newspapers and rely heavily on diplomatic reporting for their analytical write-ups, and the raw reports from the CIA's clandestine service, the Directorate of Operations. The eyes of a president with a short attention span will glaze over at nuanced multisource analysis. An ambitious CIA director holds the president's attention with human intelligence (humint) reporting that highlights CIA intelligence penetrations.

6. This analysis was gleaned from personal interviews. My informant was a bright diplomat apparently doomed by his cynicism to remote and thankless postings like Baghdad. I took him to dinner in Athens before he left, thinking his future insights on Iraq would be well worth the cost of a meal. It is just as well I never submitted the voucher to be reimbursed for his dinner. The only information about Iraq the Political Section of U.S. Embassy Athens was ever asked to obtain from the Greek Foreign Ministry was the global positioning system coordinates of the Greek embassy and ambassador's residence, so the United States could avoid bombing them by mistake.

7. David Phillips, *Losing Iraq: Inside the Postwar Reconstruction Fiasco* (New York: Westview, 2005); Bob Woodward, *Plan of Attack* (New York: Simon & Schuster, 2004), 284.

8. Businesspeople from all over the world, including the United States, took calculated risks doing business with Iraq. The French government knew that the war was going to happen. The best way to protect French oil interests and debt recovery prospects was to join in Operation Iraqi Freedom. French commercial interests were sacrificed to a mix of domestic politics and principle.

9. Judith Miller's "Illicit Arms Kept Till Eve of War, an Iraqi Scientist Is Said to Assert" was published in the *New York Times* on April 21, 2003, after a three-day delay at the request of the U.S. military. Powell and Rumsfeld issued their threats to Syria on April 15, almost certainly in response to information from that same defector. Kurtz's piece was published as "Embedded Reporter's Role in Army Unit's Actions Questioned by Military" in the *Washington Post*, June 25, 2003, C1.

10. Richard Sale, "The NSA's Tangle With Chalabi," *UPI, Washington*

*Times,* July 29, 2004, http://www.washtimes.com/upi-breaking/20040729-051231-3792r.htm.

## Chapter 15: A Look Toward the Future

1.  In the interests of full disclosure, I must confess that my father volunteered for a time for Zero Population Growth, an organization founded by the eminent Stanford doomsayer Paul Ehrlich, author of *The Population Bomb* (New York: Ballantine Books, 1968). Ehrlich underestimated the adaptability of human societies in his confident predictions of mass starvation during the 1980s. Diamond's extinct societies are not strictly parallel with the current world situation. Technological evolution, especially biotechnology, will exploit new resources and perhaps ultimately allow an indefinitely sustainable human ecosystem to develop. Existing free-market price signaling mechanisms, however, do not prevent local glitches in the supply of food or energy, with the result being cascading environmental degradation. A three-month cutoff of natural gas supplies in wintertime can lead an urban population to burn decades' worth of environmental and social capital: trees, furniture, books. In a famine, farmers eat their seed corn and breeding stock and strip the land bare. Overpopulation and social breakdown in Sudan and Afghanistan have created ghastly local moonscapes inhabitable only thanks to a steady flow of international food aid. Those moonscapes are spreading, a prospect that should horrify us more than it does.

2.  UN Economic and Social Affairs, *World Population Prospects: The 2004 Revision* (New York: UN, 2005), http://www.un.org/esa/population/publications/WPP2004/2004Highlights_finalrevised.pdf.

3.  See for example the Economist Intelligence Unit, "The World in 2005: Quality of Life Index," http://www.economist.com/media/pdf/QUALITY_OF_LIFE.pdf.

# ★ *Index* ★

# INDEX

# ★ *About the Author* ★

John Brady Kiesling, a career State Department diplomat, resigned publicly in February 2003 to protest the U.S. decision to invade Iraq. His letter of resignation, a powerful defense of diplomacy and multilateralism as the basis for U.S. leadership, was read and admired around the world.

Born in Houston, Texas, in 1957, Kiesling grew up in Los Altos, California. He graduated from Swarthmore College with a degree in ancient Greek and earned an MA in ancient history and Mediterranean archaeology at UC Berkeley. After fieldwork as an archaeologist in Spain, Greece, and Turkey, he joined the U.S. Foreign Service in 1983 under President Reagan. His first diplomatic posting was Tel Aviv as a vice consul and aide to the ambassador. He next served in Casablanca, Morocco, as economic officer, and then in Athens, Greece, as political officer. He was honored by his peers in 1994 for constructive dissent on Bosnia while serving as the Romania desk officer in Washington. He then served for two years as India desk officer. After learning Armenian, he spent 1997–99 as the political-economic counselor in Yerevan, followed by a year as deputy U.S. special negotiator for the Nagorno Karabakh conflict. His final assignment was as political counselor at the U.S. embassy in Greece, where he struggled to cope with the diplomatic consequences of the Bush administration's foreign policy.

Since 2003 he has been writing and speaking on U.S. foreign policy, including as a visiting lecturer at Princeton University. His articles and essays have been published in the *New York Review of Books, Salon.com,* and major newspapers. He lives in Athens, Greece.